INDEX NUMBERS IN THEORY AND PRACTICE

Index Numbers in Theory and Practice

R.G.D. ALLEN

First published 1975 by
THE MACMILLAN PRESS LTD
London and Basingstoke
Associated companies in New York
Dublin Melbourne Johannesburg and Madras

SBN 333 16916 6

Printed in Great Britain by
R. AND R. CLARK LTD.
Edinburgh

Contents

Preface

Index numbers are a widespread disease of modern life. . . . It is really questionable – though bordering on heresy to put the question – whether we would be any the worse off if the whole bag of tricks were scrapped. So many of these index numbers are so ancient and so out of date, so out of touch with reality, so completely devoid of practical value when they have been computed, that their regular calculation must be regarded as a widespread compulsion neurosis. M. J. Moroney (1951)

I lived with Moroney. M. C. Fessey, Business Statistics Office

There is at present, as Craig (1969) has remarked, no simple and reasonably comprehensive text on the design, construction and use of index numbers. Such references as are to be found in the standard texts on statistical theory, at various levels of difficulty, are brief and oversimplified. Sometimes the comments are more scathing than complimentary, as with the famous quotation from Moroney (1951) reproduced above. Even those who make much use of index numbers, in texts on applied economic and social statistics, do not seem willing to allocate space to an account of them. Perhaps part of the explanation of this state of affairs lies in the fact that no course in statistical methods can be expected to devote more than a few lectures and classes to index numbers. But even a few lectures need to rest on some recognised textbook for collateral or independent reading.

I have had these things in mind in writing the present text, the plan of which should be clear enough from the table of contents. In order to reach students of economics generally, and not only those who handle index numbers professionally, I have kept the text as simple as possible in mathematical terms. The subject of index numbers, however, is more extensive and sophisticated than might appear at first sight. I have not always resisted the temptation to explore far afield and not all readers will want to follow me all the way. It is just not possible to keep even a moderately comprehensive text as simple as all that.

I refer in the text to some books, and to many articles, on the theory and practice of index numbers. I have shown them as they arise in a notation which relates to the Bibliography at the end of the text, e.g. Craig (1969) and Moroney (1951). For illustrative purposes I make use of many of the more important index numbers published in this country. I make no pretence, however, to give any complete or up-to-date account of them; for this the reader must go to the sources from which the index numbers come.

I need to thank my colleagues and the secretarial staff of the Statistics Department in the London School of Economics for more help than they may realise they have given me in preparing this text for publication.

R. G. D. ALLEN

London School of Economics
July 1974

1 General Survey

1.1 Definition of Index Numbers

Ragnar Frisch began his well-known survey of index numbers with the observation:

> The problem of how to construct an index number is as much one of economic theory as of statistical technique. Frisch (1936), p. 1

It is true that some applications of index numbers are not strictly economic but occur in (more or less) distantly related subjects ranging from demography to technology. Examples are easily found: standardised birth, sickness or death-rates; crop yields. It remains true, however, that the main uses of index numbers are in economics and hence that the theory is best developed in an economic context. There is, then, little difficulty in extending the application of the index-number technique to other fields. It is important to avoid the trap of divorcing the economic and the statistical aspects of index numbers, of attempting to consider an index number in the abstract. Index numbers are essentially practical constructs. The two approaches to them, the economic and the statistical, must be used together and from the outset.

Index numbers come in pairs in economic theory, one of price and the other a matching one of quantity. In economic practice, they tend to be found paired off in this way. Sometimes one or the other is used alone; but there is almost always a mate to it in the background. Such a pair may be designed to account for the variation in a value aggregate, as when movements in aggregate expenditure of consumers are analysed into the two components of changes in prices and in real consumption. For convenience of exposition we generally refer to price index numbers in the main development of the text. It is to be remembered that practically everything that is said applies to the parallel or matching case of quantity index numbers.

Index numbers have a long history, and Kendall (1969) gives a good account of the early period. The classical definition of index numbers goes back to Edgeworth. In 1887–9 Edgeworth was secretary of a committee of the British Association set up to study methods of measuring variations in the value of money. In this capacity he wrote three lengthy memoranda, reproduced in Edgeworth (1925a), pp. 195–343. Later he gave a concise definition:

> I proposed to define an index-number as a number adapted by its variations to indicate the increase or decrease of a magnitude not susceptible of accurate measurement. Edgeworth (1925b), p. 379

The magnitude he had especially in mind was the general price level or the value (purchasing power) of money, one the reciprocal of the other. The same concept is seen in a rather more developed form in Bowley's definition:

> Index-numbers are used to measure the change in some quantity which we cannot observe directly, which we know to have a definite influence on many other quantities which we can so observe, tending to increase all, or diminish all, while this influence is concealed by the action of many causes affecting the separate quantities in various ways. Bowley (1926), p. 196

Again the non-observable quantity Bowley had in mind was an economic concept such as the value of money.

The essential feature of the definition is that it makes no attempt to get a measure or indicator of the actual level attained by the non-observable magnitude. An index number is limited to the measure of *changes* in the magnitude from one situation to another. The two situations compared are in no way restricted; they may be two time periods (e.g. two years), or two situations in a spatial sense (e.g. two regions of a country), or two groups of individuals (e.g. one and two-person pensioner families). Once again, for convenience of exposition, and since it is the most usual case in practice, we generally refer to temporal index numbers in the text. Practically all that is developed can be applied, with the appropriate adjustment of terms and notation, to comparisons between other kinds of situations.

Since index numbers measure changes, they are expressed with one selected situation as 100. This is called the *reference base* of the series of index numbers. Comparison base is an alternative term often used. In an annual series, for example, the reference base is the year taken with the level of 100 for comparison. Another year may then appear with the index number (say) 126. This means that, according to the index number used, the magnitude considered in the second year is 126% of its level in the base year. The actual level is measured in neither of the years; only the change from one year to the other, here an increase of 26%, is given by the index.

The concept of an index number is properly confined to this case of a non-observable magnitude. It is quite common, however, to see the term 'index number' applied to the variation in a magnitude which is directly measurable. It is often convenient to express the changes in such a magnitude, given (for example) as an annual series, in the form of one year as a percentage of another, of one year as showing a percentage increase or decrease over another. The reference base, that written as 100, can be any one year of the series found convenient. The result looks very much like an index number, and by extension, it is often described as such.

A simple example illustrates. The following data relate to employment in manufacturing industries in Great Britain each mid-June:

	1969	1970	1971	1972
Number of employees, 000's	8,741	8,727	8,432	8,062
Series with 1969 as 100	100	99·8	96·5	92·2
with 1971 as 100	103·7	103·5	100	95·6

From *Monthly Digest of Statistics*

The concept of employment here is simple, whatever complications may be introduced in other contexts; it is the number of employees in employment in industries classified as manufacturing. This is a measurable and observable magnitude. Moreover, in practice, it can be estimated quite closely and on a comparable basis from one year to another. The data shown are comparable, on the same basis as regards both the definition of employees and the classification of industries under manufacturing. The figures can stand on their own; the level of employment at one date, in thousands of employees. It is only as a matter of convenience that the figures are expressed with one year as reference base. Here they are shown alternatively with 1969 and with 1971 as 100, to bring out (for example) that employment fell by $3\frac{1}{2}$% from 1969 to 1971 with a further fall of more than 4% from 1971 to 1972.

It is clear from this example that a shift from one reference base to another is just an arithmetic switch. The year-to-year changes in the series are the same whatever the reference base. For example, the fall of employment from 8,432,000 in 1971 to 8,062,000 in 1972 is seen as 4·4% whether the series is taken with 1969 as reference base (a fall of 4·4% from 96·5 to 92·2) or with 1971 as base (when the decrease is explicit). The series on one reference base is simply a rescaled version of the other. If we have the series based on 1969, the arithmetic switch to 1971, as reference base, is made by dividing through by 0·965 – the 1971 figure as a ratio – or by multiplying through by the reciprocal of 0·965.

One particular manifestation of this arithmetic switch is of very extensive use. Measure all changes as ratios and only convert to percentages by multiplying by 100 at the end. Then it follows that the change calculated **forwards** from one year to a later year is the **reciprocal** of the change measured **backwards** from the later to the earlier year. This is particularly clear for a comparison between 1969 and 1971, the alternative reference bases in our illustration. The forward change is shown by the ratio of 8,432 to 8,741 or 0·965, the reciprocal of the backward change given by the ratio of 8,741 to 8,432 or 1·037. There is, in fact, a simple **general rule:**

A change between two dates in a series of figures can be shown in ratio form either forwards or backwards and one ratio is the reciprocal of the other.

The rule is thinly disguised when changes are shown in percentages:

$$1971: \frac{8,432}{8,741}\ 100 = 96·465\% \text{ of } 1969;$$

$$1969: \frac{8,741}{8,432}\ 100 = 103·665\% \text{ of } 1971$$

Here 0·96465 and 1·03665 are mutually reciprocal. A fall of just over 3·5% from 1969 to 1971 is the same thing as a rise of nearly 3·7% from 1971 to 1969.

The figures in the second or third row of the table above are quite usually described as index numbers, here with 1969 or 1971 as 100. This extended use of the term has got into the technical language and it has perforce to be accepted. Having made this note we proceed in the present text to confine the analysis to index numbers proper, as the indication of changes in a level not directly observable or measurable. The properties of the arithmetic process of switching reference base apply unchanged (**1.5** below).

Ragnar Frisch put the matter in a nutshell:

The index-number problem arises whenever we want a quantitative expression for a *complex* that is made up of individual measurements for which no common *physical* unit exists. The desire to unite such measurements and the fact that this cannot be done by using physical or technical principles of comparison only, constitute the essence of the index-number problem and all the difficulties center here. Frisch (1936), p. 1

The complex that Frisch refers to is typically a complex of prices of a range of commodities expressed in heterogeneous units, for instance p per pint, £ per dozen, £ per ton. The problem can be tackled only by switching from the perfectly sensible, but non-observable, concept of a general price level to the related, and observable, concept of changes in price levels. This is required by the Edgeworth/Bowley definition. Then, it is one thing to measure the change in a single commodity price by writing the ratio of the two prices observed. For example, when the price of milk goes up from 5p to $5\frac{1}{2}$p per pint, the second price is $(5\frac{1}{2}/5)100 = 110\%$ of the first and the price has increased by 10%. It is quite another thing to go on to conclude that the general price level for a range of commodities has increased by (say) 10%. The first is a simple ratio, even though often loosely described as an index number. It is the second which constitutes the index-number problem, as neatly summed up by Ruist:

The problem that arises is how to combine the relative changes in the prices of various commodities into a single index number that can meaningfully be interpreted as a measure of the relative change in the general price level. Ruist (1968), p. 154

Most writers on index numbers since Edgeworth's pioneer work in the 1880s have distinguished two approaches to the problem. Frisch calls the first the **stochastic approach**, where the word 'stochastic' is the adjective now generally used instead of the mouthful 'probabilistic', as corresponding to the noun 'probability'. This approach aims at a broad objective, typically the general level of prices or the value of money, without specific reference to any group or application to any set of circumstances. The other can be called the **aggregative approach** and it has reference to some aggregate and to some group specified in advance. The reference can be, for example, to the aggregative expenditure of a specified group of consumers, and the object is to say something about the net income or standard of living of the group. The specification of the group can be quite narrow (e.g. one-person pensioner families) or as wide as all consumers in the country.

Edgeworth is quite explicit in his memoranda of 1887–9. His basic approach is to develop a stochastic price index and he gives one of the main sections in his first memorandum the title:

Determination of an Index irrespective of the quantities of commodities; upon the hypothesis that there is a numerous group of articles whose prices vary after the manner of a perfect market, with changes affecting the supply of money. Edgeworth (1925a), p. 233

The hypothesis here is that monetary factors – changes in the quantity of money and in its value – show up in a proportional change in each price and hence that the influence of money is to be measured by an index number of changes in the general price level. There are, at the same time, deviations of all kinds in the movements of individual prices. They arise from the play of many non-monetary factors and they are to be regarded, from the monetary point of view, as errors of observation. The same approach is to be seen in Bowley's definition of an index number. It was on this line of approach that Edgeworth was led to plump for the unweighted geometric mean of price relatives as the preferred index number. Or, since an 'unweighted' index is (as we shall see) something of an illusion, the best bet is a geometric mean with simple weights not depending on the quantities of the commodities actually traded. The alternative approach is on aggregative lines, and Edgeworth recognises this by devoting a later section of his first memorandum (p. 247) to the case where the quantities of the commodities are brought in to define a weighted index number. Edgeworth remains faithful, however, to his first or stochastic approach; he does not pursue the alternative beyond the point of offering the weighted median as a possible index number.

In his earliest thoughts on the subject, Keynes clearly followed the Edgeworth/Bowley line and accepted the stochastic approach; see Keynes (1921), p. 213. Later, certainly by the time that he wrote the *Treatise on Money* in the late 1920s, he had completely revised his position. He rejected the stochastic approach, even for such a broad objective as the measure of changes in the value of money, and he was explicit in his statement of the case for an aggregative form of index:

> We mean by the Purchasing Power of Money the power of money to buy the goods and services on the purchase of which for puposes of consumption a given community of individuals expend their money income . . . and the appropriate index-number is of the type sometimes designated as the Consumption Index. It follows that Purchasing Power must always be defined with reference to a particular set of individuals in a given situation namely those whose actual consumption furnishes us with our standard, and has no clear meaning unless this reference has been given. Keynes (1930), p. 54

Keynes quoted Marshall in support of these views; see Marshall (1923), pp. 21, 30.

Keynes' position is now accepted as generally more relevant and appropriate than Edgeworth's. The present text, as a consequence, concentrates on the development of index numbers in aggregative forms and in the equivalent weighted versions. Some uses can still be made of the stochastic approach and of the unweighted index-number forms to which it leads. This is especially so, and indeed more so than practical index-number construction concedes, in the context of the sampling aspects of the build-up of an index number from its detailed constituents.

There is one matter always to be kept in mind in constructing and in handling index numbers of aggregative/weighted average form. The point is clear enough on the stochastic approach but tends to be overlooked in the more elaborate index numbers of aggregative types. It is simply that a price index number is an average; a single summary figure derived from a great variety of price movements. Variation of price relatives about the average, taken for the index, is just as important as the index itself. If there were no such variation, the index would be trivial; what we need to know is how much variation there is. Let Edgeworth have the last word when he observes that price index numbers:

> . . . presuppose a fairly uniform change in the price of commodities, a sporadic distribution of price-relatives about their mean. Edgeworth (1925b), p. 383

1.2 Notation

The model we deal with is complex in the sense that it involves a set of commodities and a sequence of situations. The price and the quantity bought or sold need to be specified for each commodity in each situation. A good notation is essential in such a model. This is not for purposes of algebraic manipulation but rather as a shorthand reference to the forms of index number used and as a guide in calculation of the index numbers in practice. We are concerned hardly at all with mathematical analysis in this text, but we make much use of the algebraic shorthand.

The lower-case letters p and q are used for price and quantity respectively, the capital letters P and Q being reserved for index numbers of price and quantity. Two subscripts are attached to each p and q, the first for the commodity and the second for the situation considered. So:

$$p_{it} \text{ and } q_{it}$$

represent the price and the quantity of the ith commodity in situation t. Suppose there are n commodities and k situations after the base situation 0. Write $i = 1, 2, 3, \ldots n$ and $t = 0, 1, 2, 3, \ldots k$.

As already noted, the case of temporal index numbers is used for purposes of exposition, so that $t = 0, 1, 2, 3 \ldots$ are successive periods of time. To simplify further we take the successive periods as years and so refer to year 0, year 1, and so on. All that is said applies equally to other periods, e.g. months or quarters.

The notation is specified first for two years ($t = 0, 1$) and then generalised. Two sets of prices,

$$\{p_{10}\, p_{20}\, p_{30} \cdots p_{n0}\} \quad \text{and} \quad \{p_{11}\, p_{21}\, p_{31} \cdots p_{n1}\}$$

correspond to two sets of quantities,

$$\{q_{10}\, q_{20}\, q_{30} \cdots q_{n0}\} \quad \text{and} \quad \{q_{11}\, q_{21}\, q_{31} \cdots q_{n1}\}$$

Four aggregate values can be derived, two direct (or actual) values and two cross (or computed) values. Each aggregate is the sum of products of prices and quantities, commodity by commodity. The direct-value aggregates are got by multiplying prices and quantities in one and the same year; the cross values take prices from one year and quantities from the other. To denote such aggregates, we simplify by making use of a familiar notation. For example, the actual-value aggregate of situation 0 is:

$$\sum_{i=1}^{n} p_{i0}\, q_{i0} = p_{10}\, q_{10} + p_{20}\, q_{20} + p_{30}\, q_{30} + \ldots + p_{n0}\, q_{n0}.$$

Even so the notation is awkward to handle and we seek some further simplification or shorthand.

The mathematician's answer is to use the vector/matrix notation: each value aggregate is the inner product of a price and a quantity vector and the whole set of values can be arranged as a matrix. The corresponding notation is indeed compact and precise. It is, however, unfamiliar to those with little mathematical background.

We will make do, therefore, with a compromise: a shorthand notation designed to apply whenever we can safely omit explicit reference to individual commodities. If we need to spell out for the separate commodities, we continue to use the full notation: p_{i0} and q_{i0} ($i = 1, 2, 3, \ldots n$) for prices and quantities and $\sum_{i=1}^{n} p_{i0}\, q_{i0}$ for the actual value aggregate in year 0, and similarly for other aggregates. However, whenever there is no ambiguity, we drop the subscript i; we write (for example) p_0 and q_0 for the prices and quantities, and $\sum p_0 q_0$ for the value aggregate, in year 0. The symbols $\sum p_0 q_0$ are to be read: take the sum ($\sum$) of all products of which the typical one is $p_0 \times q_0$ for some commodity.

The four value aggregates obtained from prices and quantities (p_0, q_0 and p_1, q_1) in two years can now be written in the shorthand notation and arranged in a block of two rows and two columns:

	Prices in year	Quantities in year	
		0	1
	0	$\sum p_0 q_0$	$\sum p_0 q_1$
	1	$\sum p_1 q_0$	$\sum p_1 q_1$

It is convenient to borrow one term from the matrix algebra of the mathematician. The block of values is called a *matrix*, in this case of order 2×2, and it is indicated by the square-bracket notation used for matrices. Further, the convention is adopted here in which the *rows* of the matrix correspond to *fixed prices* and the *columns* correspond to *fixed quantities* (in years 0 and 1 respectively).

The notation is easily generalised. The prices p_{ir} in year r can be combined with the quantities q_{is} in year s to give the value aggregate:

$$\sum p_r q_s = \sum_{i=1}^{n} p_{ir} q_{is} \qquad r, s = 0, 1, 2, 3, \ldots k.$$

This is a direct valuation if $r = s$, a cross valuation if $r \neq s$. The complete matrix of values is of order $(k+1) \times (k+1)$:

$$
\begin{array}{c}
\textit{Prices in year} \\
\\
\\
0 \\
1 \\
\cdots \\
k
\end{array}
\quad
\begin{array}{c}
\textit{Quantities in year} \\
0 \quad\quad 1 \quad \cdots \quad k \\
\begin{bmatrix}
\Sigma p_0 q_0 & \Sigma p_0 q_1 \cdots \Sigma p_0 q_k \\
\Sigma p_1 q_0 & \Sigma p_1 q_1 \cdots \Sigma p_1 q_k \\
\cdots & \cdots \cdots \cdots \\
\Sigma p_k q_0 & \Sigma p_k q_1 \cdots \Sigma p_k q_k
\end{bmatrix}
\end{array}
$$

The rows correspond to fixed-price valuations; the first row shows the annual sequence of quantities $(q_0, q_1, \ldots q_k)$ at the fixed prices p_0, the second row a similar sequence at the fixed prices p_1, and so on. In the same way, the columns correspond to fixed quantities valued at the annual sequence of prices $(p_0, p_1, \ldots p_k)$.

The notation extends to all kinds of sums and averages, weighted or otherwise. Consider, for example, the prices in two years 0 and 1. Form the *price relative* and use the shorthand notation wherever possible:

$$\frac{p_1}{p_0} \quad \text{for} \quad \frac{p_{i1}}{p_{i0}}(i = 1, 2, 3, \ldots n)$$

Attach weights w to these price relatives, i.e. w_i for the ith commodity $(i = 1, 2, 3, \ldots n)$. The most used average of price relatives is the *arithmetic mean*:

In *unweighted form*

$$\frac{1}{n}\Sigma\frac{p_1}{p_0} = \frac{1}{n}\left(\frac{p_{11}}{p_{10}} + \frac{p_{21}}{p_{20}} + \ldots + \frac{p_{n1}}{p_{n0}}\right)$$

and *with weights* w:

$$\frac{\Sigma w \dfrac{p_1}{p_0}}{\Sigma w} = \frac{w_1 \dfrac{p_{11}}{p_{10}} + w_2 \dfrac{p_{21}}{p_{20}} + \ldots + w_n \dfrac{p_{n1}}{p_{n0}}}{w_1 + w_2 + \ldots + w_n}$$

1.3 Choice of Formula: Stochastic Approach

The stochastic approach to index numbers has the merit of being relatively simple. Following Edgeworth, we are led quickly to the appropriate form of the index. Taking an index of prices for purposes of exposition, and a comparison of prices in two years (0 and 1), we have a simple form of index available: some unweighted mean of the

TABLE 1.1

RETAIL FOOD PRICES, AVERAGE PRICE QUOTATIONS, 1968 AND 1971–74

Item	Unit	Prices, January (d per unit) 1968	1971	1972	1973	1974	Price relatives January 1973 (% of Jan. 1968)	January 1968 (% of Jan. 1973)
Butter, N.Z.	½ lb	20	22	35½	27½	25½	137·5	72·7
Margarine, standard	,,	11	14	15	14½	18½	131·8	75·9
Lard	,,	8	11	11½	10½	17½	131·2*	76·2
Milk, ordinary	pint	10	12	13	13	13	130·0	76·9
Cheese, Cheddar	¼ lb	10¾	12¼	17½	19¼	20	179·1	55·8
Eggs, standard	each	3¾	4½	4	4	9¼	106·7	93·8*
						Sum	816·3	451·3
						Mean	136·0*	75·2

Based on Appendix Table A2

* Rounded to the nearest *even* integer on a conventional rule when the next figure is exactly 5. So 131·25 written 131·2 but 93·75 written 93·8.

price relatives (p_1/p_0) of the commodity prices observed. As a minor development, we may substitute a weighted mean with some simple weighting system which has no reference to quantities of commodities bought and sold.

The approach can be illustrated by a simple example. We seek an index of changes in the general level of retail prices of dairy produce in the period 1971–4 on 1968 as reference base. According to Edgeworth's prescription we should take 'a numerous group of articles' from amongst those classified as dairy produce. To simplify the illustration, we take only six items, those specified in Table 1.1. As some counterweight, we base the prices, in January of each year, on averages obtained by the Department of Employment in their very extensive price collection for the official index of retail prices. The averages are published in the Department of Employment *Gazette* and reproduced in Chapter 3, Appendix Table A2.

On the stochastic approach, we regard the prices of Table 1.1 as samples of all possible price observations. For convenience of the illustration, we have changed the units in which the prices are quoted from those given originally and, at the same time, we have rounded the prices to the nearest $\frac{1}{2}$d for butter, margarine, lard and milk and to the nearest $\frac{1}{4}$d for cheese and eggs. As a result the prices are written in a form easily recognised by the ordinary shopper.

An immediate caution is in order, on the effect of errors of observation and, particularly, of rounding. Price relatives are computed in Table 1.1 for each of the six items between the years 1968 and 1973. They are each shown to one decimal place, as is their sum and the arithmetic mean. Since the prices on which the relatives are based have errors of observation, including rounding, these computations are approximate. We may well decide, and indeed we would in this case, that the individual relatives and their mean can only be given accurately to the nearest whole percentage point, e.g. that the mean price relative in 1973 is 136% of 1968 and in 1968 75% of 1973, since 136·0 and 75·2 cannot be relied on to the first decimal place. However, it is necessary, and indeed standard practice, to carry at least one more figure in the computations than is needed in the result. It is better to round off at the end; too early rounding may fail to give the required accuracy in the result. Similarly, it is convenient, and again standard practice, to quote the result with the extra figure used in the computation; this allows the user to make further computations and to round off when he wishes. The means are given as 136·0 and 75·2 in Table 1.1. It is subject to the important qualification:

Figures should not be regarded as necessarily accurate to the final digit shown.

A qualification on these lines is often given in the source but, whether explicit or not, it needs always to be kept in mind.

Before pursuing the unweighted mean of price relatives, however, we can profitably spend a little time in bringing out into the open the fact that units of measurement in a collection of prices are arbitrary and conventional. There is usually no problem in handling the money unit since all prices can be reduced to a uniform specification, old pence per physical unit in this case. Even here it was necessary to convert from new pence to old pence in prices after 1971. It is in the selection of physical units that the trouble lies. The particular units selected for Table 1.1, different already from those in the source, are changed again in Table 1.2 where they need to match the units in a budget survey (ounces for all items except milk and eggs). We illustrate sufficiently by taking three particularly heterogeneous items from the total list of six: butter, milk and eggs. We also select two years for the comparison: 1968 as year 0 and 1973 as year 1.

It may be maintained that the sum of prices in each situation, $\sum p_0$ and $\sum p_1$, can be first written, and then their ratio taken:

$$I_{01} = \sum p_1 / \sum p_0 \tag{1}$$

as an appropriate index of price change. Alternatively, the form (1) can be interpreted as the ratio of the mean price in year 1 to the mean in year 0; the numerator and denominator in (1) only need division by the number of items, without change in the ratio. The separate price sums are clearly not invariant to changes in units. But the ratio (1) is invariant under some changes, e.g. if all commodities are shown by weight and the unit for all is changed from ounces to pounds. The difficulty is that some changes of units, e.g. from pints to quarts for one item and from each to dozens for another, are not of this simple proportional type. Such changes do affect the ratio (1). Hence I_{01} is not invariant to all changes of units and so not suitable as an index number of price changes.

With our three heterogeneous items as an example, we construct the table on page 14.

The alternative set of prices is exactly equivalent to the first set, and just as recognisable by shoppers. The sums of prices are quite

Prices (d *per unit*)

		Table 1.1			*Alternative*	
		1968	1973		1968	1973
Item	*Unit*	p_0	p_1	*Unit*	p_0	p_1
Butter	½ lb	20	27½	¼ lb	10	13¾
Milk	pint	10	13	pint	10	13
Eggs	each	3¾	4	doz	45	48
Sum		33¾	44½		65	74¾
$I_{01}\%$ of 1968			131·9			115·0

different and have no more than an artificial meaning. In 1968, for example, 33¾d is just the sum needed to buy ½ lb of butter, one pint of milk and one egg. At the same prices, in 1968, 65d is just the sum needed for a different lot of purchases: ¼ lb butter, one pint of milk, twelve eggs. The sums mean no more than this. Similarly, when the corresponding 1973 sums are found and the ratio I_{01} written, the result with the first set of units (131·9% of 1968) is quite different from that with the second set of units (115·0% of 1968). These are not just alternative and equally acceptable measures of the general price change. The value of I_{01} is completely at the mercy of the units selected and it is no kind of index at all.

It is to be particularly noted, in line with the Edgeworth stochastic approach, that the price relatives computed in Table 1.1 are invariant under this change, or indeed under any change, of physical units. The numerator and denominator are changed in proportion. It follows that the *mean of the ratios* (price relatives) of the three items in 1973 is invariant: $\frac{1}{3}(137·5 + 130·0 + 106·7) = 124·7\%$ of 1968. The *ratio of the means* is something quite different: $I_{01} = 131·9$ with one set of units, 115·0 with another, and still other values for further changes in units.

Our conclusion is that, for an appropriate price index on the stochastic approach, we write some average of observed price relatives. The remaining question is what particular average: arithmetic mean, geometric mean, median, or some other. We can start with the most commonly used average, the arithmetic mean, and write for a price change from year 0 to year 1:

$$AM_{01} = \frac{1}{n}\sum\frac{p_1}{p_0} \tag{2}$$

As a notation – both conventional and convenient – to be followed throughout, the order of the subscripts in (2) indicates that year 1 is being compared with year 0 as a reference base. A different arithmetic mean can be written from price relatives in the reverse direction:

$$AM_{10} = \frac{1}{n}\sum\frac{p_0}{p_1} \tag{3}$$

This is an index in which year 0 is compared with year 1 as reference base. The computation of the forms (2) and (3) from actual data is very simple in the case of the data of Table 1.1; all the work is shown in the last two columns. The forms are written as ratios so that the means of Table 1.1 need to be divided by 100:

$$AM_{01} = 1\cdot360 \quad \text{and} \quad AM_{10} = 0\cdot752$$

Index numbers, however, are commonly quoted and interpreted in percentage form, with one particular year taken as 100. Here, the two index numbers can be written:

Price index 1973 = 136·0   and   Price index 1968 = 75·2
(1968 = 100)   (1973 = 100)

We need to be flexible, sometimes writing an index as a ratio and sometimes multiplying by 100 to write it as a percentage.

We would like the forms (2) and (3) to have a property which is an extension of what we have for a simple ratio such as a price relative. A ratio in one direction is the reciprocal of that in the other direction, as illustrated in **1.1** above. For example, if a price rises from £12–15, the forward price relative is $15/12 = 1\cdot25$ and backward it is $12/15 = 0\cdot80$. These are reciprocals one of the other since $1\cdot25 \times 0\cdot80 = 1$. All that this property expresses is that percentages work in this reciprocal way, e.g. 25% up corresponds to 20% down. So all the price relatives of the last two columns of Table 1.1 are reciprocals of each other when written in ratio form, e.g. $0\cdot727 = 1/1\cdot375$.

By extension, the desirable property for index numbers of forms (2) and (3) is:

$$AM_{01} \times AM_{10} = 1 \quad \text{i.e.} \quad AM_{01} = 1/AM_{10}$$

Taking the reciprocal merely reverses the direction of the comparison, switching between the years 0 and 1 as 100. In one and the same direction, year 1 on year 0 as 100, the two forms are AM_{01} and $1/AM_{10}$. We would like these to be equal. Similarly, with year 0 on year 1 as 100, the two forms we would like to be equal are AM_{10} and $1/AM_{01}$.

In fact, the desired property, though true of individual price relatives, is *not* true of their arithmetic means. The relation which does hold, for any price relatives not all equal, is:

$$AM_{01} > 1/AM_{10} \tag{4}$$

In the trivial case where all price relatives are equal (all prices move in proportion), the inequality in (4) is replaced by equality.

The proof of this result can be conveniently set out in two steps. At the first stage, the point to appreciate is that AM_{01} and AM_{10} are not so much *unweighted* means as *equi-weighted* means. It follows that the two forms have *different* sets of equal weights and so *different* index numbers of the same price changes. AM_{01} is based on weights which assign £1 each to all commodities at year-0 prices; AM_{10} has £1 each at year-1 prices. Because of differential price movements the two forms have different weighting. At the second step, we establish that the two different index numbers are always related as in (4). A simple but formal proof is offered below. In the meantime it is important to see, more informally, why the relation must hold.

AM_{01} is based on equal weighting of commodities, £1 spent on each at year-0 prices. The relative movements of prices will have disturbed this by year 1 when more is spent on items with larger price increases than those with smaller rises. Hence AM_{01} is more influenced by items with large price rises than is the alternative index, based as it is on equal weighting in year 1. Taking changes from year 0 to year 1, we use $1/AM_{10}$ to conform with AM_{01}. The items with larger prices rises carry greater weight in AM_{01} than in $1/AM_{10}$ and so the former exceeds the latter, as stated by (4).

Table 1.1 illustrates. The index AM_{01} has equal expenditure weighting of commodities in 1968. As long as the same quantities are bought, as implied by AM_{01}, the expenditure weighting becomes unequal in 1973. But the index $1/AM_{10}$ has equal weighting in 1973. Hence butter and cheese with high price rises dominate in AM_{01}; milk and eggs with low price rises dominate in $1/AM_{10}$. In this case the difference is quite considerable since $AM_{01} = 136 \cdot 0 \%$ and $1/AM_{10} = 100/0 \cdot 752 = 133 \cdot 0 \%$. The property (4) is confirmed:

$$AM_{01} = 136 \cdot 0 > 133 \cdot 0 = 1/AM_{10}$$

with both index numbers written for 1973 on 1968 as reference base.

It is important not to confuse the relation between two *different* index numbers (and the fact that one is not the reciprocal of the other) with the rule of 1.1 above on the arithmetic switch of reference base. As between two years, such a switch in a *given* index always involves taking the reciprocal. Relation (4) itself illustrates: AM_{10} on year 1 as reference base is switched to $1/AM_{10}$ on year 0.

The relation (4) is very important. It will arise again when we consider weighted-average index numbers in **1.4** below (and, more precisely, in Chapter 2). The clue is that AM_{01} is a *base-weighted* index, i.e. equi-weighted in year 0, whereas $1/AM_{10}$ is a *current-weighted* index, i.e. equi-weighted in year 1. We shall not be surprised to find, at least for index numbers of retail prices, that the base-weighted form is larger than the current-weighted.

It is as well that the reversible property is described as desirable rather than essential; otherwise the arithmetic mean would need to be rejected out of hand. This is particularly so in view of the fact that there is an appropriate index which, as Edgeworth found, does satisfy the reversible condition. The index is the unweighted geometric mean; in our notation, with Π for product replacing $\sum$ for sum, it is:

$$GM_{01} = \sqrt[n]{\left(\Pi \frac{p_1}{p_0} \right)} \quad \text{and} \quad GM_{10} = \sqrt[n]{\left(\Pi \frac{p_0}{p_1} \right)}$$

It follows at once that the reversible property holds:

$$GM_{01} \times GM_{10} = 1 \quad \text{or} \quad GM_{01} = 1/GM_{10}$$

The computation of the geometric mean is best done from a logarithmic transform of the formula:

$$\log GM_{01} = \frac{1}{n} \sum \log \frac{p_1}{p_0}$$

i.e. take logs of the price relatives, compute the arithmetic mean and get GM_{01} as its antilog. From the data of Table 1.1:

	Price relatives		Logarithms of:	
	1973	1968		
Item	(1968 = 100)	(1973 = 100)		
	(1)	(2)	(1)	(2)
Butter	137·5	72·7	2·1383	1·8615
Margarine	131·8	75·9	2·1199	1·8802
Lard	131·2	76·2	2·1180	1·8820
Milk	130·0	76·9	2·1139	1·8859
Cheese	179·1	55·8	2·2531	1·7466
Eggs	106·7	93·8	2·0281	1·9722
		Sum	12·7713	11·2284
		Arithmetic mean	2·12855	1·8714
		Geometric mean	134·5	74·37

Hence the two index numbers as geometric means are:

Price index 1973 = 134·5   and   Price index 1968 = 74·37
      (1968 = 100)   (1973 = 100)

The one is the reciprocal of the other:

$$GM_{01} = 1·345 \quad \text{and} \quad 1/GM_{10} = 1/0·7437 = 1·345$$

It is a well known and easily established result that the arithmetic mean is greater than the geometric for any items averaged which are not all equal. This is checked in the numerical illustration: $AM_{01} = 136·0\%$ and $GM_{01} = 134·5\%$. The result is used in the following simple derivation of property (4). We have:

$$AM_{01} > GM_{01} \quad \text{and} \quad AM_{10} > GM_{10}$$

Since the geometric mean is reversible:

$$GM_{01} = 1/GM_{10} > 1/AM_{10}$$

and so:

$$AM_{01} > GM_{01} > 1/AM_{10}$$

Property (4) holds. Moreover, the geometric mean falls between the two arithmetic-mean forms.

On the strict stochastic approach, we come up with the unweighted geometric mean as the preferred form of index. We shall, in the end, reverse this decision. We adopt the arithmetic mean despite the fact that it lacks the reversible property; we reject the geometric mean despite the fact that it is reversible. The reason is that the stochastic approach makes us lose touch with the *economic* as opposed to the statistical aspects of index numbers. The geometric index does not make economic sense; the arithmetic index does. This is the theme of the following story.

1.4 Choice of Formula: Aggregative/Weighted Average Approach

The alternative approach, hastily discarded by Edgeworth but rescued by Keynes, was also explored in the context of the general price level or the value of money. It makes use both of prices and of quantities bought and sold; it develops price and quantity index numbers side by side and in the context of particular value aggregates for specified groups of individuals. The index numbers are defined

TABLE 1.2

FOOD PRICE INDEX, LOW-INCOME PENSIONER HOUSEHOLDS, 1968 AND 1973.
TWO EQUIVALENT METHODS OF COMPUTATION

Item	Unit	Budget* 1968 q	Prices, January (d per unit) 1968 p_0	1973 p_1	Cost of budget (d) at prices of: 1968 p_0q	1973 p_1q	Weight (p_0q as %) w_0	Price relatives $\frac{p_1}{p_0}$	Product $w_0\frac{p_1}{p_0}$
Butter, N.Z.	oz	7·21	2·50	3·44	18·025	24·802	17·1	137·6	2353·0
Margarine, standard	,,	3·09	1·38	1·81	4·264	5·593	4·0	131·2	524·8
Lard	,,	2·74	1·00	1·31	2·740	3·589	2·6	131·0	340·6
Milk, ordinary	pint	5·31	10·00	13·00	53·100	69·030	50·4	130·0	6552·0
Cheese, Cheddar	oz	3·71	2·69	4·81	9·980	17·845	9·5	178·8	1698·6
Eggs, standard	each	4·62	3·75	4·00	17·325	18·480	16·4	106·7	1749·9
Total					105·434	139·339	100		13218·9

Based on Appendix Table A3 and Table 1.1

* Consumption, first quarter 1968, units per head per week.

and interpreted as ratios of value aggregates and computed in equivalent form as weighted arithmetic means.

The development is most easily seen in terms of an index of retail prices, illustrated by computations from actual data. To the price data of Table 1.1, we add budget data obtained from the National Food Survey, on the consumption of dairy produce by low-income pensioner households. The budget data used are quantities consumed in the first quarter of 1968, taken from Chapter 3, Appendix Table A3. The data are assembled in Table 1.2 where we have made the two separate lots of data match in their physical units by reducing all prices (except milk and eggs) to d per oz. We have to assume, for purposes of the present calculation, that the data also match in the sense that the pensioner families providing the budgets do, on average, pay the prices derived from the price collections of the Department of Employment. Once this is granted, we have a particular value aggregate, the total expenditure on dairy produce, of the group of low-income pensioner families.

The form of price index put up for calculation is defined and interpreted as showing the changing cost, as prices change, of continuing to buy the fixed (1968) budget:

$$P_{01}(q) = \frac{\sum p_1 q}{\sum p_0 q} \tag{1}$$

where q is the fixed budget, p_0 the prices in year 0 (1968) and p_1 the prices in year 1 (1973). As before, the two subscripts in (1) show that year 1 is compared with year 0. P is used to indicate a price index, and q added in brackets to specify the particular budget fixed. By simple algebraic manipulation:

$$P_{01}(q) = \sum w_0 \frac{p_1}{p_0} / \sum w_0 \qquad (w_0 = p_0 q) \tag{2}$$

where the weights $w_0 = p_0 q$ are equal to the cost of the fixed budget in the base year 0. The two forms (1) and (2) are precisely and algebraically equivalent. The 'changing-cost' or ratio-of-aggregates definition (1) is equivalent to the weighted-average form (2).

There is one simple but important result which follows at once from the weighted-average form (2). It is that only *proportionate weights* need be used in the weighted average. All the weights w_0 for the various items can be increased or decreased in proportion (e.g. from d to £) without affecting the index; the effect on the numerator is exactly matched by the effect on the denominator. It is quite usual, and valid on this result, to take weights in percentage (or per 1,000) form. Percentage weights are used in Table 1.2.

In the numerical case of Table 1.2 each of them is computed and the results found to be identical. The actual computation is carried through with two decimal places (for prices and quantities) in order to obtain a price index correct (at least) to the nearest percentage point. The results are:

$$\text{Price index 1973} \atop (1968 = 100) = \frac{139 \cdot 339}{105 \cdot 434} \, 100 \quad \text{from the budget costs}$$

$$= \frac{13218 \cdot 9}{100} \quad \text{from the weighted average}$$

$$= 132 \cdot 2$$

The index can be compared with the unweighted arithmetic mean in 1973:

$$AM_{01} = 136 \cdot 0\% \text{ of 1968}$$

The effect of weighting is to reduce the value of the index; this is because by far the biggest weight, the biggest item in consumption of dairy produce, is provided by milk with a below-average rise in price from 1968 to 1973.

The interpretation of the result is best given from the definition (1). The cost of purchasing the given 1968 budget, of the pensioner families considered, rose by 32·2% between 1968 and 1973. The computation can be by either formula (1) or (2). Often, in practice, the proportionate value weights w_0 are better defined than the quantitative budget q; the weighted-average form (2) is then the practical one.

In the form (1), and its equivalent (2), the fixed budget q is quite arbitrary. If this means that any old budget will do, then the problem is quite trivial as well as arbitrary. It is essential that some *relevant* budget q be defined and used in the index (1). A clue is provided by the numerical illustration of Table 1.2 in which the budget q is selected as that appropriate to the base-year set of quantities q_0 and the index is the *base-weighted* form:

$$P_{01}(q_0) = \frac{\sum p_1 q_0}{\sum p_0 q_0} \tag{3}$$

For a comparison between two years only, and with year 0 selected as base, there is one alternative. That is to use the budget q_1 from the quantities of the year 1. The index is then of *current-weighted* form:

$$P_{01}(q_1) = \frac{\sum p_1 q_1}{\sum p_0 q_1} \tag{4}$$

Whereas (3) gives the changing cost, from 1968 to 1973, of buying the fixed 1968 budget, (4) gives a comparison of the cost in 1973 of the 1973 budget with the cost of this budget at the prices of 1968. Everything is completely symmetrical. It is only the fact that we have opted to go from year 0 to year 1 (forward from 1968 to 1973) that enables us to distinguish one as base-weighted and the other as current-weighted.

The budget data of the National Food Survey provide the quantities for the first quarter of 1973 as well as those of 1968. The combination both ways, on the aggregative formulae (3) and (4), is set out in Table 1.3. The index (3) is the one already got; the index (4) is the new one.

The price index 1973 (1968 = 100) is:

Base-weighted $\dfrac{139 \cdot 339}{105 \cdot 434} \; 100 = 132 \cdot 2$

Current-weighted $\dfrac{140 \cdot 456}{106 \cdot 155} \; 100 = 132 \cdot 3$

Here, unlike the simpler forms of **1.3** above, we find that the base-weighted and current-weighted forms do not differ, apart from small rounding and other errors, in this particular case.

One advantage of this approach is that the corresponding index numbers of quantity are defined and computed. Interchange of p's and q's in formulae (3) and (4) give quantity index numbers:

Base-weighted $Q_{01}(p_0) = \dfrac{\sum p_0 q_1}{\sum p_0 q_0}$ (5)

Current-weighted $Q_{01}(p_1) = \dfrac{\sum p_1 q_1}{\sum p_1 q_0}$ (6)

These come, by another permutation, from the same set of four value aggregates in the numerical case of Table 1.3. The quantity index in 1973 (1968 = 100) is:

Base-weighted $\dfrac{106 \cdot 155}{105 \cdot 434} \; 100 = 100 \cdot 7$

TABLE 1.3

FOOD CONSUMPTION AND PRICES, LOW-INCOME PENSIONER HOUSEHOLDS, 1968 AND 1973. ALTERNATIVE PRICE AND QUANTITY INDEX NUMBERS

Item	Unit	Budgets*		Prices, January (d per unit)		Products (d)			
		1968 q_0	1973 q_1	1968 p_0	1973 p_1	p_0q_0	p_0q_1	p_1q_0	p_1q_1
Butter, N.Z.	oz	7·21	6·23	2·50	3·44	18·025	15·575	24·802	21·431
Margarine, standard	,,	3·09	3·76	1·38	1·81	4·264	5·189	5·593	6·806
Lard	,,	2·74	2·66	1·00	1·31	2·740	2·660	3·589	3·485
Milk, ordinary	pint	5·31	5·47	10·00	13·00	53·100	54·700	69·030	71·110
Cheese, Cheddar	oz	3·71	3·98	2·69	4·81	9·980	10·706	17·845	19·144
Eggs, standard	each	4·62	4·62	3·75	4·00	17·325	17·325	18·480	18·480
Total						105·434	106·155	139·339	140·456

Based on Appendix Table A3 and Table 1.1.

* Consumption, first quarters, units per head per week.

Current-weighted $\dfrac{140 \cdot 456}{139 \cdot 339}$ $100 = 100 \cdot 8$

Some conclusions can now be drawn about the changes from 1968 to 1973 in the consumption of dairy produce by low-income pensioner families. The value of consumption increases by 33% from 1968 to 1973; this is not an index number since it is obtained by division from the values in 1968 (105·434d) and in 1973 (140·456d). The effect of price rises in the period is shown by one or other of the two price index numbers, i.e. 132% to the nearest percentage point. We can say that the price increase for dairy produce is 32%, little less than the rise in the value of consumption. Hence, for these families, the real consumption of dairy produce hardly varied from 1968 to 1973. A measure of the change is to be got from the two alternative index numbers of quantity, enough to say that it was a small increase of less than 1%. This kind of analysis is explored more precisely in Chapter 2.

The price index numbers (3) and (4) have a clear *economic* interpretation; the changing cost of a *fixed and specific budget* purchased by a specified group of consumers. The two index numbers differ only according to which of the two budgets, for year 0 or for year 1, is taken for costing. Equally, the quantity index in form (5) or (6) has a clear *economic* meaning. The value aggregates related are consumers' expenditures at *constant prices*, instead of at current prices. The base-weighted index, for example, compares consumers' expenditure at constant (base-year) prices. This is consumers' expenditure in real terms, as understood by the economist.

The convenient matrix notation, with the convention about rows and columns agreed upon in **1.2** above, can now be brought in, both generally and in the numerical case of Table 1.3. The 2×2 matrix of value aggregates, with the convention that prices are constant across rows and quantities fixed down columns, is in general and in the particular case:

	Value matrix *Quantities in year*			*Example* *Quantities in year*	
Prices in year	*0*	*1*	*Prices in year*	*1968*	*1972*
0	$\begin{bmatrix} \Sigma p_0 q_0 & \Sigma p_0 q_1 \\[2mm] \Sigma p_1 q_0 & \Sigma p_1 q_1 \end{bmatrix}$		1968	$\begin{bmatrix} 105 \cdot 4\text{d} & 106 \cdot 2 \\ \text{per week} & \\ 139 \cdot 3 & 140 \cdot 5 \end{bmatrix}$	
1			1972		

The price and quantity index numbers, of base-weighted and of current-weighted form, are all to be read off the 2×2 value matrix.

The computational rule is simple enough for the base-weighted forms if rather less so for the current-weighted.

To get the base-weighted index numbers, we read down the first column of the value matrix (with fixed quantities q_0) to obtain the price index, and across the first row (with fixed prices p_0) for the quantity index. Each is the ratio of the two values, in the column and row respectively. The current-weighted forms make use of the other pair of values in each case; these are in the second column of the value matrix for the price index and in the second row for the quantity index. For reasons which appear when we deal with runs of index numbers, we do well to describe the current-weighted index numbers as obtained by taking the current value (bottom right-hand corner of value matrix) and by dividing it by the corresponding value – above in the first row for the price index, to the left in the first column for the quantity index. It is all very convenient in practice.

Conventional labels are hung on the pairs of index numbers, (3) and (4) for price, (5) and (6) for quantity. The base-weighted forms are called *Laspeyres index numbers*:

$$\text{Price } P_{01}(q_0) = \frac{\sum p_1 q_0}{\sum p_0 q_0} \qquad \text{Quantity } Q_{01}(p_0) = \frac{\sum p_0 q_1}{\sum p_0 q_0} \qquad (7)$$

and the current-weighted forms are called *Paasche index numbers*:

$$\text{Price } P_{01}(q_1) = \frac{\sum p_1 q_1}{\sum p_0 q_1} \qquad \text{Quantity } Q_{01}(p_1) = \frac{\sum p_1 q_1}{\sum p_1 q_0} \qquad (8)$$

The labels come from the names of two early writers on index numbers: Laspeyres (1864) and Paasche (1874).*

It is to be noted, however, that the two-situation analysis given here is entirely symmetrical. The two years taken are completely interchangeable. The distinction between the Laspeyres index (7) and the Paasche index (8) arises only because we write the two years 0 and 1, select year 0 as the **reference base** and measure all changes of price and quantity forward from year 0 to the **current year** 1. The labels in (7) and (8) depend essentially on the order of the two subscripts in P_{01} and Q_{01}. We can just as well opt to take the comparison the other way and to select P_{10} and Q_{10}: (7) and (8) then need to be revised so

---

* The two forms were first introduced by these writers; the first occasion on which their names were used as labels was probably in Walsh (1901). Laspeyres is quite often mis-spelt as Laspeyre or with a misplaced apostrophe: Laspeyre's. There can be lax proof-reading even by the best of authors.

that the Laspeyres label goes with the q_1 (or p_1) weights, and the Paasche label with the q_0 (or p_0) weights.

This sounds confusing, and indeed it may well be so. For the moment, since the labels are in common use, we will keep them as alternative names; **Laspeyres for a base-weighted index, Paasche for a current-weighted index.** The labels become much more convenient and unambiguous when we deal with runs of index numbers over the years $t = 0, 1, 2, 3, \ldots$ Laspeyres then describes an index with a **fixed** set of weights over the years, and Paasche an index in which the **variable** set of weights is taken always from the current year.

There is often a snag in computational practice, one which precludes the calculation of the alternative index numbers of Laspeyres and Paasche forms. Consider the possibilities for a price index. In some cases, quantities are available as a budget in one year only, usually year 0, selected as the base of the price index. The computation is then limited to the calculation of only one price index in year 1; this is the Laspeyres (base-weighted) index in ratio-of-aggregates form (7). The calculation is illustrated by the first five columns of Table 1.2. In other cases, no quantities are available at all. Instead some data on the value of expenditure in the base year 0 may be available, from a source divorced from the prices and of a nature not strictly comparable with the prices. The expenditure data may, however, be good enough to give proportional weights to apply to price relatives. The Laspeyres (base-weighted) index can then be estimated as a weighted average of form (2), with $w_0 = p_0 q_0$ estimated in percentages, as illustrated by the last three columns of Table 1.2.

It follows that, though the aggregative and weighted-average computations are equivalent, the one approach or the other tends to dominate in any specific application. The *aggregative approach* is the appropriate one when dealing with consumers' expenditure by means of quantitative budgets. A price index is then a ratio of aggregates, to be interpreted as the changing cost of a fixed budget. On the other hand, the *weighted-average approach* is to be followed when value weights are estimated to apply to price relatives obtained from a price collection made for the purpose. This is the way in which the official retail price index is in fact computed. But, even when the index computed is a weighted average, the equivalent ratio-of-aggregates form is still there implicitly, supporting the weighted average and allowing the index to be interpreted as the changing cost of purchasing a fixed budget.

1.5 Runs of Index Numbers: Switching and Splicing

We pass now from the case of index numbers in two years ($t = 0$, 1) to the more general case of an indefinite sequence of years $t = 0$, 1, 2, 3, ... We start with the simplest case so that the basic problems can be seen emerging; in each year we have complete price data p_t on n commodity items and we take no account of the corresponding quantity data even if known. The price index in any year s is taken as the unweighted arithmetic mean of price relatives based on a selected year r. Generalising (2) and (3) of **1.3** above, we write

$$AM_{rs} = \frac{1}{n}\sum\frac{p_s}{p_r} \quad (r \text{ and } s = 0, 1, 2, 3, \ldots)$$

Here r and s are any integers. If r and s are the same, we have $AM_{rr} = 1$ (100%); if r and s are different, there are two index numbers according to the direction of the comparison:

$$AM_{rs} = \frac{1}{n}\sum\frac{p_s}{p_r} \quad \text{and} \quad AM_{sr} = \frac{1}{n}\sum\frac{p_r}{p_s}$$

To illustrate, use the price data of Table 1.1 for six items of dairy produce and select two alternative base years, 1968 and 1972. Two different series of price index numbers are calculated in Table 1.4. As indicated in the table, the first series consists of AM_{0t} for $t = 1, 2, 3, 4$ and here all price relatives are calculated on 1968 as 100. The second series has AM_{2t} for $t = 0, 1, 3, 4$, from price relatives based on 1972 as 100. The two series are different; they are differently based. To get from one series to the other implies a complete recalculation, a *rebasing* of the index.

There is an alternative: a purely arithmetic *switching* of the reference base from the original year to some other year, a process already illustrated (**1.1** above). This can be done with any one series, e.g. with either one or the other of the two series of Table 1.4. It does *not* change the weighting of the series and the relative magnitudes of the successive index numbers remain unaltered. Take, as our example, the first series of Table 1.4:

$$AM_{0t} \quad \text{for } t = 0, 1, 2, 3, 4 \text{ (where } AM_{00} = 1)$$

and switch the reference base (the year taken as 100) from year 0 to year 2. Divide the series through by AM_{02} and get the series:

$$AM'_{2t} = \frac{AM_{0t}}{AM_{02}} \quad \text{for } t = 0, 1, 2, 3, 4 \text{ (where } AM'_{22} = 1)$$

TABLE 1.4

FOOD PRICE QUOTATIONS, MEANS OF PRICE RELATIVES, 1968 AND 1971–4

Price relatives, January

Item	January 1968 = 100					January 1972 = 100				
	1968	1971	1972	1973	1974	1968	1971	1972	1973	1974
Butter, N.Z.	100	110·0	177·5	137·5	127·5	56·3	62·0	100	77·5	71·8
Margarine, standard	100	127·3	136·4	131·8	168·2	73·3	93·3	100	96·7	123·3
Lard	100	137·5	143·8	131·2	218·8	69·6	95·7	100	91·3	152·2
Milk, ordinary	100	120·0	130·0	130·0	130·0	76·9	92·3	100	100·0	100·0
Cheese, Cheddar	100	114·0	162·8	179·1	186·0	61·4	70·0	100	110·0	114·3
Eggs, standard	100	120·0	106·7	106·7	246·7	93·8	112·5	100	100·0	231·2
Total	600	728·8	857·2	816·3	1077·2	431·3	525·8	600	575·5	792·8
Arithmetic mean	100	121·5	142·9	136·0	179·5	71·9	87·6	100	95·9	132·1
Notation: year	0	1	2	3	4	0	1	2	3	4
Arithmetic mean	(AM_{00})	AM_{01}	AM_{02}	AM_{03}	AM_{04}	AM_{20}	AM_{21}	(AM_{22})	AM_{23}	AM_{24}

From Table 1.1

This is the same series as before (i.e. the same weighting) but re-scaled to make year 2 (AM'_{22}) as 100 instead of year 0 (AM_{00}). It is to be contrasted with the differently weighted series calculated direct on year 2:

AM_{2t} for $t = 0, 1, 2, 3, 4$ (where $AM_{22} = 1$)

These happen to have the same year as 100 but with different weighting. It would be useful if we had the property

$$AM_{2t} = \frac{AM_{0t}}{AM_{02}}$$

i.e. $AM_{02} \times AM_{2t} = AM_{0t}$

This is a circular or *transitive* property. As a particular case ($t = 0$):

$$AM_{02} \times AM_{20} = AM_{00} = 1 \qquad \text{or} \qquad AM_{02} = 1/AM_{20}$$

which is the reversible property examined in connection with property (4) of **1.3** above. For arithmetic means (though not for geometric means) the property is lacking in the transitive form as in the particular reversible form. It follows that, starting with the series AM_{0t} based on year 0, the series AM'_{2t} got by *switching* the reference base to year 2 differs from the series AM_{2t} which results from *re-basing* on year 2.

This is made clear by an examination of Table 1.4:

		1968	1971	1972	1973	1974
A	Based on 1968, 1968 = 100	100	121·5	142·9	136·0	179·5
A'	Based on 1968, switched to 1972 = 100	70·0	85·0	100	95·2	125·6
B	Based on 1972, 1972 = 100	71·9	87·6	100	95·9	132·1
B'	Based on 1972, switched to 1968 = 100	100	121·8	139·1	133·4	183·7

Here, A and A' are the same series, one being a rescaled version of the other; A' is got from A by division by 1·429 and A is got from A' by division by 0·700. In particular, 1·429 and 0·700 are reciprocal to each other (see **1.1** above). Similarly, B and B' are the same, with the same relative changes from year to year. But A' and B can be directly compared, both having 1972 = 100, and by their definition they are different index numbers (differently based). They are also seen to be different. Similarly A and B', both with 1968 = 100, are different and are seen to be different.

The conclusion is:

The arithmetical process of switching the reference base of an index from one year to another is a matter of convenience only; it does not change the index and relative values between any years are unaltered.

The second problem to consider is the splicing together of two different series of index numbers, the first on one base and the second on another base. The problem arises typically in the situation where a price index is required for a fairly long run and where two index numbers are available each covering only part of the run. If the two different series cover the run between them and if they have at least one year in common, then they can be spliced together by equating them in a common year. The question is whether this arithmetic procedure is valid.

There is such a problem for any series of magnitudes in which ratios are taken to make one year equal to 100, and not only for index numbers. The coverage or scope of the series can change over the years, producing two or more non-comparable runs which need to be spliced together. The arithmetic process of splicing, and the assumption which supports it, can be seen by pursuing an actual example already used **(1.1)**. We require a continuous series, from 1965 to 1972, of employment in manufacturing industries in Great Britain. We have at each mid-June date:

| Mid-June | Numbers of employees, 000's | | | Ratios | | | Spliced ratios |
	Pre-1966 basis	1966–9 basis	Post-1969 basis	1965 =100	1966 =100	1969 =100	1965 =100
1965	8,847			100			100
1966	8,868	8,976		100·2	100		100·2
1967		8,701			96·9		97·1
1968		8,613			96·0		96·2
1969		8,729	8,741		97·2	100	97·4
1970			8,727			99·8	97·2
1971			8,432			96·5	94·0
1972			8,062			92·2	89·8

From *Monthly Digest of Statistics*

The basis of the estimation has been changed by the Department of the Employment on two occasions in this run of eight years. To get a comparable set of figures, e.g. to estimate employment in 1972 as a percentage of that in 1965, each separate series is reduced to employment in the starting year as 100 and the three series spliced together, in 1966 and in 1969. The 1966 splice is got by multiplying 100·2 in 1966 by the next series which starts at 100 in 1966. The spliced 1969 figure is:

$$100·2 \times 97·2 = 97·4$$

A second splice is now made by multiplying this 1969 figure by the third series starting at 100 in 1969. The spliced 1972 figure is:

$$100·2 \times 97·2 \times 92·2 = 89·8$$

The final column of spliced ratios is got in this way.

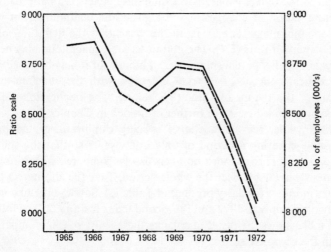

FIG. 1.1 No. of employees on three bases

The assumption on which the splicing depends is easily specified. Starting with the first (1965–6) series, we assume that it could be continued and would then move in parallel with the second (1966–9) series in the sense of showing the same percentage changes. Further, either of these series is then assumed to continue and move in parallel with the third series from 1969. Figure 1.1 illustrates, drawn on ratio scales to show parallel percentage movements. The three series are each a little higher than the previous one but assumed to be changing in parallel. The assumption is a fairly reasonable one. In any case, we generally have no alternative.

The same splicing process is needed for successive runs of annual index numbers with overlaps of at least one year. Indeed it is more frequently needed since, for a variety of reasons (**1.7** below), a given index soon gets out of date and eventually ceases to be computable at all. A substitute must then be produced, an index of different construction and of different interpretation. Though the splicing is more urgently needed, it is not strictly justified. It cannot be assumed that the first index could be continued to show parallel movements with the second index; it comes to an end simply because it cannot be continued at all.

The justification for splicing runs of index numbers rests on broader and less secure grounds. It is that each run, though different in form or interpretation (e.g. based on a different budget), is an approximate representation of changes in some given and continuing, but non-observable, magnitude. It is on this basis that the definition of an index number rests (**1.1**). The non-observable magnitude may be left as vague as the 'purchasing power of money' or it may be based on a theoretical concept of a 'true' index, as with the constant-utility index of the theory of value (**2.8** below). The implications of the splicing of index runs are further examined in Chapter 4.

Meanwhile, the arithmetic of splicing can be illustrated in an example covering a period of only a few years so that the splicing of two short runs of index numbers can be compared with runs continuously available over the whole period. Take the alternative price index numbers for dairy produce of Table 1.4. Suppose the first index is available only to 1972 and the second index from 1972. The following table shows the result of splicing these short runs in comparison with the complete series:

	1968	1971	1972	1973	1974
Spliced series:					
Series based on 1968	*100*	121·5	142·9		
Series based on 1972			*100*	95·9	132·1
Spliced series	*100*	121·5	142·9	137·0	188·8
Complete series:					
Based on 1968	*100*	121·5	142·9	136·0	179·5
Based on 1972 and switched to 1968 = 100	*100*	121·8	139·1	133·4	183·7

The splicing is done here in a single year common to the two series. In practice two runs of annual index numbers may overlap by more than one year. There is then a choice: the runs may be spliced together in any one year or over an average of years in the overlap. There is generally no unique result of the application of the splicing technique. The method is empirical and approximate, the more so the longer the period the index numbers need to cover.

1.6 Runs of Aggregative Index Numbers

It remains to provide an analysis of the main case: runs of aggregative/weighted average index numbers. For illustration, we take index numbers of price and quantity for aggregate consumers' expenditure, as for low-income pensioner families in Table 1.3 but for a comprehensive set of items and for a whole run of years. On the notation of **1.2**, computations give a matrix of direct and cross valuations of consumers' expenditure:

$$
\begin{array}{c}
\begin{array}{l}
\textit{Prices in} \\
\textit{year}
\end{array}
\quad
\begin{array}{cccc}
\textit{Quantities in year} \\
0 \quad 1 \quad 2 \quad 3 \quad \cdots
\end{array}
\\
\begin{array}{c}
0 \\ 1 \\ 2 \\ 3 \\ \cdots
\end{array}
\left[
\begin{array}{ccccc}
\sum p_0 q_0 & \sum p_0 q_1 & \sum p_0 q_2 & \sum p_0 q_3 & \cdots \\
\sum p_1 q_0 & \sum p_1 q_1 & \sum p_1 q_2 & \sum p_1 q_3 & \cdots \\
\sum p_2 q_0 & \sum p_2 q_1 & \sum p_2 q_2 & \sum p_2 q_3 & \cdots \\
\sum p_3 q_0 & \sum p_3 q_1 & \sum p_3 q_2 & \sum p_3 q_3 & \cdots \\
\cdots & \cdots & \cdots & \cdots & \cdots
\end{array}
\right]
\end{array}
$$

The key to the reading of this matrix can be described as follows. The values down the *leading diagonal*:

$$\sum p_0 q_0 \qquad \sum p_1 q_1 \qquad \sum p_2 q_2 \qquad \sum p_3 q_3 \qquad \cdots \qquad (1)$$

make a sequence of actual consumers' expenditures year by year. There is no problem of switching; the series can be expressed as a sequence of ratios with any year as 100. Nor is there any splicing problem unless for some reason the values become non-comparable, as with the employment series used above.

The values down the *first column* give a sequence which is the changing cost of the fixed consumers' budget of the base year (q_0) at successive years' prices:

$$\sum p_0 q_0 \qquad \sum p_1 q_0 \qquad \sum p_2 q_0 \qquad \sum p_3 q_0 \qquad \cdots \qquad (2)$$

Dividing through by the first value, we get the series of Laspeyres (base-weighted) price index numbers. In the same way, reading across the *first row*:

$$\sum p_0 q_0 \qquad \sum p_0 q_1 \qquad \sum p_0 q_2 \qquad \sum p_0 q_3 \qquad \cdots \qquad (3)$$

give the series of consumers' expenditure at fixed (base-year) prices instead of at current prices (1). Dividing through by the first term, we get Laspeyres (base-weighted) quantity index numbers. The computation of (2) and (3) cannot be continued indefinitely in practice. It involves the matching of prices in one year and quantities in another, a process which sooner or later becomes impossible because of changes in the complex of commodities on the market. It is here that the problems of splicing one series on another arise, to be pursued later (Chapter 4).

Meanwhile suppose that price and quantity index numbers of Laspeyres (base-weighted) form are available for consumers' expenditure over a run of years. There is then a choice of presentation which is of considerable practical importance. The price index is got from the sequence (2) by division by the *constant* base value $\sum p_0 q_0$; the quantity index is similarly written from (3) by division by the *same* constant value. So, in year t:

$$P_{0t}(q_0) = \frac{\sum p_t q_0}{\sum p_0 q_0} \quad \text{and} \quad Q_{0t}(p_0) = \frac{\sum p_0 q_t}{\sum p_0 q_0} \tag{4}$$

The alternative available is to use the numerators alone:

$$\sum p_t q_0 \quad \text{and} \quad \sum p_0 q_t$$

as indicators of price and quantity movements. These are aggregate money values but differ only from the index numbers (4) by a factor which is the same for both and constant over time. In short, to trace price movements we can stick to the value series (2), the changing cost of a fixed budget, without bothering to convert into index form. Equally, we can retain the value series (3), expenditure at constant prices, instead of the quantity index as our measure of real expenditure. This is, in fact, what economists often do.

One practical exercise of this presentational choice is in the arranging of matters so that a set of component index numbers can be aggregated into an all-item index or the other way around. There is no difficulty about values in current prices; for example, consumers' expenditure can be analysed into component expenditures on food, on drink and tobacco, on housing, and so on. The question is how to show price or quantity index numbers for such components 'adding up' to an all-items index. If the index, of base-weighted form, is shown as a run on year 0 as 100, the method of aggregation or disaggregation is not immediately apparent. The component index numbers can be combined only by means of a weighted-average computation, on a method established and illustrated in **3.2** below. Where the price or quantity index is left in the form (2) or (3), the position is far simpler. The separate sequences for components are simply added together, for each year, to give the all-items sequence. For example, take real consumption measured by the constant-price values (3). Expenditure on food, on drink and tobacco, on housing, and so on, each at constant prices, can be added together with no more difficulty than current values. This is precisely how the tables of the national accounts are set out, as illustrated in **3·8** below.

There is, however, a problem of changing the base in these Laspeyres index numbers. Suppose we wish to have year 1 as the base (as 100) instead of year 0. There are then two things, and two different things, we can do. Exactly as we found with the equiweighted arithmetic mean, we can make an arithmetic switch of *reference base* from year 0 to year 1, keeping the weights unchanged, *or* we can *rebase* the index on year 1, adjusting the weights to match. It is most important to distinguish clearly between these two operations. We have two options; we can either keep them open or decide on one or the other.

The options arise because the Laspeyres index is the basic form of aggregative/weighted average index and has a double feature built into it. Take the price index for illustration. In year t, the Laspeyres price index is $P_{0t}(q_0)$ with fixed (base) weighting. It has *fixed weights* since year 0 is taken as the fixed year in the run $t = 0, 1, 2, 3, \ldots$. It has *base weights* since year 0 is selected as the reference base. When we come to change the base from year 0 to year 1, this double feature becomes an embarrassment. We can keep one of the features, fixed or base weights, but not both.

The first option is to keep *fixed weighting*. The change of base is then an *arithmetic switch* of reference base:

$$P_{1t}(q_0) = \frac{P_{0t}(q_0)}{P_{01}(q_0)} = \frac{\sum p_t q_0}{\sum p_1 q_0} \tag{5}$$

So when we divide through by $P_{01}(q_0)$ to switch from year 0 to year 1, we keep the same relative values of the index and we retain the interpretation as the changing cost of the fixed budget q_0. We are, in fact, still operating within the confines of the first column of the value matrix, that with fixed quantities q_0.

The second option is to keep *base weighting*. As the reference base is changed from year 0 to year 1, so the weights must be changed from q_0 to q_1 to match. The index is *rebased*:

$$P_{1t}(q_1) = \frac{\sum p_t q_1}{\sum p_1 q_1} \qquad (6)$$

The index is now a new and different one and the relative values are changed. We have, in fact, shifted from the first column of the value matrix (with fixed quantities q_0) to the second column of the matrix with different fixed quantities, q_1.

We can keep our options open and call both (5) and (6) index numbers of Laspeyres form, We just need to be careful in specifying precisely what weights are used, q_0 in (5) and q_1 in (6). This is clear enough in the notation adopted here, with q_0 or q_1 shown in brackets.

On the other hand, we may wish to plump for the label Laspeyres to be applied to one or other of the two cases. If we opt for (6) as the Laspeyres index we are insisting that it is always *base-weighted*. This can be rather trying in practice in that every change in reference base, made as a matter of convenience of arithmetic, carries with it a change in weights. Hence, faced with the need to decide, we opt here for (5) as the Laspeyres index. The feature is that it has *fixed weights* and so permits arithmetic switching of reference base at will:

The Laspeyres price index for a run $t = 0, 1, 2, 3, \ldots$ has fixed weights whatever reference base is used. If the weights are the fixed quantities q_0 of year 0 and if year 1 is the reference base, the Laspeyres index in year t:

$$P_{1t}(q_0) = \frac{\sum p_t q_0}{\sum p_1 q_0}$$

always measures the changing cost of purchasing the fixed budget q_0. It is a particular case, $P_{0t}(q_0)$, when the Laspeyres index is base-weighted as well as fixed-weighted.

Nothing has been said yet about a run of Paasche index numbers and this is not accidental. The Laspeyres index is the basic form and we need to be quite precise first on what we understand it to be. Only then should we pass on to consider the related and derived form, the Paasche index. In terms of the matrix of values (aggregate expenditures), the Paasche forms are less easy to obtain than the Laspeyres forms. They are, indeed, derived forms and we need to relate the three sequences (1), (2) and (3) from the diagonal, first column and first row of the matrix. The Paasche price index in year t in relation to year 0 is:

$$P_{0t}(q_t) = \frac{\sum p_t q_t}{\sum p_0 q_t}$$

and it picks out the entry in the current expenditure sequence (1) for year t for division by the corresponding member of the fixed-price expenditure sequence (3). The Paasche index of quantity makes similar use of (1) and (2).

We shall find that the Paasche index also has a double feature – though a rather different pair – and that we need to opt between keeping the one or the other in changing base, an option which needs to be made only after we have staked our claim to a particular Laspeyres form. This is a matter we pursue in Chapters 2 and 4.

1.7 Index Numbers in Practice

Index numbers are practical constructs, essentially defined and computed to provide solutions to practical problems. One price index, for example, may be intended to serve for index-linked wage rates, another for the determination of appropriate old-age pensions and yet a third for insertion in a system of equations in a short-run econometric model of the economy. These and other index numbers are especially tricky in construction since, as we have seen, they are concerned with some concept, such as a general price level, not susceptible to direct measurement.

Practice must depend on theory. Whatever may be thought to the contrary, there can be no 'measurement without theory' in economics and the social sciences as in the physical sciences. Much of what is vague and ambiguous in index-number practice can be traced to a lack of a good theoretical basis. This is the reason for the extensive development in the present text of a theoretical framework, specifically of the aggregative/weighted average forms of index, first for the two-situation case in Chapter 2, then for runs of index numbers in Chapter 4, with plenty of illustrations in between, in Chapter 3. The development, though put in the convenient shorthand algebra of the $\sum$ notation, is not a mathematical one. The formulae are all practical ones and all backed up by a description in words of what they do.

Before embarking on this theoretical development, we must

attempt to put it in perspective by giving some account of the essential practical points to have in mind. The practical distinctions and guidance are for the most part those which arise in all applications of statistical techniques. The statistical practice of index numbers does not differ in kind, though in many ways it does in degree, from all statistical applications.

We must first lay down rather precisely what it is our index numbers are intended to measure in the particular application considered. The *concept* will usually be rather general in formulation and related to some theoretical (e.g. economic) model. It will usually call for the specification of changes in some level not directly measurable, e.g. the general level of prices. The concept needs to be made rather specific, with reference perhaps to prices paid by a particular group of individuals and hence to a specific money aggregate for the expenditure of the group. A typical task then put up for index numbers to perform is: to trace the changing cost of a specific budget appropriate to the particular group of individuals.

It is possible, however, to become too specific, to lay down specifications in too elaborate and pernickety detail. For example, the budget to be priced over time may refer to commodities pinned down to very closely defined qualities, grades and specifications. All budgets, and indeed the bases of all index numbers, get so out of date in the course of time that an index can be continued, first only with difficulty, and then not at all. With an overprecise specification, that can happen in a few months. So some balance must be struck, between a concept not sufficiently precise and one overspecified, so that we know what question the index constructed does in fact answer and so that we can continue the index for a reasonably long period, for years rather than months. It is interesting to compare the detailed construction of index numbers of retail prices in the U.S. and in the U.K. Both are quite detailed in the specifications of commodities priced, but in the U.S. the specification is pushed further than in the U.K., probably too far if it is to be followed as closely as it should be over any length of time.

With the concept sufficiently defined, the statistician needs to select a *measure* or *estimator* of the concept, from the various possible alternatives. The term 'measure' is the general one used for a translation of the concept into practical evaluation; the term 'estimator' is a more technically statistical one, with especial reference to estimation from sample data. We can conveniently keep them both. The selection of our measure/estimator is one of standard statistical practice. In the simplest case, for example, we may be attempting to get some average of price relatives such as those for 1973 (1968 = 100) in Table 1.1. It is *an* average we seek, not *the* average. We have to choose between several available: median, arithmetic mean, geometric mean, and others. The averages are different. Table 1.1 gives: median $= \frac{1}{2}(131\cdot2 + 131\cdot8) = 131\cdot5$; arithmetic mean $= 136\cdot0$; geometric mean $= 134\cdot5$. They have their well-known advantages and disadvantages. You pays your money and takes your pick.

The choice between such averages is a familiar one. We have given reasons, with reference to economic interpretation, to select the arithmetic mean generally as the measure/estimator of our index number. The choice between equi-weighting and some weighting system – and, if the latter, what weighting system – is something yet again. Here the selection, e.g. between a Laspeyres (base-weighted) and a Paasche (current-weighted) index, may well turn on the precise question put up to be answered. Change or revise the question and you may alter the selection of measure/estimator.

With the measure/estimator selected, we are faced with an extraordinary wide range of practical problems on getting actual *estimates* of our measure from data on which we can lay our hands. If we had complete and accurate data, we could just use the formula for the measure selected and so get its true value in the case considered. Our data, however, are neither complete nor accurate. Any estimate we make diverges from the true value. It is usual, and indeed most important, to distinguish two kinds of errors or divergences of estimate from true value: *sampling errors* arising from the fact that the data are a sample of the whole, and *other errors* originating in a range of factors (other than sampling) affecting the data. Sampling errors are as relevant to index numbers as to other statistical estimation; it happens that they are not as well ordered, and usually have less attention paid to them, in index-number design. Other errors again are found in all statistical application; they happen to be particularly epidemic in index-number construction. The factors at work include: inaccuracies in the data and so the use of *approximations*; the lack of some data, the fact of *incompleteness*; the non-availability of what is specified as needed and so the use of *substitutes*. The task of assessing the sampling errors turns on the sampling design – or the lack of it – adopted in the index-number construction;

the assessment of the other errors is *ad hoc*, indeed a hit-or-miss affair. We can draw up:

Guidelines to index-number construction and assessment:

The **concept** to be measured is first to be defined with sufficient precision for the purpose in hand. The **measure/estimator** is then to be selected, as appropriate as possible to the concept defined. Thirdly, the **sampling aspects** of the data used for estimation are to be examined with particular reference to getting, if possible, the standard error of the estimate. Finally, one or more **estimates** of the measure/estimator are obtained and assessed on the basis of the **approximations** used, of the **incompleteness** of the data collection and of any **substitution** made in getting the estimates.

Two illustrations will make the practical problems clear; one is a very simple illustration based on Table 1.1, and the other a sketch of the position on one of the more complicated index numbers in common use.

In the first illustration, suppose that the six dairy-produce items specified in Table 1.1 are those bought by some typical family. Define the *concept* of the index to be constructed as the average movement in price of the six items over the specified period. Select the *measure/estimator*: equi-weighted arithmetic mean of price relatives (e.g.) in 1973 (1968 = 100). Next, assume that the prices used are each an average of a large number of actual price quotations selected at random from the population of all quotations. The *standard error* of each price is then obtained, according to the nature of the sample, and hence, by well-known formulae in sampling theory, the standard error of each price relative and finally of the arithmetic mean. Finally, the *other errors* involved in the price data need to be assessed: here any inaccuracies in recording and, more particularly, the rounding in Table 1.1 to the nearest $\frac{1}{2}$ or $\frac{1}{4}$d. The errors in this particular case are substantial. For example, the price of lard should be written $11\frac{1}{2} \pm \frac{1}{4}$d in 1972 and that of eggs should be $3\frac{3}{4} \pm \frac{1}{8}$d in 1968. The effect of such rounding errors on the price relatives, and then on the arithmetic mean, depends on what correlations there are between the errors and roundings of the individual prices. Certainly the *estimate* of 136·0% given for the price index in Table 1.1 cannot be accurate to one decimal place. Indeed we should be lucky to be able to put the index at 136%. The qualification referred to at the beginning of **1.3** above is needed.

The second illustration is a brief outline of the position attained by the Department of Employment in the design and calculation of the official *General Index of Retail Prices*, with reference to the sub-group: dairy produce. The *concept* is the change over a specified period in the general level of retail prices (dairy produce) as purchased by the average 'index' family as defined by the Department of Employment; see Central Statistical Office (1967). The *measure/ estimator* is the weighted arithmetic mean of the price relatives of fourteen items of butter, margarine, lard and other cooking fat, cheese, eggs, milk (fresh and canned, dried, etc.) of which six are those shown in Table 1.1. The weights used are derived from the expenditure of the average 'index' family, as described in Central Statistical Office (1967). The *estimate* of each price relative is based on an elaborate price collection made monthly by the Department of Employment. Prices are obtained by visits to a sample of outlets (a purposive selection designed to give a representative range) in 200 selected areas (a purposive selection from five groups of towns in specified ranges of population). The price relative for each commodity is obtained as an arithmetic mean of the separate relatives calculated for each outlet, i.e. it is an average of ratios of prices and not (as in Table 1.1) the ratio of average prices. From the *sampling aspect*, the position is not such that standard errors can be calculated; the selections are purposive rather than based on a probability design. Certainly there is not as much attention to sampling in the design of the index as is desirable from the sampling-theoretic point of view. The *other errors* in the price relatives are of several kinds and some may be substantial: *approximations* in recording prices in the visits to outlets, *incompleteness* as outlets originally selected drop out over time, and *substitutions* as items sold vary over time, one brand being replaced by another (e.g. amongst branded margarines). All this is difficult to assess but the overall effect in a subgroup such as dairy produce is certainly small in view of the close control maintained over the price collection by the Department of Employment.

To link the two illustrations, we can compare the quick estimator of the increase in price of dairy produce from January 1968 to January 1973, seen in Table 1.1, with the much more elaborate calculation of the official index of retail prices. The published details of the official index show two subgroups of dairy produce, and these need to be combined. For this purpose, we obtain price relatives on

January 1968 as 100 from the published subgroup index numbers with January 1962 as 100:

	Weights 1968 (1)	Subgroup index January 1962 = 100 Jan. 1968	Jan. 1973	Relative 1973 (1968 = 100) (2)	Product (1) × (2)
Butter, etc.	12	107	147	137·4	1,648·8
Milk, cheese, eggs	39	117	165	141·0	5,499·0
Dairy produce	51				7,147·8

From *Monthly Digest of Statistics*

Even this calculation ignores one of the more sophisticated features of the index, the fact that it is a chain index. We find, on this estimation, that dairy-produce prices in January 1973, with January 1968 as 100, were $\dfrac{7,147\cdot8}{51} = 140\cdot2$. Rounding off, we estimate the price level in January 1973 as 140% of January 1968. The simple estimator of Table 1.1, as an unweighted mean of only six price relations, gives 136%.

This survey of the practical problem is enough to establish that we have a good deal to do in accommodating index-number theory to practical requirements. The practice of index numbers relates to runs over time, or with similar many-situation comparisons, e.g. between regions and/or groups. We develop the theory to deal with runs in Chapter 4. We then need to take up the practical arithmetic processes of *switching* reference bases and of *splicing* separate short runs into one long run. Other practical problems range from the development of the idea of splicing into regular chaining of index numbers, to the particular problems (e.g. estimation of seasonal variation) which arise when the run of index numbers is more frequent than annual.

There is finally for consideration, in Chapter 7, a whole range of *sampling problems*. The statistical developments of sampling distributions, of standard errors and confidence intervals tend, in application to index numbers, to break on the rock of tradition. The usual index-number construction, even in the more elaborate of official index numbers, depends heavily on purposive selection, e.g. of commodities to be priced and of retail outlets for pricing. Much more could be achieved in the way of built-in probability-sampling designs; see Allen (1964), pp. 85–6.

On the other hand, on the sampling aspects of the relation between weights and price relatives in the weighted-average form of a price index, the classical results of Bowley (1897, 1912) have stood the test of time and remain as practical today as they have ever been. Bowley himself summarised the results:

> The effect of errors of weights is small compared with that of errors of quantities when there are many quantities whose dispersion is small, no preponderant weights, and little correlation between weights and quantities. Bowley (1912), p. 84

The reference here to 'quantities' must be taken as whatever happens to be averaged in the index number, e.g. price relatives in a price index. It is easy, in general terms, to appreciate the reasons for the relative unimportance of errors in weights. See Craig (1969). The basic reason is that the weights appear in the numerator and denominator of the index so that only proportional values matter. There can be quite extensive changes in the weights with little effect on the weighted average. To get any sizeable effect, we would need to have either one or two preponderant weights with large changes, or the main changes in weights concentrated on price relatives with extreme values (e.g. large change in weight of an item with a large price increase).

With all these practical considerations in mind, the wonder is that we get anywhere near the measure of our concept with index numbers in practice. The practical data analysed in Chapter 3 do show that, with the kind of case found in most published index numbers, we can get near to the measure of some relevant concept. It may not be precisely the concept we start with; we often need to reframe our question in the light of the answer our index-number estimator provides. It may be that we have alternative answers, as with different types of average or with Laspeyres and Paasche forms. But, in most cases, the answers come close enough for sensible conclusions. At the same time, some of the data of Chapter 3 have been selected to illustrate that, if we are not careful, and if we try to cut corners, we can land ourselves a long way off a sensible answer.

We come back to the point we made early in this survey of practice. Index-number construction has all the problems of the application of statistical techniques, but to a higher degree than most. Part of the trouble may lie in the fact that index numbers are attempting something more difficult than usual – the measure of some concept rather vaguely defined and not capable of direct observation. Another part of the high degree of difficulty may be because sampling techniques are not so applicable, and certainly not as much used as they might be, in index-number design.

1.8 The Irving Fisher Tests

This general survey is appropriately rounded off by short accounts of two theoretical approaches to the problem of index numbers, one statistical and one economic. The economic-theoretic view of index numbers is taken in the next section and pursued in Chapter 2; it is a useful approach but it must not be followed very far. The statistical approach now considered briefly is concerned with Irving Fisher's search for the 'ideal' index on certain statistical criteria. It is now mainly of historical interest but the 'ideal' formula, obvious enough when written down, is of considerable practical use.

We have seen (**1.5** above) that the unweighted arithmetic mean, as a possible index-number form, does not possess a desirable property, that of being transitive. So, for any selected bases, years 0 and 1, and for any current year t, we know that:

$$AM_{01} \times AM_{1t} \neq AM_{0t}$$

For example, with only two years ($t = 0, 1$) the reversal property does not hold:

$$AM_{01} \times AM_{10} \neq 1$$

and with three years ($t = 0, 1, 2$) the circular property fails:

$$AM_{01} \times AM_{12} \neq AM_{02}$$

The properties fail for other forms of index numbers. These facts suggest an investigation of what properties index numbers should have and which form best satisfies them. Such an investigation was carried out exhaustively by Irving Fisher early in the inter-war period; see Fisher (1922).

The tests proposed can be conveniently classified under three heads. In the first two, the tests are expressed here for a run of years and in terms of a price index. They can be applied equally to the corresponding quantity index. The third head is concerned with the relation between corresponding price and quantity index numbers.

The *first category* has three tests which should be passed by any reasonably constructed index, and are passed by all the standard unweighted and weighted forms of index P_{st} (s and $t = 0, 1, 2, \ldots$):

(i) *Identity Test*: $P_{tt} = 1$
i.e. when one year is compared with itself, the index shows 'no change'.

(ii) *Proportionality Test*: $P_{st} = \lambda$ when $p_t = \lambda p_s$ for each item, i.e. when all prices move in proportion, so does the index.

(iii) *Change-of-units Test*: P_{st} is invariant under any change in the money or physical units in which individual prices are measured.

The *second category* concerns the transitive property in its two manifestations:

(iv) *Time-reversal Test*: $P_{st} = 1/P_{ts}$ ($s \neq t$, s and $t = 0, 1, 2, \ldots$)

(v) *Circular Test*: $P_{0s} \times P_{st} = P_{0t}$ ($s \neq t$, s and $t = 1, 2, \ldots$)

The unweighted arithmetic mean fails both (iv) and (v) as do all the weighted arithmetic means (aggregative forms) described as Laspeyres and Paasche. All these types of index number make economic sense, but they are not transitive. A simple index which does satisfy the tests is the unweighted geometric mean. But this makes little or no economic sense and, in any case, the tests are again failed if some fixed weighting is introduced. Irving Fisher got to his 'ideal' index by 'crossing' standard forms of index number and by concluding that the 'cross', which best measures up to the tests while having economic sense, is the geometric mean between the Laspeyres and Paasche forms. For two years, 0 and 1, we write:

$$\text{Ideal price index: } PI_{01} = \sqrt{\{P_{01}(q_0) \times P_{01}(q_1)\}} \tag{1}$$

All the above tests are passed with the exception of (v), the circular test. If this test is passed, the implication is that the price index over a period P_{0t} does not depend on how prices develop over time, in the intermediate years (p_0 to p_t via $p_1, p_2, \ldots$).

This test is a very severe one; indeed, in economic terms, we have every reason to expect that the course of prices over time does matter. To go to the other extreme, we may assume that an index at time t depends on the whole course of prices and quantities over the period from 0 to t; we are led to the concept of the 'integral' index and its practical realisation as a chain index (Chapter 5).

The *last test* is concerned with matching price and quantity index numbers. For two years, 0 and 1, suppose P_{01} and Q_{01} are matched in the sense that one is obtained from the other by interchanging p's and q's in the formula. Suppose that $V_{01} = \sum p_1 q_1 / \sum p_0 q_0$ is the change in actual aggregate value from year 0 to year 1. Then:

(vi) *Factor-reversal Test*: $P_{01} \times Q_{01} = V_{01}$

    i.e. the two index numbers between them account for the value change.

Neither the unweighted arithmetic nor the unweighted geometric mean passes this test. For Laspeyres and Paasche forms:

$$P_{01}(q_0) = \frac{\sum p_1 q_0}{\sum p_0 q_0} \text{ matches } Q_{01}(p_0) = \frac{\sum p_0 q_1}{\sum p_0 q_0} \text{ (Laspeyres)}$$

and $P_{01}(q_1) = \dfrac{\sum p_1 q_1}{\sum p_0 q_1}$ matches $Q_{01}(p_1) = \dfrac{\sum p_1 q_1}{\sum p_1 q_0}$ (Paasche)

It is easily checked from the formulae that they fail test (vi):

$$P_{01}(q_0) \times Q_{01}(p_0) \neq P_{01}(q_1) \times Q_{01}(p_1) \neq V_{01}$$

But equally it is easy to find forms which do satisfy test (vi). It is only necessary to 'cross' Laspeyres with Paasche, instead of 'matching' them. So:

$$P_{01}(q_0) \times Q_{01}(p_1) = P_{01}(q_1) \times Q_{01}(p_0) = V_{01} \tag{2}$$

This is a very important property of Laspeyres and Paasche forms:

The change in actual value V_{01} is precisely accounted for either by the Laspeyres price index with the Paasche quantity index or by the Paasche price index with the Laspeyres quantity index.

Indeed, as we shall see later in our theoretical development, this is one of the double features of the Paasche form. The basic form is the Laspeyres; the Paasche form is derivative and dependent on the Laspeyres form selected. One property of the Paasche form $P_{01}(q_1)$ is that it shows the changing cost of the current budget q_1, by analogy with the Laspeyres $P_{01}(q_0)$ as the changing cost of the fixed budget q_0. The other property of the Paasche price index is that it satisfies (2) so that it is to be got by dividing the value change by the Laspeyres quantity index:

$$P_{01}(q_1) = V_{01} / Q_{01}(p_0)$$

Similarly, the Paasche quantity index is the value change deflated by the Laspeyres price index:

$$Q_{01}(p_1) = V_{01}/P_{01}(q_0)$$

It follows immediately from (2), and this was decisive in Irving Fisher's search for the ideal index, that the form (1) satisfies the factor-reversal test.

Our conclusion is that the ideal index does make economic sense, being a cross between the basic aggregative index numbers, and it does pass all the tests with the single exception of the one which must be regarded as optional in an economic context: the circular test (v). The test approach does not have the central theoretical importance given to it by Irving Fisher. Rather it is 'a convenient tool for judging the comparative merits of various formulae that suggest themselves' as is observed by Frisch (1936), p. 7. The ideal form is of some considerable practical use. If we wish to link together a price index between two years 0 and 1 (e.g. as part of a larger chain over time), and if we have price and quantity data in both years, then the Laspeyres and Paasche price index numbers can both be computed, and their geometric mean by (1) is the 'ideal' link we seek.

1.9 The Economic-theoretic Approach

The point has been stressed that index numbers are an economic as well as a statistical construct. We have had regard to the point all along, in broad and general terms. The question can now be asked: can index numbers be defined as an economic-theoretic concept? The answer is that this can be done certainly in one branch of economic theory and for one type of index. This index is a measure of price changes to an individual consumer, assumed to be a utility-maximiser under conditions of an unchanged preference map in the theory of consumer choice. In short, an economic-theoretic index can be sought as a *constant-utility price index* defined and specified in the context of the *theory of value*. To the price index, there corresponds a quantity index, the deflation of the actual value change by the constant-utility price index. This corresponding quantity index is the index of *real income* or real consumption.

The theory of consumer choice, and hence the constant-utility price index, is strictly to be confined to an individual consumer with a fixed preference (indifference) map. To go from these limiting confines to wider problems requires an act of faith rather than an application of economic theory. For one thing, preference maps will change over time, but this is a familiar kind of problem for index numbers. We are used to constructing approximate index numbers on shifting sands. What is more critical is that we wish to define, specify and apply price index numbers for groups of individuals. To make economic-theoretic sense here we need to take on trust the existence of a group or average preference map, to permit interpersonal utility comparisons. And so we proceed at our own risk to an analysis of consumers' expenditure, as one aggregative constituent of the gross domestic product (GDP), by means of a consumers' price index and a corresponding index of real consumption. We are at even greater peril in proceeding to analyse GDP, as a comprehensive aggregate of expenditures, in the same way into real GDP by deflation by a price index described, in the official national income *Blue Book*, as 'home costs per unit of output'. If we reach this point, we are far from the theory of value.

The definition of a constant-utility price index is clear enough, given only the preference map of an individual consumer as a system of convex *indifference surfaces* in n-dimensional commodity space. On any one indifference surface, the combinations of quantities of commodities consumed leave the consumer with equal utility or satis-faction. He is indifferent between budgets lying on one indifference surface. So, given two price situations p_0 and p_1 and the budget q_0 actually purchased in situation 0, we first specify the indifference surface on which q_0 lies (selected at price p_0) and then go on to specify that budget $\bar{q}_1$ which would be purchased at price p_1 and keep the consumer on the same indifference surface. The definition follows:

$$\text{Constant-utility price index } I_{01}(q_0) = \frac{\sum p_1 \bar{q}_1}{\sum p_0 q_0}$$

as the changing cost of remaining on one and the same indifference surface (as specified by q_0). The notation $I_{01}(q_0)$ indicates that the price index is a function of the indifference level q_0 of the consumer. At different levels of real income the price index $I_{01}(q_0)$ changes. The constant-utility price index depends on the constant utility level selected.

The preference (indifference) map of the individual consumer is conceptually an observable phenomenon. In practice, it cannot be observed just by use of recorded price/quantity data; we cannot know, from such data alone, what is the indifference level of the consumer in each of two situations. We certainly cannot find the budget $\bar{q}_1$ which is indifferent to the starting budget q_0 as the prices change from p_0 to p_1. Hence the form $I_{01}(q_0)$ is not a practical index-number formula. What it does is to provide a basis for judging how close we are to a 'true' index; it gives the target at which we aim. We can hope to approximate to this true index, or at least to get bounds between which the true index lies, by use of actual price and quantity data. This is a problem to be pursued in **2.8**.

So much has been recognised for some considerable time in the development of the theory of value. More recently a parallel has been sought in the theory of production. Can real output be obtained by deflation with a theoretical price index? The concept here is a constant-resources price deflator as analysed in **2.9**.

2 Theory: The Two-situation Case

2.1 The Problem

The given data are sets of observations of prices and quantities for n commodities (goods and services). The data relate to specified groups (e.g. of buyers or sellers) in defined markets or geographical areas and for particular time periods. It is convenient, but not essential, to think of a specified group of consumers purchasing the goods and services and to describe the set of quantities as a *budget* for the group of consumers. This, at least, serves to keep the economic aspect of index numbers clearly in mind.

The problem is to derive index numbers to show changes in the general level of prices and/or quantities between specified and comparable situations by means of changes in aggregate values appropriate to the group of consumers. Comparable situations are those which differ in one material respect with other specifications fixed. There are three types of comparable situations, involving comparisons of:

(i) two time periods for a given consumer group in a given area;
(ii) two areas for a given consumer group in one time period;
(iii) two consumer groups for a given area in one time period.

For example, if we are tracing changes in the general level of prices and/or consumption of pensioner households, then (i) might be a comparison of all pensioner households in England and Wales between 1968 and 1972; (ii) might be a comparison of all pensioner households in 1972 between England and Wales on the one hand and Scotland on the other; (iii) might be a comparison of one-person with two-person pensioner households in England and Wales in 1972.

The theory developed here applies, with no more than routine adaptions, to all comparisons, whether over time, over areas or over groups. However, as in **1.2** above, we opt to use temporal index numbers, the most usual case, for purposes of exposition and, for convenience, we refer to the time periods as years. Hence our two situations are year 0 and year 1.

On the notation of **1.2**, we have n commodities and we write prices and quantities in year 0 as: p_{i0} and q_{i0} ($i = 1, 2, 3, \ldots n$). For brevity, we write the value aggregate:

$$\sum_{i=1}^{n} p_{i0} q_{i0} = \sum p_0 q_0$$

The prices and quantities in year 1 are then written with the appropriate change of subscript and there are four value aggregates arranged in the *value matrix*:

Prices in year	Quantities in year	
	0	1
0	$\left[\sum p_0 q_0 \right.$	$\left. \sum p_0 q_1 \right]$
1	$\left[\sum p_1 q_0 \right.$	$\left. \sum p_1 q_1 \right]$

The *leading diagonal* shows actual values; off-diagonal elements are computed cross-valuations. The rows are values at *fixed prices* and the *columns* are valuations of *fixed quantities*.

For temporal, as for the other two types of index number, there is complete symmetry, just two situations compared one with the other. That one situation is written year 0 and the other year 1 is only a matter of selecting and attaching labels for identification. Once we have the labels, however arbitrarily selected, we can go further, again in the interests of exposition. One of the years is earlier and one later. Let us agree to the convention that year 0 is the *earlier* and year 1 the *later* year. But note that comparisons can still be either way and that we now have a ready way of distinguishing them. We speak of the comparison from year 0 to year 1 as *forward*, i.e. year 1 in relation to year 0. Equally, the *backward* comparison is from year 1 to year 0, or year 0 in relation to year 1. When we come to write index numbers, the order of the subscripts makes the distinction; so P_{01} and Q_{01} are forward and P_{10} and Q_{10} are backwards index numbers of price and quantity.

2.2 Basic Concept: Laspeyres (base-weighted) Index

In the following development, price and quantity index numbers are introduced in parallel. There is, however, only one basic concept and the price index can be got from the quantity index, or conversely, simply by an interchange of p's and q's.

The basic index-number concept and notation, on the aggregative approach, are supplied by the *definition*:

$$P_{01}(q) = \frac{\sum p_1 q}{\sum p_0 q} \quad \text{and} \quad Q_{01}(p) = \frac{\sum p q_1}{\sum p q_0} \tag{1}$$

for the price index with an arbitrary fixed budget q and the quantity index with an arbitrary fixed set of prices p. The index numbers (1) are the *forward* forms from year 0 to year 1. The corresponding *backward* forms are:

$$P_{10}(q) = \frac{\sum p_0 q}{\sum p_1 q} \quad \text{and} \quad Q_{10}(p) = \frac{\sum p q_0}{\sum p q_1}$$

obtained by simply reversing the subscripts.

These forms have arbitrary weights. As long as q (or p) remains fixed, the forward and backward index numbers are the reciprocals of each other. They have, however, little or no further significance: they are intended simply to set the stage. When we come to select appropriate weights, in the two-situation case, we have just two obvious choices: the weights from year 0 or from year 1. The selection for our basic form is the simple one: choose the weights from the same year that we use as the starting year of the comparison. The basic form of index number is then written with base weights. It appears together with three variants:

Laspeyres (base-weighted) Index Numbers

Forward	Price	$P_{01}(q_0) = \dfrac{\sum p_1 q_0}{\sum p_0 q_0}$	(2)
	Quantity	$Q_{01}(p_0) = \dfrac{\sum p_0 q_1}{\sum p_0 q_0}$	(3)
Backward	Price	$P_{10}(q_1) = \dfrac{\sum p_0 q_1}{\sum p_1 q_1}$	(4)
	Quantity	$Q_{10}(p_1) = \dfrac{\sum p_1 q_0}{\sum p_1 q_1}$	(5)

It must be stressed that there is only one basic form, which we can write for prices as (2). Then (4) comes by interchanges of 0 and 1 for a backward comparison; (3) and (5) come from (2) and (4) respectively by interchange of p's and q's.

It must also be stressed that the name Laspeyres is attached as a traditional label indicating that the form is base-weighted. To identify the basic property in each of (2)–(5), observe that the subscript attached to the weights in brackets is the same as the *first* subscript attached to P or Q, i.e. 0 in (1) and (2) and 1 in (4) and (5). This process of attaching the Laspeyres label, as noted in **1.4** above, is a convenient but arbitrary one. It depends on the selection of one of the two symmetric situations as a base for weighting. The convention here is that we go forward from the earlier year 0 as base, and so backward from year 1 as base in the reverse comparison. In a forward index from year 0, the Laspeyres index uses year 0 weights; in a backward index from year 1, weights from year 1 are taken in the Laspeyres form.

As noted in **1.5** above, the appropriate use of the Laspeyres label is not in the symmetric two-situation case, but in a run of index numbers. The Laspeyres form is then better regarded as fixed-weighted. In its turn, this involves the distinction between two types of base. The *weights base* is the year to which the weights, fixed in the Laspeyres index, are chosen to relate. The *reference base* is the year selected as the unity in the index, or as the 100 when in percentage form. In the two-situation case, the two bases are identical in the Laspeyres index; whatever year we start from in the comparison, that is the year for the weights. This 'tight' situation is opened up (as indicated in **1.5**) when the theory of runs of index numbers is developed in Chapter 4.

2.3 Derived Concept: Paasche (current-weighted) Index

To each Laspeyres index there corresponds a second index to which the label Paasche is attached. It can be described (as in **1.4**) as current-weighted in the sense that the weights come, not from the year from which the comparison starts, but from the other year. This other (or non-base) year can be called the current year, as indeed it will be when a run of index numbers is taken, and so the index appears as current-weighted. There are again four variants according as the index is one of price or quantity and as it is forward or backward.

The derivation of the Paasche index can be done in two ways, producing the same result in the two-situation case. It is important to be clear on the two derivations since the distinction becomes critical in the theory of Chapter 4 on runs of index numbers. The derivations are worked out for the forward price index; the others follow as variants as before.

The first derivation starts from the forward Laspeyres price index $P_{01}(q_0) = \sum p_1 q_0 / \sum p_0 q_0$ from the year 0 to the current (and later) year 1. Instead of selecting the base weights q_0, opt for the other available weights, i.e. the current weights q_1. Making the substitution, write:

$$P_{01}(q_1) = \frac{\sum p_1 q_1}{\sum p_0 q_1}$$

as the forward current-weighted index of prices to be given the Paasche label.

The second derivation starts from the recorded change in value forward from year 0 to year 1:

$$V_{01} = \frac{\sum p_1 q_1}{\sum p_0 q_0}$$

and then takes the forward Laspeyres quantity index $Q_{01}(p_0) = \sum p_0 q_1 / \sum p_0 q_0$ as the appropriate measure of the change in quantity. The *corresponding* measure of the change in price when multiplied by $Q_{01}(p_0)$ gives V_{01}. This price index is the *deflated* value:

$$\frac{V_{01}}{Q_{01}(p_0)} = \frac{\sum p_1 q_1}{\sum p_0 q_0} \bigg/ \frac{\sum p_0 q_1}{\sum p_0 q_0} = \frac{\sum p_1 q_1}{\sum p_0 q_1}$$

which is the index $P_{01}(q_1)$ got by the first derivation.

Hence, the definition of the derived Paasche index has the two equivalent expressions:

$$P_{01}(q_1) = \frac{\sum p_1 q_1}{\sum p_0 q_1} = \frac{V_{01}}{Q_{01}(p_0)} \tag{1}$$

From the first expression, it is properly called a current-weighted index. From the second, it is seen to be the price index which 'matches' the Laspeyres quantity index, in the sense that the two between them account for the recorded value:

$$V_{01} = P_{01}(q_1) \times Q_{01}(p_0)$$

The current-weighted version appears together with its three variants:

Paasche (current-weighted) Index Numbers

    Forward   **Price** $P_{01}(q_1) = \dfrac{\sum p_1 q_1}{\sum p_0 q_1}$ (2)

$$\text{Quantity} \qquad Q_{01}(p_1) = \frac{\sum p_1 q_1}{\sum p_1 q_0} \qquad (3)$$

Backward   **Price** $\qquad P_{10}(q_0) = \dfrac{\sum p_0 q_0}{\sum p_1 q_0} \qquad (4)$

$$\text{Quantity} \qquad Q_{10}(p_0) = \frac{\sum p_0 q_0}{\sum p_0 q_1} \qquad (5)$$

All come from one form, (4) from (2) by interchange of 0 and 1, the other two by interchange of p's and q's. Moreover, they are all to be regarded as derived from the corresponding Laspeyres forms. So $P_{01}(q_1)$ comes from $P_{01}(q_0)$ by changing weights from base year to current year, and similarly for each variant. Alternatively, $P_{01}(q_1)$ comes by dividing V_{01} by $Q_{01}(p_0)$; equally $Q_{01}(p_1)$ comes by the deflation of the value change V_{01} by the price index $P_{01}(q_0)$. There are similar derivations for the backward forms.

The current-weighted index numbers have Paasche as a traditional label. They can again be identified, through their current-weighted property, by observing that the subscript to the weights in brackets agrees with the *second* subscript attached to P or Q. This subscript is 1 for the forward index from comparison base 0 to current year 1 in forms (2) and (3). For the backward index numbers, (4) and (5), the subscript is 0.

2.4 Properties of Laspeyres and Paasche Forms

The index numbers are defined in terms of ratios of value aggregates. If the quantities are called a budget, then each of the aggregates is immediately interpreted as the cost of, or the expenditure on, a certain budget at certain prices. An index, as a ratio of aggregates, is then to be interpreted as a changing cost or expenditure between the two years, the budget being fixed for a price index, and prices being fixed for a quantity index. So the basic Laspeyres forms are interpreted: the price index is the changing expenditure on the fixed q_0 budget as prices change; the quantity index is the changing expenditure at fixed p_0 prices as the budget changes. The Paasche forms have similar interpretations.

The definitions and interpretations can be summarised in convenient tabular form. There are altogether eight different index numbers in the two-year comparison, on the $2 \times 2 \times 2$ scheme of

Laspeyres/Paasche, Price/Quantity and Forward/Backward. The four forward index numbers are:

FORWARD LASPEYRES AND PAASCHE FORMS
(year $0 = 100$)

Index number		Weights	Formula: $100 \times$	Interpretation
Price:	Laspeyres	q_0	$P_{01}(q_0) = \dfrac{\sum p_1 q_0}{\sum p_0 q_0}$	Changing expenditure on q_0 budget
	Paasche	q_1	$P_{01}(q_1) = \dfrac{\sum p_1 q_1}{\sum p_0 q_1}$	Changing expenditure on q_1 budget
Quantity:	Laspeyres	p_0	$Q_{01}(p_0) = \dfrac{\sum p_0 q_1}{\sum p_0 q_0}$	Changing expenditure at p_0 prices
	Paasche	p_1	$Q_{01}(p_1) = \dfrac{\sum p_1 q_1}{\sum p_1 q_0}$	Changing expenditure at p_1 prices

The four backward index numbers are got by interchanging years 0 and 1.

The properties of the Laspeyres and Paasche forms now developed are all of relevance to the design and computation of index numbers in practice. The first properties follow immediately from the derivation of the Paasche as shown in (1) of **2.3** above. If the change in actual value from year 0 to year 1 is V_{01}, then the Paasche price index is V_{01} divided by the Laspeyres quantity index and the Paasche quantity index similarly is V_{01} deflated by the Laspeyres price index. Together there are two alternative splits of the value change into price and quantity components:

$$P_{01}(q_0) \times Q_{01}(p_1) = P_{01}(q_1) \times Q_{01}(p_0) = V_{01} \tag{1}$$

These properties are an immediate consequence of the aggregative-ratio forms of the various index numbers:

$$\frac{\sum p_1 q_0}{\sum p_0 q_0} \times \frac{\sum p_1 q_1}{\sum p_1 q_0} = \frac{\sum p_1 q_1}{\sum p_0 q_1} \times \frac{\sum p_0 q_1}{\sum p_0 q_0} = \frac{\sum p_1 q_1}{\sum p_0 q_0} \tag{2}$$

A general expression of the properties has been given in **1.8** and their practical uses can now be followed up briefly.

One use is an example of the familiar statistical exercise in which alternative measures are available to serve one general purpose. As an average of a distribution, for example, we may use either or both of the median and the arithmetic mean; and the extent to which the two diverge tells us something about the distribution. So, here (1) gives alternative expressions of what part of a recorded change in value is due to price changes and what part to real changes. The price element is represented by the Laspeyres price index, or alternatively by the Paasche index. The corresponding real change is then shown by the Paasche quantity index, or alternatively by the Laspeyres index. We have a close approximation to a single estimate of the split if the Laspeyres and Paasche forms differ little. In any case we would look for some combination or 'cross' between the two forms as a good single estimate, a matter pursued in **2.6** below. If the two forms of index do diverge considerably, then we would like to know why, a question examined in **2.7**.

Another use of (1) and (2) helps in any search for saving on computational work. To get both Laspeyres and Paasche forms of the price and/or quantity index requires the computation of two cross-valuations: $\sum p_1 q_0$ and $\sum p_0 q_1$. In many cases, this raises difficult problems and it may even be not practical at all. Our result tells us, however, that a 'matching' pair of prices and quantity index numbers can be got from just one cross-valuation. The equations (2) show how the two cross-valuations appear separately. So, if we compute the base budget at current prices $\sum p_1 q_0$, then we get, first, the Laspeyres price index $P_{01}(q_0) = \sum p_1 q_0 / \sum p_0 q_0$ by dividing by the base value, and then an implied quantity index of Paasche form by deflation of the recorded value change: $Q_{01}(p_1) = V_{01}/P_{01}(q_0)$. On the other hand, if we compute only the fixed-price value (at year 0 prices) of the current budget q_1 (i.e. $\sum p_0 q_1$), then a different pair of 'matching' index numbers follows: first the Laspeyres quantity index and then the implied Paasche price index.

To sum up:

If the Laspeyres price index $P_{01}(q_0)$ is computed from the cross-valuation $\sum p_1 q_0$, there is an implied quantity index of Paasche form by deflation of the change in value: $Q_{01}(p_1) = V_{01}/P_{01}(q_0)$. Conversely, if $\sum p_0 q_1$ is computed, the Laspeyres quantity index $Q_{01}(p_0)$ has an implied Paasche price index: $P_{01}(q_1) = V_{01}/Q_{01}(p_0)$.

The practical choice, as illustrated in Chapters 3 and 4 below, is often for the second of these procedures. The only computations made are fixed-price (year 0) valuations of all budgets. The basic index is then the Laspeyres quantity index and there is an implied price index of Paasche form.

As a computational guide to the calculation of index numbers when both cross-values are used, first compute the four valuations (two direct and two cross) and arrange in the *value matrix* set out in **2.1** above. The Laspeyres index numbers (weights of year 0) follow from the first column (for prices) and from the first row (for quantities) by dividing the first entry into the second in each case. For the Paasche forms, pick out the second diagonal element $(\sum p_1 q_1)$ and divide by the entry above it (for prices) and to the left (for quantities). The results of the calculation can be arranged conveniently in a matrix:

Index year 1 (Year 0 = 100)	Laspeyres		Paasche	
Price	$\dfrac{\sum p_1 q_0}{\sum p_0 q_0}$	100	$\dfrac{\sum p_1 q_1}{\sum p_0 q_1}$	100
Quantity	$\dfrac{\sum p_0 q_1}{\sum p_0 q_0}$	100	$\dfrac{\sum p_1 q_1}{\sum p_1 q_0}$	100

The remaining properties are developed on the basis of the alternative method of computing aggregative index numbers by weighing price or quantity relative, instead of by computing the value matrix. The method is illustrated in **1.4** in the simple case of Table 1.2. The algebra is simple and direct for the Laspeyres form:

$$P_{01}(q_0) = \frac{\sum p_1 q_0}{\sum p_0 q_0} = \frac{\sum p_0 q_0 \dfrac{p_1}{p_0}}{\sum p_0 q_0} = \frac{\sum w_0 \dfrac{p_1}{p_0}}{\sum w_0}$$

and

$$Q_{01}(p_0) = \frac{\sum p_0 q_1}{\sum p_0 q_0} = \frac{\sum p_0 q_0 \dfrac{q_1}{q_0}}{\sum p_0 q_0} = \frac{\sum w_0 \dfrac{q_1}{q_0}}{\sum w_0}$$

(3)

where the same base values, $w_0 = p_0 q_0$, item by item, are used as weights for both prices and quantity index numbers. So:

The Laspeyres (base-weighted) index of prices or quantity is the weighted arithmetic mean of price or quantity relatives, the weights being the base values $w_0 = p_0 q_0$, item by item.

Attempting a similar piece of algebra for the Paasche forms, we have:

$$P_{01}(q_1) = \frac{\sum p_1 q_1}{\sum p_0 q_1} = \frac{\sum p_0 q_1 \dfrac{p_1}{p_0}}{\sum p_0 q_1} = \frac{\sum w_{01} \dfrac{p_1}{p_0}}{\sum w_{01}} \qquad (w_{01} = p_0 q_1)$$

$$Q_{01}(p_1) = \frac{\sum p_1 q_1}{\sum p_1 q_0} = \frac{\sum p_1 q_0 \dfrac{q_1}{q_0}}{\sum p_1 q_0} = \frac{\sum w_{10} \dfrac{q_1}{q_0}}{\sum w_{10}} \qquad (w_{10} = p_1 q_0)$$

The result is not very useful since the weights are now of 'crossed' form and different from the price to the quantity index. A neater result is got from the reciprocals:

$$\left.\begin{array}{l} \dfrac{1}{P_{01}(q_1)} = \dfrac{\sum p_0 q_1}{\sum p_1 q_1} = \dfrac{\sum p_1 q_1 \dfrac{p_0}{p_1}}{\sum p_1 q_1} = \dfrac{\sum w_1 \dfrac{p_0}{p_1}}{\sum w_1} \\[3ex] \dfrac{1}{Q_{01}(p_1)} = \dfrac{\sum p_1 q_0}{\sum p_1 q_1} = \dfrac{\sum p_1 q_1 \dfrac{q_0}{q_1}}{\sum p_1 q_1} = \dfrac{\sum w_1 \dfrac{q_0}{q_1}}{\sum w_1} \end{array}\right\} \qquad (4)$$

where the current values, $w_1 = p_1 q_1$ item by item, provide the weights in both cases. So:

The reciprocal of the Paasche (current-weighted) index of price or quantity is the weighted arithmetic mean of the backward price or quantity relatives, the weights being the current values, $w_1 = p_1 q_1$ item by item.

The parallel between (3) and (4) is clear. The weighted mean of the Laspeyres form is an average of the *forward* relatives with *base-value* weights. The weighted mean of the *reciprocal* of the Paasche form is an average of the *backward* relatives with *current-value* weights. The significance of this is brought out in the following section.

2.5 Forward and Backward Index Numbers

There are two more results which follow immediately from the aggregate forms of index numbers. From the way in which the Paasche is derived from the basic Laspeyres form:

$$P_{01}(q_0) \times P_{10}(q_0) = P_{01}(q_1) \times P_{10}(q_1) = 1 \qquad (1)$$

as is seen at once when spelt out:

$$\frac{\sum p_1 q_0}{\sum p_0 q_0} \times \frac{\sum p_0 q_0}{\sum p_1 q_0} = \frac{\sum p_1 q_1}{\sum p_0 q_1} \times \frac{\sum p_0 q_1}{\sum p_1 q_1} = 1$$

The result (1) shows that the backward index of one type is the reciprocal of the forward index of the other type:

$$\frac{\sum p_0 q_0}{\sum p_1 q_0} = P_{10}(q_0) = 1/P_{01}(q_0) = 1 \left/ \frac{\sum p_1 q_0}{\sum p_0 q_0} \right. \qquad (2)$$

and similarly for $P_{10}(q_1)$ as the reciprocal of $P_{01}(q_1)$. Both (1) and (2) can be expressed similarly in terms of quantity index numbers. So:

The Laspeyres and Paasche index forms are related so that the reciprocal of the forward Laspeyres index is the backward Paasche index and the reciprocal of the forward Paasche index is the backward Laspeyres index.

It is this result which accounts for the particular way in which the weighted-average version of the Paasche index is set out in (4) of **2.4**. The reciprocal of $P_{01}(q_1)$ is first identified as $P_{10}(q_1)$ and this in its turn is expressed as a weighted average with $w_1 = p_1 q_1$ weights.

It is to be noticed here that the reciprocal of an index has a simple meaning in practical terms. Any price index P_{01} shows the change in prices from year 0 to year 1 in ratio or percentage terms. Its reciprocal expresses the same change taken backwards from year 1 to year 0. The reciprocal is no more than an *arithmetic switch* of the two years related in an index of given form. For example, $P_{01} = 1 \cdot 25$ has reciprocal $0 \cdot 80$ and this simply states that the particular price movement can be expressed alternatively: year-1 prices are 125% of those of year 0 and year-0 prices are 80% of those of year 1. A 25% increase forward is equivalent to a 20% decrease backward.

The result (2) can be reinterpreted. The Laspeyres price index forward from year 0 is $P_{01}(q_0)$. Its reciprocal uses the same fixed budget q_0 but prices it backward from year 1. By (2) this is the backward Paasche form $P_{10}(q_0)$. The forward Paasche and backward Laspeyres forms are similarly related. Hence, a switch of reference base is an arithmetic process, that of taking the reciprocal, but by (2) it happens to convert a forward Laspeyres into a backward Paasche index or conversely.

This conclusion is of limited use in the two-situation case but it comes into its own when extended to apply to runs of index numbers. In any particular run we may go backwards as well as forwards from a base year and we then find it very convenient to switch at choice from one reference base to another.

2.6 Fisher Ideal Index

The Laspeyres and Paasche forms of aggregative index numbers can be conveniently checked against the Fisherian tests of **1.8**. The first three tests cause no trouble. Of the other three, the Circular Test refers to more than two situations and does not apply here. The tests to consider are the others: the Time-reversal and the Factor-reversal Tests. The position is similar on each. The *Time-reversal Test* requires for the Laspeyres and Paasche index numbers of price change from year 0 to year 1:

$$P_{01}(q_0) \times P_{10}(q_1) = 1 \quad \text{and} \quad P_{01}(q_1) \times P_{10}(q_0) = 1$$

i.e. $\quad P_{10}(q_1) = 1/P_{01}(q_0) \quad$ and $\quad P_{10}(q_0) = 1/P_{01}(q_1)$

Neither condition is satisfied. Instead, (1) and (2) of **2.5** show that the forms are 'crossed' in the sense that the reversal of a Laspeyres index is of Paasche form and conversely. All this is true equally of the quantity index numbers.

The *Factor-reversal Test* requires:

$$P_{01}(q_0) \times Q_{01}(p_0) = P_{01}(q_1) \times Q_{01}(p_1) = V_{01}$$

Property (1) of **2.4** shows that the price and quantity index numbers are not matched in this way. They are again 'crossed'; the Laspeyres price index goes with the Paasche quantity index and conversely.

The fact that the two forms operate in this way suggests that some 'cross' of them will come up with the desired properties. It turns out that the 'cross' to take is the geometric mean, a position reached so laboriously by Irving Fisher in 1922. The Laspeyres and Paasche forms separately fail the tests; together, in their geometric mean, they pass. The form so defined is the *Fisher Ideal Index*, first of price and then of quantity:

$$PI_{01} = \sqrt{\{P_{01}(q_0)P_{01}(q_1)\}} \quad \text{and} \quad QI_{01} = \sqrt{\{Q_{01}(p_0)Q_{01}(p_1)\}}$$

The formal algebraic proofs that they pass the tests are as follows. First for the Time-reversal Test:

$$\begin{aligned} PI_{01} \times PI_{10} &= \sqrt{\{P_{01}(q_0)P_{01}(q_1)\}} \times \sqrt{\{P_{10}(q_1)P_{10}(q_0)\}} \\ &= \sqrt{\{P_{01}(q_0)P_{10}(q_0)\}} \times \sqrt{\{P_{01}(q_1)P_{10}(q_1)\}} = 1 \end{aligned}$$

by (1) of **2.5**. The price index therefore satisfies the test. In the same way the quantity index is found to pass the test. Again for the Factor-reversal Test:

$$\begin{aligned} PI_{01} \times QI_{01} &= \sqrt{\{P_{01}(q_0)P_{01}(q_1)\}} \times \sqrt{\{Q_{01}(p_0)Q_{01}(p_1)\}} \\ &= \sqrt{\{P_{01}(q_0)Q_{01}(p_1)\}} \times \sqrt{\{P_{01}(q_1)Q_{01}(p_0)\}} \\ &= \sqrt{V_{01}} \times \sqrt{V_{01}} = V_{01} \end{aligned}$$

by (1) of **2.4** and the test is passed.

A limited answer is now provided to a question posed in **2.4**. The separate Laspeyres and Paasche forms between them lead to alternative splits of the value change into price and quantity components. If a single answer is needed – so much due to price and so much to quantity changes – then the Ideal Index is a consistent one to use:

$$PI_{01} \times QI_{01} = V_{01}$$

This is not to say that the Ideal form is the 'true' index. Even if there is such an index, the Ideal form may be no nearer to it than either the Laspeyres or the Paasche index is on its own.

The Fisher Ideal Index is only one possible 'cross' of the Laspeyres and Paasche forms. There are others with similar properties and Stuval (1957) suggests at least one quite practical alternative.

2.7 Statistical Relation between Laspeyres and Paasche Forms

Start again with the alternative splits of the value change given by (1) of **2.4**. It follows that the ratio of the Paasche to the Laspeyres form is the same for price and for quantity index numbers:

$$\frac{P_{01}(q_1)}{P_{01}(q_0)} = \frac{Q_{01}(p_1)}{Q_{01}(p_0)} \tag{1}$$

This is checked at once by substitution of the aggregative formulae for the index numbers. Whatever divergence arises between the two index forms for prices also appears for the quantity index. The problem is to get a measure of the divergence.

This problem is examined here in statistical terms, using the item-by-item distributions of, and correlation between, price and quantity relatives. The results are due to Bortkiewicz (1922, 1924) in his classic papers on the structure of price index numbers.

All the statistical measures used here are in weighted form with base-year values, $w_0 = p_0 q_0$, as weights item by item. All relatives and index numbers take year 1 in comparison with year 0. The weighted means of relatives are to be identified by (3) of **2.4** as Laspeyres price and quantity index numbers:

$$P_{01}(q_0) = \sum w_0 \frac{p_1}{p_0} \bigg/ \sum w_0 \quad \text{and} \quad Q_{01}(p_0) = \sum w_0 \frac{q_1}{q_0} \bigg/ \sum w_0 \tag{2}$$

The corresponding weighted variances are:

$$\sigma_p{}^2 = \sum w_0 \left\{ \frac{p_1}{p_0} - P_{01}(q_0) \right\}^2 \Big/ \sum w_0 \quad \text{and}$$

$$\sigma_q{}^2 = \sum w_0 \left\{ \frac{q_1}{q_0} - Q_{01}(p_0) \right\}^2 \Big/ \sum w_0 \tag{3}$$

Finally, the weighted covariance times $\sum w_0$ is:

$$\sum w_0 \left\{ \frac{p_1}{p_0} - P_{01}(q_0) \right\} \left\{ \frac{q_1}{q_0} - Q_{01}(p_0) \right\}$$

$$= \sum w_0 \frac{p_1 q_1}{p_0 q_0} - P_{01}(q_0) \sum w_0 \frac{q_1}{q_0} - Q_{01}(p_0) \sum w_0 \frac{p_1}{p_0} + P_{01}(q_0) Q_{01}(p_0) \sum w_0$$

$$= \sum w_0 \frac{p_1 q_1}{p_0 q_0} - P_{01}(q_0) Q_{01}(p_0) \sum w_0 \qquad \text{by (2)}$$

Divide through by $\sigma_p \sigma_q \sum w_0$ to get the weighted correlation coefficient r between price and quantities:

$$r = \frac{\sum w_0 \frac{p_1}{p_0} \frac{q_1}{q_0}}{\sigma_p \sigma_q \sum w_0} - \frac{P_{01}(q_0)}{\sigma_p} \frac{Q_{01}(p_0)}{\sigma_q} \tag{4}$$

Use $w_0 = p_0 q_0$ and (1) of **2.4** to give:

$$\frac{\sum w_0 \frac{p_1}{p_0} \frac{q_1}{q_0}}{\sum w_0} = \frac{\sum p_1 q_1}{\sum p_0 q_0} = V_{01} = P_{01}(q_1) Q_{01}(p_0)$$

This brings in the Paasche price index. Substituting in (4):

$$r = \frac{P_{01}(q_1)}{\sigma_p} \frac{Q_{01}(p_0)}{\sigma_q} - \frac{P_{01}(q_0)}{\sigma_p} \frac{Q_{01}(p_0)}{\sigma_q} = \frac{P_{01}(q_0)}{\sigma_p} \frac{Q_{01}(p_0)}{\sigma_q} \left\{ \frac{P_{01}(q_1)}{P_{01}(q_0)} - 1 \right\}$$

Rearrangement gives the required common ratio (1) of the Paasche to the Laspeyres index numbers:

$$\frac{P_{01}(q_1)}{P_{01}(q_0)} = \frac{Q_{01}(p_1)}{Q_{01}(p_0)} = 1 + r \frac{\sigma_p}{P_{01}(q_0)} \frac{\sigma_q}{Q_{01}(p_0)} \tag{5}$$

To interpret (5), note that the operative term is the *coefficient of correlation r* between price and quantity relatives, multiplied by two *coefficients of variation*, i.e. the standard deviations from (3) as ratios of the means (2). The coefficients of variation are positive so that the sign of r is sufficient to fix the *direction* of the divergence of the

Paasche from the Laspeyres index. The Paasche index is the greater if $r > 0$ and the Laspeyres index if $r < 0$. So:

The Paasche price index is greater than the Laspeyres if prices and quantities tend to move in the same direction between years 0 and 1; the Laspeyres index is the greater if prices and quantities tend to go in opposite directions.

From (1) it follows that the direction of the divergence of the quantity index numbers is the same as that of the price index numbers.

The *extent* of the divergence, in whichever direction it is, depends partly on the strength of the correlation r and partly on the dispersion of the price and quantity relatives as shown up in the coefficients of variation. Something can be said about this. In the classic problem of the purchasing power of money, for example, the level of either the Laspeyres or the Paasche price index is settled primarily by monetary factors while the divergence between the two forms depends more on non-monetary influences working on the spread of price relatives about the 'norm'. The typical situation is that the two forms drift apart over time. The gap between them can grow very quickly in periods of great change; see Allen (1963).

A good deal more can be said about the direction of the divergence. Distinguish two situations:

Case: $P_{01}(q_1) > P_{01}(q_0)$. The Paasche index of price (and equally of quantity) is the greater. The statistical condition is $r > 0$, movements of prices and quantities tending to be in the same direction. The economic condition is that the market is dominated by suppliers so that the typical reaction to a price rise is an increase in supplies and in sales. Examples are exporters selling on a large international market and farmers selling on a market comprising both home-produced and imported foodstuffs; the Paasche index is to be expected to exceed the Laspeyres for export prices and for prices received by farmers.

Case: $P_{01}(q_1) < P_{01}(q_0)$. The Laspeyres index is the greater both for prices and for quantities. Here $r < 0$; prices and quantities tend to move in opposite directions. The typical economic case is the demand-dominated market where buyers set the pace, buying less as prices rise and more as prices fall. The leading example is the market for consumer goods; the Laspeyres form of the retail price index, and equally of the index of volume of retail sales, is generally the greater of the two forms.

2.8 Economic Theory: Constant-utility Price Index

An economic-theoretic support for index-number construction can be supplied in one important case: the constant-utility price index and the corresponding index of real consumption. The economic basis is to be sought in the theory of consumer choice for an individual assumed to be a utility-maximiser with an unchanged preference map. The subject was introduced in **1.8** and now comes up for more extended development. The analysis is given for two situations which are typically two points of time. Further, for expository purposes, it is expressed in the two-goods case making it possible to use illustrative diagrams in two dimensions.

Take q_1 and q_2 as the quantities purchased of the two goods. The consumer's *preference map*, illustrated in Fig. 2.1, comprises two sets of intersecting curves in the plane Oq_1q_2. It is across this map, that we trace the changing purchases of the consumer as he maximises utility in the face of variations in his income and of movements in market prices. Saving is assumed away in the analysis so that income and expenditure on the two goods are the same.

One of the sets of curves is a system of *indifference curves*, taken as non-intersecting and convex to the origin. Combinations of

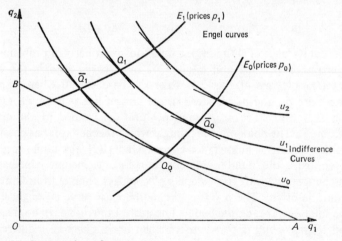

FIG. 2.1 Consumer's preference map

purchases shown by points on one of the curves are indifferent to the consumer and correspond to a particular level of utility, i.e. to one and the same value of real income/expenditure. Figure 2.1 shows a sequence of indifference curves shifting away from the origin as the utility level rises: u_0, u_1, u_2, ... The other set of curves cuts across the indifference curves and shows how purchases vary as income increases at constant market prices. These are *Engel curves*, one for each value of relative market prices, and Fig. 2.1 shows two of them: E_0 for fixed prices in one of the two situations taken and E_1 for fixed prices in the other situation.

Behind the preference map there lies an ordinal *utility function* $u = u(q_1, q_2)$ giving the set of indifference curves in the form: $u(q_1, q_2)$ = constant. The value of the constant is the utility level of the particular indifference curve taken, e.g. u_0 for the first curve of Fig. 2.1. The consumer operates under the constraint of balancing his budget, given his income y and the market prices p_1 and p_2. So: $p_1 q_1 + p_2 q_2 = y$. This appears in the diagram as a *budget line* with negative slope to Oq_1 given by the price ratio p_1/p_2 and shifting away from the origin as income y increases.

The model of consumer choice is to be written in alternative but equivalent forms on the *duality approach* following Houthakker (1952), Hicks (1956) and McKenzie (1957). Given the market price p_1 and p_2, the consumer determines purchases q_1 and q_2 so that:

$$\max u = u(q_1, q_2) \qquad \text{given} \qquad y = p_1 q_1 + p_2 q_2 \tag{1}$$

or $$\min y = p_1 q_1 + p_2 q_2 \qquad \text{given} \qquad u = u(q_1, q_2) \tag{2}$$

The equivalence of (1) and (2), a well-known property of problems of constrained maxima and minima, is most easily seen in the diagrammatic terms of Fig. 2.1. Take the base year 0 when market prices are p_{10} and p_{20}. Under (1), the budget line is fixed, at AB in Fig. 2.1, with slope p_{10}/p_{20} and position determined by the given income y_0. The point on AB is sought which reaches as far as possible up the system of indifference curves. Under (2), the utility level is given, fixing the initial indifference curve u_0. As income y increases, the budget line with given slope p_{10}/p_{20} moves parallel to itself away from the origin. The point on the indifference curve is sought with the smallest y, i.e. on the budget line nearest the origin. In both cases the optimal point is Q_0 where a budget line touches an indifference curve.

The optimal purchases q_1 and q_2 under (1) are given in terms of p_1, p_2 and y, the demand functions. They can be written either in the quantities or in the corresponding expenditures:

$$\begin{aligned}\text{Demand by quantity: } & q_1 = q_1(p_1, p_2, y) \text{ and } q_2 = q_2(p_1, p_2, y)\\ \text{by expenditure: } & y_1 = y_1(p_1, p_2, y) \text{ and } y_2 = y_2(p_1, p_2, y)\end{aligned} \quad (3)$$

where $y_1 = p_1 q_1$ and $y_2 = p_2 q_2$. The maximised utility level follows, named by Houthakker (1952):

$$\text{Indirect utility function: } u = u(p_1, p_2, y) \quad (4)$$

At the optimal position the arguments q_1 and q_2 of the utility function can be replaced by p_1, p_2 and y, the arguments of the indirect utility function.

Precisely the same optimal purchases are obtained under (2) but the demand functions (3) then involve u instead of y. The advantage of this approach lies in the fact that the minimised value of y is given in terms of the prices and of u:

$$\text{Expenditure function: } y = y(p_1, p_2, u) \quad (5)$$

Since the optimum is the same, the functions (4) and (5) are simply inverse to each other.

At given market prices the *Engel curve* is specified by (3) as y varies. With (3) in quantitative form an Engel curve such as E_0 is given across the preference map of Fig. 2.1. Alternatively, Engel curves can be written in the expenditures versions of (3), i.e. y_1 and y_2 as functions of y and subject to the constraint $y_1 + y_2 = y$. Such Engel curves, with special reference to the linear case, are examined by Allen and Bowley (1935). It was Engel (1857) who first found that expenditure on food as a proportion of income declined as income rose at constant prices. This situation obtains, in the linear case, when for (e.g.) the first good $y_1 > 0$ at $y = 0$. This is the case described by Allen and Bowley as a necessary as opposed to a luxury good. Accounts of Engel curves and of the forms they can assume are provided by Prais and Houthakker (1955), by Leser (1963) and by Brown and Deaton (1972).

The *constant-utility price index* follows as in **1.8** as the ratio of two expenditures given at optimal positions for different market prices but on one and the same utility level. The index appears in alternative forms on the duality approach. That based on the model (2) is the more immediate since it specifies minimum expenditure at a given utility level. The other and equivalent form from the maximum-utility model (1) can be pursued subsequently and in diagrammatic terms in relation to Laspeyres and Paasche index numbers.

At the prices p_{10} and p_{20} of the base year 0, the optimal purchases give an expenditure $p_{10}q_{10} + p_{20}q_{20}$ at the utility level u_0. Similarly, at the prices of the current year 1, the expenditure is $p_{11}q_{11} + p_{21}q_{21}$ at the utility level u_1. There is one constant-utility price index for each utility level to be obtained directly from the expenditure function (5). The two index numbers defined at the utility levels of years 0 and 1 are:

$$\text{Constant-utility price index: } I_{01}(u_0) = \frac{y(p_{11}, p_{21}, \ldots u_0)}{y(p_{10}, p_{20}, \ldots u_0)} \left.\begin{array}{c} \\ \\ \end{array}\right\}$$
$$I_{01}(u_1) = \frac{y(p_{11}, p_{21}, \ldots u_1)}{y(p_{10}, p_{20}, \ldots u_1)} \left.\begin{array}{c} \\ \\ \end{array}\right\} \tag{6}$$

where provision is made for the obvious extension to more than two goods. The denominator of $I_{01}(u_0)$ is the actual (optimal) expenditure of the base year, i.e. $p_{10}q_{10} + p_{20}q_{20} + \ldots$ also extended to more than two goods. On the other hand, it is the numerator of $I_{01}(u_1)$ which is an actual expenditure, that of the current year.

Switch now to the maximum-utility model (1) and assume that the *actual* purchases in year 0 are the optimal values given by the point Q_0 in Fig. 2.1 where the given budget line AB touches the indifference curve at the (maximised) utility level u_0. For comparison, take the prices (but nothing more) from the current year 1 and pick out the *hypothetical* purchases which would be made at these prices and still retain the utility level u_0 as optimum. These are given by the co-ordinates $\bar{q}_{11}$ and $\bar{q}_{21}$ of the point $\bar{Q}_1$ on the indifference curve u_0 where the tangent has slope p_{11}/p_{21}. The ratio of the expenditure at $\bar{Q}_1$ to the actual expenditure at Q_0 is the constant-utility index:

$$I_{01}(u_0) = \frac{\sum p_1 \bar{q}_1}{\sum p_0 q_0} \tag{7}$$

where the extension to more than two goods is again made and adapted to the usual $\sum$ notation.

Even apart from the problems arising from aggregation over groups of consumers, the hypothetical purchases $\bar{q}_1$ are not observable and the most that can be expected is to get one or more bounds of the true index $I_{01}(u_0)$. An upper bound, but not a lower, can be found at once. Since the utility-maximising consumer would select

$\bar{q}_1$ rather than q_0 at prices p_1, the first costs less than the second at these prices:

$$\sum p_1 \bar{q}_1 < \sum p_1 q_0$$

In terms of Fig. 2.1, the tangent at $\bar{Q}_1$ and the parallel line through Q_0 are both budget lines at prices p_1 and, since the indifference curve is convex, the former is nearer the origin than the latter. The income attached to the former ($\sum p_1 \bar{q}_1$) must be less than that ($\sum p_1 q_0$) of the other budget line. So, from (7):

$$I_{01}(u_0) < \frac{\sum p_1 q_0}{\sum p_0 q_0} = P_{01}(q_0) \quad \text{Laspeyres} \tag{8}$$

The upper bound sought is the Laspeyres index, base-weighted on year 0.

The whole process can be repeated starting from the point Q_1 on the utility level u_1 achieved in year 1 and jobbing back to the prices of year 0. The hypothetical point $\bar{Q}_0$ on the indifference curve u_1 gives optimal purchases at year-0 prices but at the utility level u_1. Write these purchases $\bar{q}_0$ and it follows as before that $\sum p_0 \bar{q}_0 < \sum p_0 q_1$. The constant-utility price index at the utility level u_1 is then:

$$I_{01}(u_1) = \frac{\sum p_1 q_1}{\sum p_0 \bar{q}_0} > \frac{\sum p_1 q_1}{\sum p_0 q_1} = P_{01}(q_1) \quad \text{Paasche} \tag{9}$$

and a lower bound is obtained, the current-weighted Paasche index.

The results (8) and (9) provide one bound each for two different true index numbers of price. The position can be summarised:

$$\left. \begin{array}{ccc} \dfrac{\sum p_1 q_1}{\sum p_0 q_1} & < & I_{01}(u_1) \\[4mm] & I_{01}(u_0) & < & \dfrac{\sum p_1 q_0}{\sum p_0 q_0} \\[4mm] \text{Paasche} & \text{Two different} & \text{Laspeyres} \\ \text{index} & \text{true indexes} & \text{index} \end{array} \right\} \tag{10}$$

Neither the indirect utility function nor the expenditure function is observable from price/quantity data. The true price index cannot be estimated, therefore, either from formula (6) or from the alternative (7). This is why we seek refuge in the Laspeyres or Paasche bound of (10). There is one possible way out. If a specific form can be assumed for the utility function, including one or more parameters to be estimated from price/quantity data, then the constant-utility price index can be derived from (6). It is a matter of straightforward mathematics to get the index, and to get it explicitly as a function either of the utility level u or of the consumer's income y, once the utility function is specified. Of the many possible forms of the utility function, the most popular and certainly the most convenient is that developed by Geary (1950) and Stone (1954, 1956). It has the advantage of making demand expenditure (3) a linear function of all prices and income. It is the form appropriate to the *linear expenditure system* of Stone (1954) and it is developed for use in a particular application later (Chapter 6).

If we are driven back to the result (10), lacking an explicit utility function, what can we do in practice? The development of the theory summarised here was spread over a long period of time, from Konüs (1924) and Haberler (1927), through Frisch (1936) to Klein and Rubin (1948) and later writers. The practical thought was always that, though the Laspeyres and Paasche bounds applied in theory to separate true index numbers, there should be a strong presumption that any one true index could be pinned down between both bounds. The two cases of 2.7 can be brought in here. The situation of particular reference to the constant-utility price index is that of a demand-oriented market. The Laspeyres index is to be expected to be greater than the Paasche form – so leaving room for the true index, at either utility level, to fall in between them.

What we need in practice, broadly speaking, is first to know that Laspeyres and Paasche index numbers are not far apart in a two-period comparison, and then to have a reasonable expectation that the true index numbers based on one period and on the other are not very different. The first is a matter of observation. The second can be a fairly safe guess if the periods compared are neither unusual nor far apart.

The question that remains is whether an index of real consumption can be defined to match the constant-utility price index. As long as the preference map of the consumer is unchanged, the question can be answered by writing the quantity index implied by a specified price index. Write the change V_{01} in total expenditure in alternative forms:

$$V_{01} = \frac{\sum p_1 q_1}{\sum p_0 q_0} = \frac{y(p_{11}, p_{21}, \ldots u_1)}{y(p_{10}, p_{20}, \ldots u_0)}$$

The second of these makes use of the extended version of the expenditure function (5). Take the price index $I_{01}(u_0)$ at the constant utility level u_0 as a deflator of V_{01} and use the alternative expressions (6) and (7) for the purpose. So:

$$\text{Implied index of} \atop \text{real consumption:} \quad \frac{V_{01}}{I_{01}(u_0)} = \frac{y(p_{11}, p_{21}, \ldots u_1)}{y(p_{11}, p_{21}, \ldots u_0)} \tag{11}$$

and

$$= \frac{\sum p_1 q_1}{\sum p_1 \bar{q}_1} > \frac{\sum p_1 q_1}{\sum p_1 q_0} = Q_{01}(p_1) \quad \text{Paasche} \tag{12}$$

Here, (11) is a direct use of the expenditure function and a straightforward comparison of constant-price valuations; it is in line with the usual definition of a quantity index. The expenditures are here at the fixed prices of the current year 1; they are those required to attain first the utility level u_0 and then u_1. The index is a measure of the increase in (ordinal) utility from u_0 to u_1. The result (12) goes on to show that the Laspeyres upper bound of the price index is matched by a Paasche lower bound of the implied quantity index. The two bounds, $P_{01}(q_0)$ and $Q_{01}(p_1)$, themselves multiply to V_{01}.

The deflation of V_{01} by the alternative price index, i.e. $I_{01}(u_1)$ at the constant-utility level u_1, provides another implied index of real consumption. Corresponding results to (11) and (12) show that it compares expenditures at the constant prices of year 0 and that it has the Laspeyres upper bound $Q_{01}(p_0)$.

The matching pair of the constant-utility price index $I_{01}(u_0)$ and the real-consumption index given by (11) and (12) can be interpreted, in the two-goods case, as a couple of steps across the preference map of Fig. 2.1. The current purchases of the point Q_1 are reached from the base purchases of Q_0 by going first along the indifference curve u_0 to $\bar{Q}_1$ and then along the Engel curve E_1 to Q_1 at constant prices of year 1. The first step is the *substitution effect*; it involves the price index $I_{01}(u_0)$ and unchanged real consumption. The second step is the *income effect*, tracing the change in real consumption at constant (current) prices. The other matching pair of index numbers comprises the price index at the constant-utility level u_1 and the real-consumption index at constant (base) prices. They are shown by two different steps across the preference map: the first from Q_0 to $\bar{Q}_0$ for the income effect at base prices along the Engel curve E_0, the second from $\bar{Q}_0$ to Q_1 for the substitution effect at the constant-utility level u_1.

Note that these alternative paths across the preference map merge into a unique direction of change as the finite steps of Fig. 2.1 tend to infinitesimal movements from Q_0. The elasticity of consumer demand is then the unambiguous sum of income and substitution effects, the familiar Slutsky result of value theory; see Hicks (1946).

In conclusion, it is to be emphasised that the whole development is based on the assumption of an unchanged preference map. When the tastes of the consumer vary over time, the position and shape of the indifference curves change. If the Engel curves are then taken over time across the shifting preference map, they may become twisted out of all recognition. A treatment of simple versions of the problem of changing consumer tastes is left over to Chapter 7.

2.9 Economic Theory: Constant-resources Price Deflator

An economic-theoretic analysis of the output or supply side of the market can be given on rather similar lines. The following development turns on a somewhat conventional representation of the technology of the whole economy, in which the factors of production are assumed to be used always in fixed proportions while outputs are produced in continuously variable amounts. The technology of the economy can then be expressed as a single relation:

$$f(x_1, x_2, \ldots x_n, u) = 0 \tag{1}$$

between the outputs (the x's) of the n goods produced and the level u of usage of the factors in their given proportions. The relation (1) is to be regarded as giving the minimum usage of resources for each specified bundle of outputs $(x_1, x_2, \ldots x_n)$. It could equally show the maximum bundle of outputs for a given usage of resources.

It is possible to think of u as the number of composite units of the factors employed. Such a composite unit need not be specified explicitly, however, and it may be better to take the variable u as an ordinal concept, like utility, representing the scale of usage of the resources of the economy.

In the two-outputs case illustrated by Fig. 2.2, assume that (1) gives u uniquely in terms of the two outputs:

$$u = u(x_1, x_2) \tag{2}$$

For a constant value of u, (2) is shown as a curve in output space: the *production-frontier curve*. Given the factor usage, what can be got out of the technology in the way of outputs is confined within this curve. Hence, the bundles of outputs (x_1, x_2) given by points on

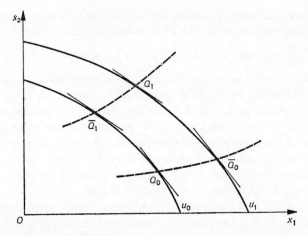

FIG. 2.2 Production-frontier map

the curve are to be taken as the same *real output*, the most to be got from the given resources. A whole set of such curves is obtained by varying the given resources as a parameter: the *production-frontier map* of Fig. 2.2. Each curve of the map represents real output from one level of resources; we move outwards across the map as the level of resources increases. It is assumed that the curves are non-intersecting and concave to the origin.

Given output prices, π_1 and π_2, and the usage u of resources, the determination of outputs x_1 and x_2 is a problem of the constrained maximum of the value of output m:

$$\max m = \pi_1 x_1 + \pi_2 x_2 \quad \text{given} \quad u = u(x_1, x_2)$$

The optimal outputs are shown by the point where the line $\pi_1 x_1 + \pi_2 x_2 = m$, with slope given by the prices, touches the production frontier u. The maximised output value m is the constant of the line.

The analysis now proceeds exactly as in **2.8** and it is illustrated in Fig. 2.2. Consider two situations, taken as years 0 and 1. When output prices are ruling market prices, write them as p's instead of π's; when outputs are optimal (actual or hypothetical), write q's instead of x's. The notation is then in the usual form for index numbers. In year 0 with resources u_0, a typical price is p_0 and the corresponding output q_0; u_1, p_1 and q_1 are the values in year 1. The change in value of output from year 0 to year 1 is to be split into price and real-output components. The alternatives are: first to determine $\bar{q}_1$ at prices p_1 but on the level of real output u_0; second to find $\bar{q}_0$ at prices p_0 but on the level of real output u_1. Then:

$$\sum p_1 \bar{q}_1 > \sum p_1 q_0 \quad \text{and} \quad \sum p_0 \bar{q}_0 > \sum p_0 q_1 \tag{3}$$

Both follow in the same way. For example, the first expresses the fact that, at prices p_1, output $\bar{q}_1$ is optimal and so greater in value than the non-optimal q_0. In Fig. 2.2, the line through Q_0, parallel to the tangent to the production frontier u_0 at $\bar{Q}_1$, lies below this tangent because of the concavity of the production frontier. The inequalities are in the opposite direction to those of **2.8** simply because the production-frontier map is concave as compared with the convex curves of the indifference map of the consumer.

The definitions of alternative constant-resources price deflators now follow, as do the implied measures of real output got by deflating the value change:

$$V_{01} = \frac{\sum p_1 q_1}{\sum p_0 q_0}$$

They can be written:

Constant-resources price deflator

at resources level u_0: $\quad I_{01}(u_0) = \dfrac{\sum p_1 \bar{q}_1}{\sum p_0 q_0} > \dfrac{\sum p_1 q_0}{\sum p_0 q_0}$ Laspeyres $\qquad$ (4)

at resources level u_1: $\quad I_{01}(u_1) = \dfrac{\sum p_1 q_1}{\sum p_0 \bar{q}_0} < \dfrac{\sum p_1 q_1}{\sum p_0 q_1}$ Paasche $\qquad$ (5)

Real-output index

implied by $I_{01}(u_0)$: $\quad \dfrac{V_{01}}{I_{01}(u_0)} = \dfrac{\sum p_1 q_1}{\sum p_1 \bar{q}_1} < \dfrac{\sum p_1 q_1}{\sum p_1 q_0}$ Paasche $\qquad$ (6)

implied by $I_{01}(u_1)$: $\quad \dfrac{V_{01}}{I_{01}(u_1)} = \dfrac{\sum p_0 \bar{q}_0}{\sum p_0 q_0} > \dfrac{\sum p_0 q_1}{\sum p_0 q_0}$ Laspeyres $\qquad$ (7)

The Laspeyres and Paasche bounds come directly from (3). For the price deflator, they can be arranged:

$$\left.\begin{array}{ccc} \dfrac{\sum p_1 q_1}{\sum p_0 q_1} & > & I_{01}(u_1) \\[2ex] & I_{01}(u_0) & > & \dfrac{\sum p_1 q_0}{\sum p_0 q_0} \end{array}\right\} \tag{8}$$

| Paasche index | Two different price deflators | Laspeyres index |

The inequalities here are in the opposite direction to those on the demand side, in (10) of **2.8**. To have a reasonable expectation that both deflators lie between the Laspeyres and Paasche index numbers, we need the Paasche index to be greater than the Laspeyres. The analysis of **2.7** shows that this is to be expected in a supply-dominated market.

The fact that there are alternative splits of the value change from year 0 to year 1 is clear in terms of Fig. 2.2; they show up in alternative routes from point Q_0 to point Q_1. One route is over $\bar{Q}_1$, a first step at constant real output on the deflator $I_{01}(u_0)$ and a second step of increasing real output at constant prices p_1. The other route proceeds through $\bar{Q}_0$; increasing real output at constant prices p_0 is followed by a step at constant real output with the aid of the deflator $I_{01}(u_1)$.

Though illustrated in the two-outputs case, the analysis is quite general and the results (3) to (8) hold for any number of outputs. The production-frontier map comprises a set of surfaces in the n-dimensions of output space, one surface for each level of resources. The curves along which real output expands at fixed prices, shown broken in Fig. 2.2, remain as curves across the set of surfaces.

The deflation of output into real terms is a process essentially dependent on the technology of the economy. It follows that technological changes between years 0 and 1 affect the deflation process. There are two choices: *either* stick to year-0 technology, use the price deflator (4) and switch if need be to the Laspeyres index as a lower bound; *or* make comparisons on the basis of year-1 technology with the aid of a price deflator (5) and its Paasche upper bound. The corresponding measures of real output are the Paasche form (6) on the first choice and the Laspeyres form (7) on the second.

The economist is quite used to thinking of real output as valued at some constant prices. His natural choice is then the Laspeyres-type index of real output (7) and the matching deflator is that of Paasche form (5). If he makes this choice, then he should remember that his Paasche index exaggerates the true price increase in the deflation, and hence that he is understating increases in real output. There is something to be said for the opposite choice. A Laspeyres price deflator understates price rises and so does not fall into the trap of understating real output; see Fisher and Shell (1972).

3 Illustrations

3.1 Introduction

The object of this chapter is to analyse either published index numbers or data from which index numbers may be computed, and so to illustrate the two-situation theory of Chapter 2. At the same time the ground is prepared for the later developments of Chapters 4 and 5 on the theory and practice of runs of index numbers. The important problems in practice have to do with runs and the material assembled here can be called upon later to illustrate them.

The data from the official sources used are for the most part set out in the appendix to this chapter; the calculations performed on the data are shown in the text. All the index numbers, being of Laspeyres and Paasche forms, may be computed as ratios of aggregates and/or in the equivalent weighted-average form. The range of economic subjects illustrated is quite extensive and the topics, though interrelated, can be conveniently put in two blocks.

The first block of topics is that of retail prices and personal or family consumption, an area which has some theoretical backing in the theory of value (2.8). Here, in addition to the much-used index of retail prices calculated from market price quotations by the Department of Employment (Appendix Tables A1 and 2), price index numbers of more limited scope are calculated, specifically those relating to the consumption by pensioner families (Table A3). Quantity index numbers, showing changes in the volume of consumption, are also derived. Among them is an index which may be regarded as matching a large chunk of the retail price index: the volume of retail sales.

The second block of data, in Appendix B, deals with the main aggregates of the national income accounts: Gross Domestic Product (GDP) and its broad constituents. The national accounts are a complex double-entry jigsaw in current-value terms. Index numbers play their part in reducing money aggregates to real terms and in tracing the corresponding price changes. We start with some small pieces of the jigsaw: merchandise imports and exports. The same kind of problems are then found to arise in building up to total GDP; they are just writ larger. In the end, two broad, and largely independent, lines of attack on the measurement of real GDP are followed and three different measures result. These correspond to the three concepts of the national income: as expenditure, as output and as income generated.

In relating the two topics, we find, for example, that the retail price index of the first area is to be compared with the index of consumer prices thrown up in the national accounts; and this is one of the illustrations of runs of index numbers used later in Chapter 6. As the analysis proceeds we bring in additional index numbers to supplement our findings. Examples are the official index of retail sales and that of wholesale prices.

In 1.7 we wondered why in using index numbers in practice, we got anywhere near answers to the broad questions posed. We do, indeed, sometimes get a long way off target. To keep things in perspective, however, we do find that the occasional 'flops' are more than counterbalanced by success stories. The following analysis will illustrate both. It will, indeed, throw up results of some general interest; these must be regarded here as by way of a bonus. The purpose of the exercise is still to illustrate the design and calculation of economic index numbers.

3.2 Weighted-Average Index: Retail Prices

A good example of the method of computation of an index as a weighted average is the index of retail prices calculated monthly by the Department of Employment; it is one of the most familiar of all economic indicators. The weighted-average form is adopted since the index is designed to use prices and quantities/expenditures drawn from different sources. There are no comprehensive data on prices and quantities which are good enough matches to multiply out to value aggregates. The prices are those actually quoted at retail, obtained by the Department in a special price collection each month. Comparability over time being essential, each price quotation obtained from each source is used to give an individual price relative on the base date and these are averaged to provide relatives for each commodity item, carefully specified for inclusion in the index. Against this, the budget expenditures item by item, averaged over a wide group of families specified for the index, come from a separate source, the continuous Family Expenditure Survey conducted by the Department. The index then follows by weighting the price relatives with the budget expenditures item by item.

Before 1962 the index was an almost 'straight' example of a Laspeyres (base-weighted) index. Since 1962 it has become rather more sophisticated, the leading example of a chain index as developed in Chapter 5. The weights are budget expenditures averaged over three years and brought annually up to date in a year-to-year chaining. To accommodate this in the present context, consider the index as running monthly for one year at a time, each a Laspeyres (base-weighted) form. In the period covered by Appendix Table A1, there is one index based on January 1971, another based on January 1972, a third on January 1973. The first, running to January 1972, has weights which are expenditures of the 'index' families averaged over the three years to June 1970 and repriced at January 1971. The lag between the budgets and the base prices is incidental here; we regard them as base weights w_0. The second index is similarly weighted with budget expenditures (averaged over three years to June 1971) at January 1972 prices. The third index has weights from a budget over three years to June 1972 at January 1973 prices.

In the following exercises it would be exceedingly tedious to carry out the calculations for each of the twelve months for which each base-weighted index runs. It is quite enough to illustrate with one or two months in each case. The months selected are the three January dates (in 1972, 1973 and 1974) each in comparison with the preceding January. In addition the intermediate July dates (in 1972 and 1973) are used to give a different seasonal picture.

The first exercise is to show how the all-items index is put together from the eleven group-index numbers and how a group index is got from constituent subgroups. The advantage of the base-weighted form is that this build-up is achieved by treating the group (or subgroup) index numbers as price relatives, to be weighted with the group (or subgroup) weights (see 1.7). The algebraic proof is simply a manipulation with the $\sum$ notation. It is enough to take two groups: A, comprising m commodities ($i = 1, 2, \ldots m$) with total weights $w_a = \sum_{i=1}^{m} w_{i0}$ and price index

$$I_a = \frac{1}{w_a} \sum_{i=1}^{m} w_{i0} \frac{p_{i1}}{p_{i0}}$$

and B, comprising n–m commodities ($i = m + 1$, $m + 2$, ... n) with total weights w_b and index I_b similarly written. Then the overall index I is:

$$I = \frac{1}{w} \sum_{i=1}^{n} w_{i0} \frac{p_{i1}}{p_{i0}} \quad \text{where } w = \sum_{i=1}^{n} w_{i0} = w_a + w_b$$

So: $\quad (w_a + w_b)I = \sum_{i=1}^{m} w_{i0} \frac{p_{i1}}{p_{i0}} + \sum_{i=m+1}^{n} w_{i0} \frac{p_{i1}}{p_{i0}} = w_a I_a + w_b I_b$

i.e. $\qquad I = \frac{w_a I_a + w_a I_b}{w_a + w_b} \quad$ as required

The reconstruction of the all-items index from the groups is shown in Table 3.1 and that of the food group from the constituent subgroups in Table 3.2. The weights are taken direct from Table A1. They are to be applied to price relatives, each expressed on the previous January as 100. The published index numbers of Table A1 are all chained back to January 1962; to yield the required price relatives, they have to be 'dechained' by simple division of the index numbers at the two dates concerned. The results are entered in Tables 3.1 and 3.2. Finally, at the foot of each of these tables, the weighting process is set out in detail for each index, giving the sums of products of weights and price relatives. The resulting index numbers, on division by the sum of the weights, are entered in the penultimate row of the main part of each table in comparison with the links in the chain from published figures.

The calculation of the index in January 1972 (Jan. 1971 = 100), first for food and then for all-items, illustrates the arithmetical work. The sum of products (1) × (4) divided by the sum of weights (1) in Table 3.2 gives:

$$\text{Food index} = \frac{27{,}899}{250} = 111{\cdot}60 \quad \text{in January 1972 (Jan. 1971 = 100)}$$

as entered in the penultimate row of the main part of the table. It can be checked against the published index numbers appropriately dechained from Table A1 and taken to two decimal places:

$$\frac{163{\cdot}9}{147{\cdot}0} 100 = 111{\cdot}50 \quad \text{in January 1972 (Jan. 1971 = 100)}$$

There is agreement within the margin of error arising from rounding in the calculations. In the same way, from Table 3.1,

TABLE 3.1

GENERAL RETAIL PRICE INDEX, 1971–4

Groups	Weights, January 1971 (1)	1972 (2)	1973 (3)	Price relatives Jan. 1971 = 100 Jan. 1972 (4)	Jan. 1972 = 100 July 1972 (5)	Jan. 1973 (6)	Jan. 1973 = 100 July 1973 (7)	Jan. 1974 (8)
Food	250	251	248	111·50	103·23	110·07	107·87	120·12
Alcoholic drink	65	66	73	101·85	103·37	105·97	100·61	101·65
Tobacco	59	53	49	99·86	100·00	102·31	99·58	100·42
Housing	119	121	126	108·89	106·60	113·98	104·86	110·45
Fuel and light	60	60	58	110·22	102·73	106·00	98·32	105·78
Durables	61	58	58	104·38	101·88	104·42	103·81	109·78
Clothing	87	89	89	106·46	103·22	107·39	105·31	113·49
Transport	136	139	135	107·51	103·23	105·01	103·83	109·79
Miscellaneous goods	65	65	65	109·92	100·78	102·17	102·24	107·30
Services	54	52	53	108·64	103·03	108·53	108·02	112·24
Meals out	44	46	46	112·93	105·15	110·01	112·99	120·66
All items: from groups	1000	1000	1000	108·19	103·29	107·75	104·87	111·95
as published				108·16	103·27	107·74	104·90	111·97

	(1) × (4)	(2) × (5)	Products (2) × (6)	(3) × (7)	(3) × (8)
Food	27,875·0	25,910·7	27,627·6	26,751·8	29,789·8
Alcoholic drink	6,620·2	6,822·4	6,994·0	7,344·5	7,420·4
Tobacco	5,891·7	5,300·0	5,422·4	4,879·4	4,920·6
Housing	12,957·9	12,898·6	13,791·6	13,212·4	13,916·7
Fuel and light	6,613·2	6,163·8	6,360·0	5,702·6	6,135·2
Durables	6,367·2	5,909·0	6,056·4	6,021·0	6,367·2
Clothing	9,262·0	9,186·6	9,557·7	9,372·6	10,100·6
Transport	14,621·4	14,349·0	14,596·4	14,017·0	14,821·6
Miscellaneous goods	7,144·8	6,550·7	6,641·0	6,645·6	6,974·5
Services	5,866·6	5,357·6	5,643·6	5,725·1	5,948·7
Meals out	4,968·9	4,836·9	5,060·5	5,197·5	5,550·4
Total	108,188·9	103,285·3	107,751·2	104,869·5	111,945·7

From Appendix Table A1

TABLE 3.2

INDEX OF RETAIL FOOD PRICES, 1971–4

Subgroups	Weights, January			Price relatives				
				Jan. 1971=100	Jan. 1972=100		Jan. 1973=100	
	1971	1972	1973	Jan. 1972	July 1972	Jan. 1973	July 1973	Jan. 1974
	(1)	(2)	(3)	(4)	(5)	(6)	(7)	(8)
Bread, etc.	37	36	33	108·3	103·0	105·9	106·1	125·7
Meat and bacon	65	64	73	111·0	109·3	125·6	111·1	125·0
Fish	8	9	8	121·0	102·6	115·8	110·9	145·0
Butter, etc.	11	14	10	138·3	91·0	83·1	100·7	114·3
Milk, cheese, eggs	37	39	36	114·9	92·6	101·9	106·7	122·4
Tea, etc.	14	13	12	102·4	101·6	104·6	98·5	100·0
Sugar, etc.	23	23	21	109·9	99·4	100·6	94·4	105·6
Fruit	13	13	14	113·7	106·0	118·0	118·5	119·7
Vegetables	25	24	25	107·1	113·8	112·6	118·1	119·1
Other food	17	15	16	107·0	103·9	106·5	98·8	108·0
All food:								
from subgroups	250	251	248	111·60	103·14	110·10	107·67	120·09
as published				111·50	103·23	110·07	107·87	120·12

	(1) × (4)	(2) × (5)	Products (2) × (6)	(3) × (7)	(3) × (8)
Bread, etc.	4,007	3,708	3,812	3,501	4,148
Meat and bacon	7,215	6,995	8,038	8,110	9,125
Fish	968	923	1,042	887	1,160
Butter, etc.	1,521	1,274	1,163	1,007	1,143
Milk, cheese, eggs	4,251	3,611	3,974	3,841	4,406
Tea, etc.	1,434	1,321	1,352	1,182	1,200
Sugar, etc.	2,528	2,286	2,314	1,982	2,218
Fruit	1,478	1,378	1,534	1,659	1,676
Vegetables	2,678	2,731	2,702	2,952	2,978
Other food	1,819	1,662	1,704	1,581	1,728
Total	27,899	25,889	27,635	26,702	29,782

From Appendix Table A1

$$\text{All-items index} = \frac{108,188 \cdot 9}{1,000} = 108 \cdot 19 \qquad \begin{array}{l} \text{in January 1972} \\ \text{(Jan. 1971} = 100) \end{array} \qquad (1)$$

which checks (to one decimal place) against the published index numbers:

$$\frac{159 \cdot 0}{147 \cdot 0} \ 100 = 108 \cdot 16 \qquad \text{in January 1972 (Jan. 1971} = 100) \qquad (2)$$

The results of successive calculations of (1) are entered in the penultimate row and of (2) in the last row of the main part of Table 3.1.

It is to be particularly stressed that the weighting process needs to be carried out for each dechained index, base-weighted on each successive January. It cannot be done on the published index as it stands since the weights are changed annually. The dechaining is a necessary process; there is no short cut. It is dictated by the chain form adopted for the index since 1962.

Equally it is to be stressed that, once annual index numbers are got by the weighting process of Table 3.1 and 3.2, the published forms chained back to 1962 are reproduced by the splicing process (**1.5** above) done regularly every January, i.e. by cumulative multiplication. With the present data, start from the published all-items index of 147·0 in January 1972 and chain on the subsequent links. Within rounding errors, the same chain index is got by use of the weighted averages such as (1) or the published links such as (2). For January 1972 with January 1962 = 100, the two chainings are:

From (1): $147 \cdot 0 \times 1 \cdot 0819 = 159 \cdot 04$

From (2): $147 \cdot 0 \times 1 \cdot 0816 = 159 \cdot 0$ as published

and continuing:

Date	All-items index (Jan. 1962=100) From weighted averages		As published
1972 Jan.	$147 \cdot 0 \times 1 \cdot 0819$	$= 159 \cdot 04$	159·0
July	$147 \cdot 0 \times 1 \cdot 0819 \times 1 \cdot 0329$	$= 164 \cdot 27$	164·2
1973 Jan.	$147 \cdot 0 \times 1 \cdot 0819 \times 1 \cdot 0775$	$= 171 \cdot 36$	171·3
July	$147 \cdot 0 \times 1 \cdot 0819 \times 1 \cdot 0775$		
	$\times 1 \cdot 0487$	$= 179 \cdot 71$	179·7
1974 Jan.	$147 \cdot 0 \times 1 \cdot 0819 \times 1 \cdot 0775$		
	$\times 1 \cdot 1195$	$= 191 \cdot 84$	191·8

This exercise is not just a check on the chain form of the official index; it serves to show how the pieces of the jigsaw fit together and so how to remove one or more of them. The base-weighted form has the property that a group or subgroup index can be treated as a price relative, to be multiplied by the group or subgroup weight, and this goes for subtraction as well as for addition.

A further exercise makes use of this fact in a process of stripping down a given index to eliminate sections which are not required. Two examples illustrate; the first excludes housing from the all-items index and the second eliminates fruit and vegetables from the food index. The calculation again proceeds with separate base-weighted index numbers, each valid for twelve months. There are, in these illustrations, three such index numbers and the data and computations of Table 3.1 and 3.2 are to be rearranged as follows. Reference numbers indicate columns of Table 3.1 or 3.2; the all-items index numbers are those from published data.

Index based on:	All items	Housing	All excl. housing	All food	Fruit	Vegetables	All food excl. fruit and vegetables
Jan. 1971							
Weights (1)	1,000	119	881	250	13	25	212
Products							
(1) × (4)	108,160	12,958	95,202	27,899	1,478	2,678	23,743
Jan. 1972							
Weights (2)	1,000	121	879	251	13	24	214
Products							
(2) × (5)	103,270	12,899	90,371	25,889	1,378	2,731	21,780
(2) × (6)	107,740	13,792	93,948	27,635	1,534	2,702	23,399
Jan. 1973							
Weights (3)	1,000	126	874	248	14	25	209
Products							
(3) × (7)	104,900	13,212	91,688	26,702	1,659	2,952	22,091
(3) × (8)	111,970	13,917	98,053	29,782	1,676	2,978	25,128

Division of the products by the weights gives the index numbers with and without the excluded items:

Index	Date	All-items index All	Excl. Housing	Food index All	Excl. fruit and vegetables
Jan. 1971 =100	Jan. 1972	108·2	108·1	111·6	112·0
Jan. 1972 =100	July 1972	103·3	102·8	103·1	101·8
	Jan. 1973	107·7	106·9	110·1	109·3
Jan. 1973 =100	July 1973	104·9	104·9	107·7	105·7
	Jan. 1974	112·0	112·2	120·1	120·2

If such index numbers are required with January 1962 as 100, as published, the calculations need to be taken back year by year to January 1962 and the resulting index numbers chained together (see **5.4**). Again there is no short cut; the exercise cannot be carried out on the published index with its set of weights changed annually.

The separate (annual) index numbers are usually enough in themselves. So, in the present illustrations, it is clear that the exclusion of the particular items has sometimes had little effect; at other times the increase in retail prices has been lower without them.

3.3 Retail Sales: Value and Volume

It is not possible to be very precise on the quantity index which corresponds to the index of retail prices. The nearest is an index representing the real-consumption levels of all consumers, arising in national income accounting, but this is of wider coverage than the 'index' families of the retail price index. On the other hand, a substantial part of the index of retail prices, that relating to prices in retail shops of all kinds, is covered by the data on retail sales published by the Department of Trade and Industry. It is important to be clear on the scope of retail sales. They comprise all commodities sold through retail shops, valued at market prices, with instalment purchases included at the full prices at the time of the transaction. They exclude meals out, all housing, fuel and light, all services and such sales of drink and tobacco as take place through non-retail outlets (e.g. pubs and restaurants). Of total consumers' expenditure of £24,000mn in 1966, a little more than £11,000mn is through retail shops and rather less than £13,000mn through other channels.

The Department of Trade regularly obtains returns of retail sales by value from a substantial sample of businesses in retail trade. No analysis of sales by commodities is asked for, so that the Department's figures can be shown by types of retail business but cannot be made to match the commodity grouping of the retail price index. The Department calculates an index of sales by volume by deflation of the value figures for various types of business by price index numbers estimated for the purpose, using the commodity analysis for the base year given by the Census of Distribution. The price index numbers are essentially of Laspeyres form, currently with 1971 weighting; the resulting volume index is, therefore, of Paasche form. This follows from property (1) of **2.3** above. The alternative Laspeyres volume index requires the calculation of sales at 1971 prices, not possible in the absence of commodity details of sales year by year.

In view of this rather rough and ready method, the question can be explored whether we cannot do as well by estimating a price index for retail sales, as part of the general index of retail prices, and using it to deflate the total value of retail sales. The attempt is carried out in Table 3.3. The retail price index has eleven groups (see Table 3.1); only six are relevant to retail sales and of these, two

TABLE 3.3

RETAIL SALES, ESTIMATED PRICE INDEX, 1966–73

Groups

	Food	Alcoholic drink	Tobacco	Durables	Clothing	Miscellaneous goods	Weighted average
Weights*							
1971	48·6	3·2	6·9	11·8	16·9	12·6	100
Prices† (1971 = 100)							
1966	74·3	79·7	87·2	79·2	83·1	70·7	77·0
1967	76·2	82·1	87·2	80·5	84·5	71·5	78·5
1968	79·2	83·2	90·6	83·6	85·8	78·3	81·6
1969	84·2	89·2	97·8	87·4	89·0	83·2	86·4
1970	90·0	94·2	98·4	93·1	93·6	89·8	91·7
1971	100	100	100	100	100	100	100
1972	108·9	104·1	100·7	103·8	107·3	105·6	106·9
1973	125·3	107·5	101·9	109·8	117·3	108·5	117·8

From *Monthly Digest of Statistics* (based on General Retail Price Index)

* % distribution of 1971 weights of Retail Price Index; drink weight reduced by 75% and tobacco weight by 40%.

† Group index numbers of Retail Price Index (Jan. 1962 = 100) switched to 1971 = 100.

(drink and tobacco) are given reduced weights (roughly estimated). The group index numbers are used, the published figures (on Jan. 1962 = 100) being switched by division to average 1971 as 100. The weighting of these price relatives into a price index appropriate to retail sales is done in Table 3.3, and the results transferred to Table 3.4. Here the official calculation of the volume index, with the implicit price index to match, is compared with that obtained by deflation of the value series by the price index we have constructed. Both price index numbers are (broadly) of Laspeyres form, and both those of volume are of Paasche form.

The results are not very close. Generally, the reconstructed price index runs ahead of that implied in the official calculations. Equally, the volume index as got in our calculations runs below the official index of volume. The comparison, however, is not too bad in the

TABLE 3.4

RETAIL SALES BY VOLUME, 1966–73

| | Published | | | Estimated (Table 3.3) | |
Index (*1971* = 100)	*Value index* (1)	*Volume index* (2)	*Implied price index:* (1)/(2) (3)	*Price index* (4)	*Implied volume index:* (1)/(4) (5)
1966	72·7	92·8	78·3	77·0	94·4
1967	75·3	94·6	79·6	78·5	95·9
1968	80·4	97·2	82·7	81·6	98·5
1969	84·9	97·3	87·3	86·4	98·3
1970	91·4	99·0	92·3	91·7	99·7
1971	100	100	100	100	100
1972	112·0	105·8	105·9	106·9	104·8
1973	126·9	110·7	114·6	117·8	107·7

From *Trade and Industry* and Table 3.3

sense that the general movements from year to year broadly correspond. The conclusion is that the kind of reconstruction shown in Table 3.3 is too rough to give results which are at all precise. If there is no alternative, the exercise may be worth while in disclosing the general changes from year to year.

3.4 The Use of Price Quotations

The price collection made monthly by the Department of Employment, for the index of retail prices, includes some hundreds of price quotations obtained for each food item in the index and from a variety of shops in 200 areas of the country. The Department publishes monthly in its *Gazette* the averages of the actual prices obtained, in pence per unit, for a list of food items which is extensive but not comprehensive. Appendix Table A2 shows these average prices for particular food subgroups: dairy produce, fruit and vegetables.

As an exercise in reconstruction, we can calculate a price index for each of the subgroups by combining price relatives from Table A2 with section weights of the retail price index. The latter are the subgroup weights given in Table A1, but in more detail. The results can be compared with the published subgroup figures to see how

RETAIL FOOD PRICES, AVERAGE PRICE QUOTATIONS, 1971–4

Price relatives

Subgroup	Item	Jan. 1971 =100 Jan. 1972 Items	Jan. 1971 =100 Jan. 1972 Mean	Jan. 1972 =100 July 1972 Items	Jan. 1972 =100 July 1972 Mean	Jan. 1972 =100 Jan. 1973 Items	Jan. 1972 =100 Jan. 1973 Mean	Jan. 1973 =100 July 1973 Items	Jan. 1973 =100 July 1973 Mean	Jan. 1973 =100 Jan. 1974 Items	Jan. 1973 =100 Jan. 1974 Mean
Butter, etc.	Butter, N.Z.	162·9		87·3		76·2		92·5		93·8	
	Danish	147·9	155·4	89·6	88·5	78·9	77·6	94·0	93·2	97·7	95·7
	Margarine, standard	105·7		98·0		98·0		106·8		128·1	
	Lower-priced	112·8	109·2	94·7	96·3	94·7	96·3	105·6	106·2	130·4	129·2
	Lard		103·2		92·5		93·9		112·1		163·6
Milk, cheese, eggs	Milk, ordinary		105·0		90·9		100·0		100·0		100·0
	Cheese, Cheddar		142·7		108·0		109·7		100·9		105·0
	Eggs, large	91·5		79·5		94·9		139·9		216·1	
	standard	88·6		78·4		99·0		140·6		230·1	
	medium	87·3	89·1	78·2	78·7	102·8	98·9	145·3	141·9	231·2	225·8
Fruit	Apples, cooking	135·7		137·2		169·2		127·3		81·8	
	dessert	115·3		103·0		128·8		115·3		89·7	
	Pears, dessert	119·4		105·3		136·8		117·6		98·4	
	Oranges	114·0		98·9		111·8		102·4		117·2	
	Bananas	115·9	120·1	101·0	109·1	104·9	130·3	125·7	117·7	125·7	102·6
Vegetables	Potatoes, white	107·5		127·9		123·3		117·0		109·4	
	red	110·4	109·0	132·1	130·1	117·0	120·1	112·9	114·9	112·9	111·2
	Tomatoes	108·1		94·2		100·0		98·3		116·8	
	Mushrooms	112·2		113·9		111·9		108·0		148·7	
	Cabbage, greens	110·3		131·4		109·3		129·8		147·9	
	hearted	108·2	95·1	85·7	84·7	91·3	109·6	86·5	95·3	133·5	114·8
	Cauliflower	109·7		200·0		119·0		206·4		117·0	
	Carrots	94·1		150·0		147·9		131·7		106·3	
	Onions		107·1		129·2		113·2		126·8		128·4

From Appendix Table A2

TABLE 3.6

FOOD PRICE INDEX, FOUR SUBGROUPS, 1971-4

Subgroup	Section	Weights, January			Price relatives				
					Jan. 1971 = 100	Jan. 1972 = 100		Jan. 1973 = 100	
		1971	1972	1973	Jan. 1972	July 1972	Jan. 1973	July 1973	Jan. 1974
		(1)	(2)	(3)	(4)	(5)	(6)	(7)	(8)
Butter, etc.	Butter	7	10	6	155·4	88·5	77·6	93·2	95·7
	Margarine	2	2	2	109·2	96·3	96·3	106·2	129·2
	Lard	2	2	2	103·2	92·5	93·9	112·1	163·6
	Subgroup	11	14	10	137·5	90·2	82·6	99·6	116·0
Milk, cheese, eggs	Milk	24	26	24	105·0	90·9	100·0	100·0	100·0
	Cheese	4	6	6	142·7	108·0	109·7	100·9	105·0
	Eggs	9	7	6	89·1	78·7	98·9	141·9	225·8
	Subgroup	37	39	36	108·5	91·3	101·3	107·1	121·8
Dairy Produce	Total	48	53	46	115·1	91·0	96·4	105·5	120·5
Fruit	Subgroup	13	13	14	120·1	109·1	130·3	117·7	102·6
Vegetables	Potatoes	9	8	9	109·0	130·1	120·1	114·9	111·2
	Tomatoes	4	3	3	95·1	84·7	109·6	95·3	114·8
	Other	12	13	13	107·1	129·2	113·2	126·8	128·4
	Subgroup	25	24	25	105·9	123·9	115·0	118·7	120·6
Fruit and Vegetables	Total	38	37	39	110·7	118·7	120·4	118·4	114·1

Products

		(1) × (4)	(2) × (5)	(2) × (6)	(3) × (7)	(3) × (8)
Butter, etc.	Butter	1,087·8	885·0	776·0	559·2	574·2
	Margarine	218·4	192·6	192·6	212·4	258·4
	Lard	206·0	185·0	187·8	224·2	327·2
	Subgroup	1,512·2	1,262·6	1,156·4	995·8	1,159·8
Milk, cheese, eggs	Milk	2,640·0	2,363·4	2,600·0	2,400·0	2,400·0
	Cheese	570·8	648·0	658·2	605·4	630·0
	Eggs	801·9	550·9	692·3	851·4	1,354·8
	Subgroup	4,012·7	3,562·3	3,950·5	3,856·8	4,384·8
Dairy Produce	Total	5,524·9	4,824·9	5,106·9	4,852·6	5,544·6
Fruit	Subgroup	1,561·3	1,418·3	1,693·9	1,647·8	1,436·4
Vegetables	Potatoes	981·0	1,040·8	960·8	1,034·1	1,000·8
	Tomatoes	380·4	254·1	328·8	285·9	344·4
	Other	1,285·2	1,679·6	1,471·6	1,648·4	1,669·2
	Subgroup	2,646·6	2,974·5	2,761·2	2,968·4	3,014·4
Fruit and Vegetables	Total	4,207·9	4,392·8	4,455·1	4,616·2	4,450·8

From Department of Employment *Gazette* for Weights; Table 3.5 for price relatives (means) near we get. It is not an idle exercise since we may be driven to use this kind of calculation to supplement the official index numbers as published. We may, for example, be able to discover something of the make-up of a subgroup index, to see whether this item or that is mainly responsible for price movements over a particular period.

At the outset, we should note two differences between our reconstruction and the actual computation of the retail price index. One is the incidence of incomplete data (as examined briefly in **1.7** above) since the price quotations represent only a partial and a somewhat biased coverage of all the food items in the index. The other is that we are compelled to use a substitute estimator of price relatives. The official price relative for one item (e.g. Danish butter) is got first by writing a price relative (ratio of prices) for each individual quote obtained and then by averaging over all quotations. In our exercise, we get the price relative (e.g. for Danish butter) by taking the ratio of average prices at two dates. The difference is between the average of price ratios and the ratio of price averages. There is a case to be made out for the ratio of averages (see **7.1**) but it happens not to be the estimator used in the official index.

Subject to these limitations, we proceed to the first stage in the exercise, the estimation of price relatives written from the average prices of Appendix Table A2. This is shown in Table 3.5. The means are taken for the items which fall in the various sections of the official index, i.e. two kinds of butter, two kinds of margarine, one lard quote, and so on. These means are transferred to Table 3.6, in which are also entered the published section weights of the official index. The weighting of the price relatives is carried through to produce estimates of the subgroup index numbers.

For example, in January 1972 on January 1971 as 100, the subgroup index numbers for butter, etc. and for milk, cheese, eggs are got from sums of products divided by sums of weights:

$$\text{Butter, etc. } \frac{1,512 \cdot 2}{11} = 137 \cdot 5; \text{ Milk, cheese, eggs } \frac{4,012 \cdot 7}{37} = 108 \cdot 5$$

These calculated index numbers are inserted in the relevant subgroup rows of Table 3.6. Other subgroup index numbers are obtained similarly, as are the index numbers for dairy produce and for fruit and vegetables, each the amalgamation of two subgroups.

The results of the exercise are displayed below in comparison with the published index numbers. The latter come from Table 3.2, with subgroup index numbers also combined in pairs by use of the relevant weights.

Index	Date	Butter, etc.	Milk, cheese, eggs	All dairy produce	Fruit	Veget-ables	All fruit and vegetables
From price quotations							
Jan. 1971							
=100	Jan. 1972	137·5	108·5	115·1	120·1	105·9	110·7
Jan. 1972	July 1972	90·2	91·3	91·0	109·1	123·9	118·7
=100	Jan. 1973	82·6	101·3	96·4	130·3	115·0	120·4
Jan. 1973	July 1973	99·6	107·1	105·5	117·7	118·7	118·4
=100	Jan. 1974	116·0	121·8	120·5	102·6	120·6	114·1
As published							
Jan. 1971							
=100	Jan. 1972	138·3	114·9	120·2	113·7	107·1	109·4
Jan. 1972	July 1972	91·0	92·6	92·2	106·0	113·8	111·1
=100	Jan. 1973	83·1	101·9	96·9	118·0	112·6	114·5
Jan. 1973	July 1973	100·7	106·7	105·4	118·5	118·1	118·2
=100	Jan. 1974	114·3	122·4	120·6	119·7	119·1	119·3

The comparison shows up one success and one complete 'flop'. The index for butter, etc. is closely reproduced, with differences little more than 1 % at their greatest; the price quotations appear to provide adequate coverage. The index for milk, cheese, eggs does equally well after January 1972, due in no small part to the stability in the price of milk, but is far too low in January 1972. The same holds for the combined dairy-produce index. On the other hand, the attempt to reconstruct the published index for fruit and vegetables from the price quotations, available and selected for the purpose, is a failure. The coverage of price quotations is inadequate, omitting such diverse items as most seasonal vegetables and all canned or dried fruit and vegetables.

The exercise is just good enough to disclose the influence of some particular items within the broad movements of prices of subgroups. A dominating factor is clearly the rise and fall of butter prices in the period. Another factor is the opposed movement of prices of tomatoes, low in July when most vegetables are dear. In any case, the dispersion of the price relatives of vegetables in the summer (July) is so great that the price index for vegetables must be regarded as uncertain if not unstable then.

3.5 Aggregative Index Numbers: Some Practical Problems

No calculations have yet been made of price and/or quantity index numbers as ratios of value aggregates. For this, matching price and quantity data are needed, or at least matching quantity and expenditure figures. An attempt is now made to make use of such data for retail prices and consumption. At the same time the effects of imperfections in the data are shown up: specifically, incomplete data from a single source, and non-comparable material drawn from different sources.

The data used are again for the food subgroups considered in **3.4**. The main source is the National Food Survey (NFS) based on an annual sample of some 8,000 households making weekly returns on food consumption and expenditure. The results are published in annual reports by the National Food Survey Committee for the Ministry of Agriculture. To limit the scope of the calculations, and to show results for a smaller group than so far examined, a group of low-income pensioner households, distinguished in the survey, is selected for the exercise. These are, in fact, the main group excluded by the lower cut-off point of the 'index' families for the retail price index. Other groups are picked up in **3.6**.

The period of the comparison needs close specification. The returns of the NFS each relate to one week but they are spread throughout the year. It is possible to average the returns to obtain results, not only for years, but for shorter periods, taken in the NFS down to quarters. The comparisons here are over the period from 1968 to 1972 and 1973, and data for the first quarter of each year are used.

As supplementary data, the average price quotations published by the Department of Employment are available for use, as in **3.4**, but taken over the longer period from 1968. It is convenient to continue to take prices in January, in each of the years 1968, 1972 and 1973. This is not a precise matching of data but it is not unreasonable to relate consumption in the first quarter to January prices.

The source data used are given in Appendix Table A2 for price quotations and Table A3 for NFS material.

The calculations of aggregative index numbers of price and quantity should be based on comparable data taken from one source only, the NFS data. The difficulty is that the data are incomplete since they lack any information on actual prices paid by the families making returns. Indeed it would not be a practicable proposition to attempt to get prices quoted and paid, in all their variety, in a household survey. The problem is not an unusual one and a further example of it is examined in **3.7**.

One way out of the difficulty is to use a substitute estimator for prices: *unit values* obtained for each item by dividing expenditure by quantity bought or consumed. These are shown in Table 3.8 for the NFS data. The money expenditure does correspond to the quantity, being obtained from a single set of returns, and the ratio is a surrogate for average price and in the same units (e.g. pence per lb). But changes in unit values are imperfect and often biased estimators of price changes. This is because unit values change, not only when the consumer has to pay a different price, but also when he switches his purchases between the various grades, brands or qualities available to him on the market. So the unit value of consumption of margarine, in pence per lb, even when calculated for only one family, reflects two things. One is the price as stamped on a particular brand of margarine; the other is the way in which the family distributes its purchases between different brands. All price quotations could remain unchanged and yet unit value can increase as a consequence of a switch of purchases from cheaper to more expensive brands of (presumably) better quality. Unit values are to be used for prices with due caution, and index numbers calculated from them are to be carefully labelled as such.

A second way out of the difficulty of the lack of prices in the NFS data is to import price quotations (Table A2) to match as far as possible the quantities consumed as given in the NFS material. This is done in Table 3.9. A new difficulty now arises, that the prices are those paid by consumers generally and not specifically by low-income pensioners. There is, moreover, the practical difficulty that the NFS data are given in a rather coarse classification of commodities (e.g. all fruit) so that we need to get round our general ban on averaging heterogeneous prices. The limited departure from rectitude forced upon us is to take the means of price quotations in some 'mixed bags' of commodities in the NFS groupings. It is clearly a pretty rough job.

As a check on these two attempts at a solution of the problem, and as a fall-back in case both fail, we revert to the equivalent weighted-average form of index. In effect here we give up the quantities, provided by the NFS data on consumption of low-income pensioners, as impossible to match with prices. Instead we use the NFS to provide only the expenditures of these households, the basic weights of our index number to be applied to price relatives showing changes in prices over time as given by the supplementary data on price quotations. This is an example of a commonly used practice of calculating a price and/or quantity index by getting relatives from a special collection of prices and/or quantities and by weighting them with expenditures picked up from another source. This procedure, followed in the retail price index as in other official index numbers, is much less influenced by the coarse classification of expenditures by commodities as long as the prices and/or quantities come in fine and accurate detail for the calculation of the relatives. This is so if only because of Bowley's result on errors in weights (**1.7**).

The weighted-average calculations are carried out in Table 3.10. The work, however, is set out in such a way that the various (direct and cross) value aggregates are estimated for comparison with the corresponding aggregates of Tables 3.8 and 3.9. It is only a matter of keeping separate the numerators and denominators of the weighted averages.

In tabulating the calculations of the index numbers, adopt a convenient algebraic notation for prices and quantities and hence for value aggregates. The periods used in the exercise are the first quarter (in NFS data) or January (price quotations) of each of three years indicated by a subscript:

1968: subscript 0;   1972: subscript 1;   1973: subscript 2

So p_0, p_1, p_2 are the prices of an item, and q_0, q_1, q_2 the quantities consumed, at the three dates. Value aggregates are then written in the usual notation; for example, $\sum p_2 q_0$ is the aggregate of the 1968 quantities at 1973 prices.

The first task is to assemble the material on price quotations in the form needed for Tables 3.9. and 3.10. This involves taking the means of prices (in d per unit) for multiplication by NFS quantities (Table 3.9) and for writing price relatives (% of January 1968) to which NFS expenditure weights are applied (Table 3.10). One small but troublesome difficulty is to be noticed. In NFS data, the subgroup butter, etc. is shown in some detail in the quantities consumed but only in total in expenditure (except in 1973). Hence Table 3.9, in which only quantities are taken from the NFS, is in more detail than the other two. To match this, the means of prices are to be shown in detail for butter, etc., but the price relatives only for the subgroup. The calculations are given in Table 3.7.

The three separate exercises in estimating value aggregates, from which index numbers can later be derived, are now set out in suc-

FOOD PRICE QUOTATIONS: MEANS OF PRICES AND PRICE RELATIVES, 1968 AND 1972-3

Subgroup	Item	Prices (d per lb)* — p_0 Jan. 1968		p_1 Jan. 1972		p_2 Jan. 1973		Price relatives (% of Jan. 1968) — p_1/p_0		p_2/p_0	
		Items	Mean	Items	Mean	Items	Mean	Items	Mean	Items	Mean
Butter, etc.	Butter, N.Z.	40·3		71·5		54·5		177·4		135·2	
	Danish	47·8	44·05	76·3	73·9	60·2	57·35	159·6		125·9	
	Margarine, standard	22·0		29·8		29·2		135·5		132·7	
	Lower-priced	16·6	19·3	26·4	28·1	25·0	27·1	159·0		150·6	
	Lard		16·1		22·8		21·4	141·6	154·6	132·9	135·5
Milk, cheese, eggs	Milk, ordinary		10·0		13·2		13·2		132·0		132·0
	Cheese, Cheddar		43·0		69·8		76·6		162·3		178·1
	Eggs, large	51·9		57·1		54·2		110·0		104·4	
	standard	46·5	46·6	49·0	49·6	48·5	48·9	105·4	106·2	104·3	104·9
	medium	41·4		42·7		43·9		103·1		106·0	
Fruit	Apples, cooking	18·4		15·6		26·4		84·8		143·5	
	dessert	22·1		23·3		30·0		105·4		135·7	
	Pears, dessert	22·1		22·8		31·2		103·2		141·2	
	Oranges	15·0	18·7	18·7	20·2	20·9	26·0	124·7	109·1	139·3	138·7
	Bananas	16·0		20·4		21·4		127·5		133·8	
Vegetables	Potatoes, white	3·8		4·3		5·3		113·2		139·5	
	red	4·5	4·15	5·3	4·8	6·2	5·75	117·8	115·5	137·8	138·6
	Tomatoes	30·7		42·5		46·6		138·4		151·8	
	Mushrooms	58·0		69·2		69·2		119·3		119·3	
	Cabbage, greens	8·8		10·1		11·3		114·8		128·4	
	hearted	6·6		8·6		9·4		130·3		142·4	
	Cauliflour	18·6		25·2		23·0		135·5		123·7	
	Carrots	6·8		7·9		9·4		116·2		138·2	
	Onions	8·2	19·7	9·6	24·7	14·2	26·2	117·1	124·5	173·2	139·6

From Appendix Table A2

* Except milk (*d* per pint) and eggs (*d* per doz)

TABLE 3.8

FOOD CONSUMPTION AND UNIT VALUES, LOW-INCOME PENSIONER HOUSEHOLDS, 1968 AND 1972–3

Subgroup	Item	Unit	Consumption, 1st quarter (Units per head per week)			Unit values, 1st quarter (d per unit)		
			1968 q_0 (1)	1972 q_1 (2)	1973 q_2 (3)	1968 P_0 (4)	1972 P_1 (5)	1973 P_2 (6)
Dairy Produce	Butter, etc.	oz	13·04	12·87	12·65	2·078	3·174	2·553
	Milk	pint	5·31	5·11	5·47	10·085	13·865	13·097
	Cheese	oz	3·71	3·86	3·98	2·898	4·619	5·095
	Eggs	each	4·62	4·49	4·62	4·082	4·655	4·857
Fruit and Vegetables	Fresh fruit	oz	16·64	16·85	16·16	0·992	1·160	1·386
	Other fruit	,,	4·92	5·93	5·16	1·423	1·717	1·870
	Potatoes	,,	43·39	42·49	48·08	0·245	0·245	0·307
	Other vegetables	,,	34·72	35·62	39·32	0·826	1·053	1·033

Subgroup	Item		Products, (4) × (d per head per week)			Products, (5) ×			Products, (6) ×		
			(1) P_0q_0	(2) P_0q_1	(3) P_0q_2	(1) P_1q_0	(2) P_1q_1	(3) P_1q_2	(1) P_2q_0	(2) P_2q_1	(3) P_2q_2
Dairy Produce	Butter, etc.		27·10	26·74	26·29	41·39	40·85	40·15	33·29	32·86	32·29
	Milk		53·55	51·53	55·16	73·62	70·85	75·84	69·55	66·93	71·64
	Cheese		10·75	11·19	11·53	17·14	17·83	18·38	18·90	19·67	20·28
	Eggs		18·86	18·33	18·86	21·51	20·90	21·51	22·44	21·81	22·44
	Total		110·26	107·79	111·84	153·66	150·43	155·88	144·18	141·27	146·65
Fruit and Vegetables	Fresh fruit		16·51	16·72	16·03	19·30	19·54	18·75	23·06	23·35	22·39
	Other fruit		7·00	8·44	7·34	8·45	10·18	8·86	9·20	11·09	9·65
	Potatoes		10·77	10·39	11·78	10·77	10·39	11·78	13·50	13·04	14·78
	Other vegetables		28·67	29·42	32·48	36·56	37·51	41·40	35·87	36·80	40·63
	Total		62·95	64·97	67·63	75·08	77·62	80·79	81·63	84·28	87·45

From Appendix Table A3

FOOD CONSUMPTION AND PRICES, LOW-INCOME PENSIONER HOUSEHOLDS, 1968 AND 1972-3

Subgroup	Item	Consumption, first quarter (lbs per head per week)*			Mean prices, January (d per lb)*		
		1968 q_0 (1)	1972 q_1 (2)	1973 q_2 (3)	1968 P_0 (4)	1972 P_1 (5)	1973 p_2 (6)
Dairy Produce	Butter	0·451	0·362	0·389	44·05	73·9	57·35
	Margarine	0·193	0·256	0·235	19·3	28·1	27·1
	Lard	0·171	0·186	0·166	16·1	22·8	21·4
	Milk	5·31	5·11	5·47	10·0	13·2	13·2
	Cheese	0·232	0·241	0·249	43·0	69·8	76·6
	Eggs	0·385	0·374	0·385	46·6	49·6	48·9
Fruit and Vegetables	Fruit	1·3475	1·424	1·3325	18·7	20·2	26·0
	Potatoes	2·749	2·656	3·005	4·15	4·8	5·75
	Other vegetables	2·170	2·226	2·4575	19·7	24·7	26·2

Products (d per head per week)

Subgroup	Item	$(1)\times(4)$ p_0q_0	$(2)\times(4)$ p_0q_1	$(1)\times(5)$ p_1q_0	$(2)\times(5)$ p_1q_1	$(3)\times(4)$ p_0q_2	$(1)\times(6)$ p_2q_0	$(3)\times(6)$ p_2q_2
Dairy	Butter	19·87	15·95	33·33	26·75	17·14	25·86	22·31
	Margarine	3·72	4·94	5·42	7·19	4·54	5·23	6·37
	Lard	2·75	2·99	3·90	4·24	2·67	3·66	3·55
	Milk	53·10	51·10	70·09	67·45	54·70	70·09	72·20
	Cheese	9·98	10·36	16·19	16·82	10·71	17·77	19·07
	Eggs	17·94	17·43	19·10	18·55	17·94	18·83	18·83
	Total	107·36	102·77	148·03	141·00	107·70	141·44	142·33
Fruit and Vegetables	Fruit	25·20	26·63	27·22	28·76	24·92	35·04	34·64
	Potatoes	11·41	11·02	13·20	12·75	12·47	15·81	17·28
	Other vegetables	42·75	43·85	53·60	54·98	48·41	56·85	64·39
	Total	79·36	81·50	94·02	96·49	85·80	107·70	116·31

From Appendix Table A3 and Table 3.7

* Except milk (pints and d per pint) and eggs (doz and d per doz).

TABLE 3.10

FOOD PRICE INDEX, LOW-INCOME PENSIONER HOUSEHOLDS, 1968 AND 1972-3

| Subgroup | Item | Expenditure, first quarter (d per head per week) | | | Mean of price relatives (% of Jan. 1968) | | Ratios | | Products | |
		1968 w_0 (1)	1972 w_1 (2)	1973 w_2 (3)	1972 $\frac{p_1}{p_0}$ (4)	1973 $\frac{p_2}{p_0}$ (5)	(2)/(4) p_0q_1	(3)/(5) p_0q_2	(1)×(4) p_1q_0	(1)×(5) p_2q_0
Dairy Produce	Butter, etc.	27·10	40·85	32·29	154·6	135·5	26·42	23·83	41·90	36·72
	Milk	53·55	70·85	71·64	132·0	132·0	53·67	54·27	70·69	70·69
	Cheese	10·75	17·83	20·28	162·3	178·1	10·99	11·39	17·45	19·15
	Eggs	18·86	20·90	22·44	106·2	104·9	19·68	21·39	20·03	19·78
	Total	110·26	150·43	146·65			110·76	110·88	150·07	146·34
Fruit and Vegetables	Fruit	23·51	29·72	32·04	109·1	138·7	27·24	23·10	25·65	32·61
	Potatoes	10·77	10·39	14·78	115·5	138·6	9·00	10·66	12·44	14·93
	Other vegetables	28·67	37·51	40·63	124·5	139·6	30·13	29·10	35·69	40·02
	Total	62·95	77·62	87·45			66·37	62·86	73·78	87·56

From Appendix Table A3 and Table 3.7

cessive tables. The first is Table 3.8 making use only of NFS data on an entirely comparable basis. Here the classification is necessarily coarse, and unit values need to be used as substitutes for prices. For both reasons the index numbers of price and quantity to be got from the calculations are less accurate than we would like them to be.

The second exercise is done in Table 3.9 in which the price means are lifted from Table 3.7 and applied to NFS quantities on consumption. The data are in more detail in the butter, etc. subgroup and the NFS quantities are converted to different units in order to match the prices. The weakness of the calculation lies mainly in the non-comparable data used and also in the fact that price means need to be taken for 'mixed bags' of commodities.

The last exercise is a weighted-average calculation, NFS expenditure weights being applied to price relatives from Table 3.7. It is laid out in Table 3.10 in such a way that estimates of value aggregates are obtained rather than their ratios as weighted averages The actual index numbers are derived later when the results of all three exercises are assembled. Meanwhile, it is important to be clear how the aggregates of Table 3.10 are to be interpreted in the weighted-average context. Consider the base-weighted price index in 1972:

$$\frac{\sum p_1 q_0}{\sum p_0 q_0} = \frac{\sum w_0 \dfrac{p_1}{p_0}}{\sum w_0} = \frac{\text{sum of col. (1)} \times (4)}{\text{sum of col. (1)}}$$

and the corresponding current-weighted form $\sum p_1 q_1 / \sum p_0 q_1$ as the reciprocal of:

$$\frac{\sum p_0 q_1}{\sum p_1 q_1} = \frac{\sum w_1 \dfrac{p_0}{p_1}}{\sum w_1} = \frac{\sum w_1 / \dfrac{p_1}{p_0}}{\sum w_1} = \frac{\text{sum of col. (2)}/(4)}{\text{sum of col. (2)}}$$

The four aggregates in these two ratios are shown separately in Table 3.10. They serve equally to give the quantity index numbers to match the price forms. It is to be noticed that one cross-valuation, $\sum p_1 q_0$, is estimated simply by applying the price relatives of col. (4) to the weights of col. (1). The other cross-valuation could be estimated equally simply by writing a new column of price relatives p_0/p_1 as the reciprocals of the relatives of col. (4) and applying them to the weights of col. (2). It saves time and space to achieve the same result by *dividing* the weights of col. (2) each by the price relative p_1/p_0 already written in col. (4).

The results of the three exercises are assembled in the value

TABLE 3.11

VALUE MATRICES, LOW-INCOME PENSIONER HOUSEHOLDS, 1968 AND 1972–3

Values (d per head per week)

Cases: Table	First quarter	Subscript	Dairy Produce Quantities			Fruit and Vegetables Quantities		
			q_0	q_1	q_2	q_0	q_1	q_2
3.8	1968	0						
	1972	1						
Unit Values (prices)	1973	2						
		p_0	110·26	107·79	111·84	62·95	64·97	67·63
		p_1	153·66	150·43	155·88	75·08	77·62	80·79
		p_2	144·18	141·27	146·65	81·63	84·28	87·45
3.9 Prices		p_0	107·36	102·77	107·70	79·36	81·50	85·80
		p_1	148·03	141·00	..	94·02	96·49	..
		p_2	141·44	..	142·33	107·70	..	116·31
3.10 Prices		p_0	110·26	110·76	110·88	62·95	66·37	62·86
		p_1	150·07	150·43	..	73·78	77·62	..
		p_2	146·34	..	146·65	87·56	..	87·45

From Tables 3.8, 3.9, 3.10

matrices of Table 3.11. There is one matrix for the subgroup dairy produce and another for the subgroup fruit and vegetables, and each pair is estimated by each of the three methods of Tables 3.8, 3.9 and 3.10. The matrices are of order 3×3 since three dates are compared.

TABLE 3.12

INDEX NUMBERS, LOW-INCOME PENSIONER HOUSEHOLDS, 1968 AND 1972–3

Cases: table	First quarter index (First quarter 1968 = 100)		Unit value or Price index		Quantity index	
			Base-weighted	Current-weighted	Base-weighted	Current-weighted
Dairy	3·8	1972	139·4	139·6	97·8	97·9
Produce		1973	130·8	131·1	101·4	101·7
	3·9	1972	137·9	137·2	95·7	95·3
		1973	131·7	132·2	100·3	100·6
	3·10	1972	136·1	135·8	100·5	100·2
		1973	132·7	132·3	100·6	100·2
Fruit and	3·8	1972	119·3	119·5	103·2	103·4
Vegetables		1973	129·7	129·3	107·4	107·1
	3·9	1972	118·5	118·4	102·7	102·6
		1973	135·7	135·6	108·1	108·0
	3·10	1972	117·2	117·0	105·4	105·2
		1973	139·1	139·1	99·9	99·9

From Tables 3.8, 3.9, 3.10

The computational procedure of **2.4** is applied to each value matrix to give index numbers of price and quantity in Laspeyres and Paasche forms for the first quarter of 1972 and 1973 with the first quarter of 1968 as 100. One numerical example serves to illustrate the procedure. The whole complex of index numbers is shown in Table 3.12. As the example, take index numbers for *dairy produce* on the method of Table 3.8, got from the top left-hand matrix of Table 3.11. The two base-weighted (Laspeyres) index numbers come by division of entries in the first column of the matrix for unit value and in the first row for quantity:

Laspeyres index (first quarter 1968 = 100)

First quarter:	Unit value	Quantity
1972	$\dfrac{153\cdot66}{110\cdot26}100 = 139\cdot4$	$\dfrac{107\cdot79}{110\cdot26}100 = 97\cdot8$
1973	$\dfrac{144\cdot18}{110\cdot26}100 = 130\cdot8$	$\dfrac{111\cdot84}{110\cdot26}100 = 101\cdot4$

The corresponding current-weighted (Paasche) forms come from the division of a diagonal entry in the matrix by the matching entry in the first row for unit value and in the first column for quantity.

Paasche index (first quarter 1968 = 100)

First quarter:	Unit value	Quantity
1972	$\dfrac{150\cdot43}{107\cdot79}\,100 = 139\cdot6$	$\dfrac{150\cdot43}{153\cdot66}\,100 = 97\cdot9$
1973	$\dfrac{146\cdot65}{111\cdot84}\,100 = 131\cdot1$	$\dfrac{146\cdot65}{144\cdot18}\,100 = 101\cdot7$

One incidental point can be noticed. If the object is to get index numbers all on one base date as 100, as in the numerical example above, then the whole of the 3×3 value matrix is not used. The entries in the middle of the last row and column are the cross-valuations $\sum p_2 q_1$ and $\sum p_1 q_2$, neither being needed. These entries may be left blank as in the matrices on the last two methods in Table 3.11. To illustrate the fact that the entries can be computed if needed, they are obtained in Table 3.8 and included in the matrices on the first method in Table 3.11. It is from these entries that index numbers relating the first quarter of 1973 to that of 1972 are to be derived. They are not given explicitly here since they are incidental in the present exercise.

Table 3.12 is intended to illustrate different methods of getting *approximate estimates* of index numbers from data which are imperfect in some respect or other. Any choice between the methods depends a good deal on whether or not unit values are acceptable as surrogates for prices. If a group of commodities varies little in composition and quality over the time period considered, then unit values change in much the same way as prices and there is no problem. The difficulties arise when there are considerable shifts in the make-up of a commodity group. To fix ideas, suppose that prices and quantities are measured in a physical unit such as lbs, that both are increasing over time and that there is also an improvement in the average quality, in that purchases include an increasing proportion of items of higher quality (e.g. more of the better brands of margarine costing more per lb). A 'pure' price index, based on price quotations with given weighting, must then go with a quantity index which uses not only the physical units (lbs) but also reflects the quality improvement. On the other hand, a unit-value index, which matches a quantity index based on physical units (lbs), will reflect quality changes as well as 'pure' price movements. The question is: which index, that of price or that of quantity, should reflect the fact of improvement in quality?

So, if it is acceptable for us to group quality changes in with price movements, then the first method of Table 3.8 is to be preferred with its advantage of using matching data from one source. But it may well be that it is the quantity movements which should include quality changes (e.g. in assessing the standard of living). Then the NFS data need to be supplemented by the (strictly) non-comparable price data to permit the second or third method to be used in estimating a price index as opposed to one of unit values.

For *fruit and vegetables* there is little choice. An earlier analysis (**3.4**) discloses that the particular price quotations available for the present exercise are quite inadequate for the purpose. It is a matter of accepting the unit-value method or nothing. For *dairy produce*, there is an effective choice since the price quotations are reasonably adequate for the job. Of the two price index numbers, there is little doubt that the weighted-average method of Table 3.10 produces a more reliable index with these coarsely classified data. There is a lot to be said for the standard practice of averaging price relatives with expenditure weights; it avoids the problem of trying to match quantities and actual prices averaged over a 'mixed bag' of items. From 1968 to 1972 the index numbers appear to tell a consistent story: an increase of about 36% in 'pure' prices, and a larger increase in excess of 39% in unit values with a considerable quality improvement swept in. Unfortunately the results for the comparison of 1968 with 1973 do not follow this pattern; either we must accept that there has been a quality deterioration after 1972, or errors in the data are clouding the issue.

Though substantive results cannot be expected from this exercise, some comments are in order on what the index numbers show. One observation is clear enough; in this material over a five-year period all the base-weighted (Laspeyres) forms are quite close to the current-weighted (Paasche) forms. While this cannot be relied upon completely, even in the short period, it does illustrate the fact that close agreement between the two forms is often found. We must not exaggerate the difference between the Laspeyres and the Paasche index. We need quite a large shift in weights (relative expenditures) to get a significant difference. It can happen, but not often, in the short run; it must be expected to arise as time goes on. Further, with the two forms close together, the expected bias (here that the Laspeyres form exceeds the Paasche) will also be small and swallowed up in the imperfections of, and errors in, the data. So it is here; Table 3.12 shows sometimes the Laspeyres form and sometimes the Paasche as the larger.

Another consequence of the closeness of the Laspeyres and Paasche forms is that there is close agreement between the alternative split of the change in expenditure into price and quantity components by property (1) of **2.4** above. One illustration is enough: changes between 1968 and 1972 in dairy-produce expenditure by these pensioner families. Expenditure increases by 36·4% from 110·26 (d per head per week) in 1968 to 150·43 in 1972, as shown in Table 3.11. The alternative splits of the expenditure change from Table 3.12 (price effect first):

$$1·364 = 1·361 \times 1·002 = 1·358 \times 1·005 \quad \text{by the price method}$$
$$\text{(Table 3.10)}$$
$$\text{and} \ 1·364 = 1·394 \times 0·979 = 1·396 \times 0·978 \quad \text{by the unit-value method}$$
$$\text{(Table 3.8)}$$

Hence by rounding off percentage increases, we get the same results from the alternative splits. We can say without ambiguity that low-income pensioners increased their expenditure on dairy produce by 36½% from 1968 to 1972, almost all (36%) being due to a price increase, leaving very little (not more than ½%) for an increase in real consumption *including* a quality improvement. If we throw the quality change with that in prices in the unit-value index, then the two together account for more than the expenditure change and real consumption *excluding* quality improvement has shown a slight decline.

3.6 Retail Price Index: Pensioner Households

Following recommendations by the Cost of Living Advisory Committee (1968), the Department of Employment has calculated separate index numbers of retail prices since 1969 both for one-person and for two-person pensioner households. These households have three-quarters or more of their income from pensions and, as such, are excluded from the group of 'index' families for the general index of retail prices. The new index numbers are designed to match the general index; they are published quarterly (not monthly) and they are again chain-based on January 1962 as 100 with weights estimated from average expenditures of the relevant families, as obtained from the Family Expenditure Survey. They differ only in one main particular: the housing group of prices is excluded. This is because rents of pensioner households are commonly paid as a supplement to their pensions. The index numbers have a direct application in an assessment of the level of pensions.

A quick comparison is made here between the published index numbers for pensioners and the general retail price index. For this purpose, housing is excluded from the general index on the method displayed at the end of **3.2**:

RETAIL PRICE INDEX IN FIRST QUARTER

| | *January 1962* =100 | | | *1972* | *1973* |
	1971	*1972*	*1973*	*(1971* =100*)*	*(1972* =100*)*
Pensioner households:					
One-person	148·5	162·5	175·3	109·4	107·9
Two-person	148·4	161·8	175·2	109·0	108·3
General index:					
All items	147·9	159·7	172·4	108·0	108·0
All except housing	146·0	157·4	168·7	107·8	107·2

The year-to-year changes shown are obtained by division of the index numbers on January 1962; they are between first quarters in the respective years. The two pensioner index numbers are quite close to each other but over time they have diverged upwards from the general index (excluding housing). This is mainly because pensioners lay out their budgets in different proportions, with different weighting in the index numbers calculated for them. It is also partly because they pay different prices and face different price movements over time.

Each official pensioner index is published in disaggregated form only to the group level and, even then, only once a year. The weights of the index numbers are, however, given in more detail, and some light – although not enough – can be thrown on the influence of the factors making for differences between pensioner and general index numbers. If we assume away differential price movements (though not differential price levels) i.e. if we assume that prices paid by pensioners move on average as prices generally, we may apply the different sets of weights to the general subgroup index numbers of retail prices (Table 3.2). The calculations are for two-person pensioners and general families, and for the block of four subgroups

TABLE 3.13

FOOD PRICE INDEX, TWO-PERSON PENSIONER AND GENERAL INDEX HOUSEHOLDS, 1971–4

	Weights*						Price relatives				
	Two-person pensioners			General index			Jan. 1971 =100	Jan. 1972 = 100		Jan. 1973 = 100	
Subgroup	1971 (1)	1972 (2)	1973 (3)	1971 (4)	1972 (5)	1973 (6)	Jan. 1972 (7)	July 1972 (8)	Jan. 1973 (9)	July 1973 (10)	Jan. 1974 (11)
Butter, etc.	24	30	21	12½	16	11½	138·3	91·0	83·1	100·7	114·3
Milk, cheese, eggs	72	74	69	42	44	41	114·9	92·6	101·9	106·7	122·4
Fruit	20	22	23	15	15	16	113·7	106·0	118·0	118·5	119·7
Vegetables	38	39	41	28	27	28½	107·1	113·8	112·6	118·1	119·1
Total	154	165	154	97½	102	97					

	Products									
	Jan. 1971=100		Jan. 1972=100				Jan. 1973=100			
	(1)×(7)	(4)×(7)	(2)×(8)	(2)×(9)	(5)×(8)	(5)×(9)	(3)×(10)	(6)×(10)	(3)×(11)	(6)×(11)
Butter, etc.	3,319	1,729	2,730	2,493	1,456	1,330	2,115	1,158	2,400	1,314
Milk, cheese, eggs	8,273	4,826	6,852	7,541	4,074	4,484	7,362	4,375	8,446	5,018
Fruit	2,274	1,706	2,332	2,596	1,590	1,770	2,726	1,896	2,753	1,915
Vegetables	4,070	2,999	4,438	4,391	3,073	3,040	4,842	3,366	4,883	3,394
Total	17,936	11,260	16,352	17,021	10,193	10,624	17,045	10,795	18,482	11,641

From Department of Employment *Gazette* for weights; Table 3.2 for price relatives

* January; out of total weight (excl. housing) of 1000.

making up dairy produce, fruit and vegetables, as shown in Table 3.13.

Look first at the effect of the differential weighting within this food block on the price index, i.e. the influence of the fact that pensioners devote more of their budget to purchases of dairy produce than of fruit and vegetables. Calculate a price index for the four subgroups taken together as, for example, the pensioner index in January 1972 (Jan. 1971 = 100):

$$\frac{17,936}{154} = 116\cdot5$$

Putting all such index numbers together, we have:

PRICE INDEX:
DAIRY PRODUCE, FRUIT AND VEGETABLES

Index Jan. 1971	Date	Two-person pensioners	General index
= 100	Jan. 1972	116·5	115·5
Jan. 1972	July 1972	99·1	99·9
= 100	Jan. 1973	103·2	104·2
Jan. 1973	July 1973	110·7	111·3
= 100	Jan. 1974	120·0	120·0

The main effect is that arising from the larger relative weight for dairy produce in pensioner budgets. It happens that the prices of dairy produce, notably butter and cheese, rose rapidly to early 1972 and then either fell or tapered off. The pensioner index was pushed up above the general index in January 1972 and then fell rather more rapidly than the general movement in 1972 and 1973.

The second effect to look for arises because this block of food purchases looms much larger (by more than 50%) in the pensioner budget as a whole. The result is that a high price index (as in January 1972) for these foods carries through and pushes the pensioner all-items index above that for the general 'index' families. Indeed, the price index for all items (except housing) rose from January 1971 to January 1972 by 9% for pensioners and by a little below 8% for general families. (These figures are given above for a comparison from first quarter to first quarter; they are about the same from January to January.) We can pursue a little further on observing that, with total weights set at 1,000, each all-items index can be analysed into subgroups a, b, c, ...

$$\sum \frac{w_0}{1,000} \frac{p_1}{p_0} = \underset{a}{\sum \frac{w_0}{1,000} \frac{p_1}{p_0}} + \underset{b}{\sum \frac{w_0}{1,000} \frac{p_1}{p_0}} + \underset{c}{\sum \frac{w_0}{1,000} \frac{p_1}{p_0}} + \ldots$$

The sums on the right, for subgroups, are given by the figures (all divided by 1,000) in the 'products' columns of Table 3.13 if carried all the way down to the all-items total. We may, therefore, pick out the contribution to the all-item (excluding housing) index of particular subgroups by taking the relevant sum of products (divided by 1,000). In January 1972 (Jan. 1971 = 100), the pensioner index of 109 has a contribution from dairy produce, fruit and vegetables of 17,936/1,000 = 17·9. The corresponding contribution in the general index is 11,260/1,000 = 11·3 to an all-items figure of under 108. These foods more than account for the difference between the pensioner and the general index. In terms of price movements, all the other groups and subgroups must balance out, with a little in favour of the pensioners.

The published index numbers for pensioners are temporal indices, i.e. they show price changes over time for each group of pensioners separately. In first quarter 1972, for example, the price rises from January 1962 for all items (except housing) are 62·5% for one-person pensioner households, 61·8% for households of two pensioners and only 57·4% for the general run of 'index' families. What is important here is that such figures say nothing about the level of prices paid by pensioners in comparison with other families. We know that prices are rising faster for pensioners but not whether they are higher or lower than prices paid by others. The index numbers are *not* inter-group indices; they do *not* show whether or not pensioners are paying higher prices than other households.

It remains to examine here the way in which non-temporal index numbers are constructed. The illustration below relates to *inter-group* indices; it continues and completes the analysis above by comparing the level of prices paid by one group of households with those paid by other groups. Of even more interest are *inter-regional* indices comparing price levels between one region or area and another. The Retail Prices Index Advisory Committee (1971) has made some specific proposals in this direction. There is, first, a quite conventional proposal that temporal index numbers should be constructed region by region. They would show, for example, whether London prices are rising faster than Scottish. The second and more experimental proposal is that inter-regional index numbers should be designed and computed to compare the level of prices, at one and the same date, in one region in comparison with another. It is such an index which would show (e.g.) whether and by how much London prices are higher than those in Scotland.

These proposals are not yet implemented. Meanwhile the nature of the problem of the construction of non-temporal index numbers can be illustrated quite well in the inter-group case.

The data used in the illustration are quantities and unit values from NFS material, analysed exactly as in Table 3.8 but limited (for convenience only) to dairy produce. The difference is that consumption and prices paid (unit values) are compared, not for three dates, but for three income-groups of families. Low-income pensioners are again taken and for comparison, two higher-income groups. These are specified in Table 3.14 which sets out the calculations for the first quarter of 1972 and then, as a repeat exercise, for the first quarter of 1973. All prices are now in new pence.

The base year of a temporal index is selected mainly on grounds of convenience. There is even less to guide the selection for an inter-group index; it is quite immaterial which of the three groups A, B and C of Table 3.14 is the 'base' of the index and which are left to be treated as 'current' situations. One group is to be compared with another as regards the level of prices paid and in all possible combinations. Since some selection must be made, the groups B and C are taken here in comparison with the pensioner group A as reference base.

It is by no means evident in general terms in which direction prices paid vary from low-income to high-income families. Pensioners and other low-income groups may pay lower prices since they need to economise, but equally they may pay higher prices in view of the small quantities they purchase. The answer to the question of how the balance is struck, at least for prices of dairy produce, is to be sought in data such as those of Table 3.14.

All possible aggregates, both direct valuations such as $\sum p_a q_a$ and cross-valuations such as $\sum p_a q_b$, are calculated and arranged in two value matrices of order 3×3, one for each of the two dates taken:

VALUE MATRICES, p PER HEAD PER WEEK

	First quarter 1972 Quantities consumed by:			First quarter 1973 Quantities consumed by:		
Dairy produce	A	B	C	A	B	C
Unit values paid by group:						
A	62·68	59·75	64·75	61·10	55·43	56·85
B	60·50	57·66	61·31	60·06	54·50	55·86
C	65·10	62·04	65·89	63·14	57·33	58·75

TABLE 3.14

CONSUMPTION AND PRICES, THREE GROUPS OF HOUSEHOLDS,* 1972 AND 1973

Date	Item	Unit	Consumption (units per head per week)			Unit values (p per unit)		
			Group A q_a	Group B q_b	Group C q_c	Group A p_a	Group B p_b	Group C p_c
First quarter, 1972	Butter, etc.	oz	12·87	11·05	10·33	1·3225	1·2624	1·3698
	Milk	pint	5·11	5·15	5·38	5·7769	5·6019	6·1190
	Cheese	oz	3·86	3·50	4·65	1·9249	1·9714	2·1118
	Eggs	each	4·49	4·46	5·02	1·9399	1·7848	1·7928
First quarter, 1973	Butter	oz	6·23	4·99	5·70	1·4029	1·3547	1·3807
	Margarine	,,	3·76	3·16	1·91	0·8484	0·8418	0·8691
	Lard	,,	2·66	1·95	1·26	0·5714	0·5846	0·6349
	Milk	pint	5·47	5·18	5·35	5·4570	5·4189	5·6991
	Cheese	oz	3·98	3·64	4·03	2·1231	2·0659	2·2481
	Eggs	each	4·62	4·27	4·33	2·0238	1·9555	2·0485

Products

	d per head per week	p_aq_a	p_aq_b	p_aq_c	p_bq_a	p_bq_b	p_bq_c	p_cq_a	p_cq_b	p_cq_c
First quarter, 1972										
Butter, etc.	"	17·02	14·61	14·98	16·25	13·95	13·04	17·63	15·14	14·15
Milk	"	29·52	29·75	31·08	28·63	28·85	30·14	31·27	31·51	32·92
Cheese	"	7·43	6·74	8·95	7·61	6·90	9·17	8·15	7·39	9·82
Eggs	"	8·71	8·65	9·74	8·01	7·96	8·96	8·05	8·00	9·00
Total Dairy Produce	"	62·68	59·75	64·75	60·50	57·66	61·31	65·10	62·04	65·89
First quarter, 1973										
Butter	"	8·74	7·00	8·00	8·44	6·76	7·72	8·60	6·89	7·87
Margarine	"	3·19	2·68	1·62	3·17	2·66	1·61	3·27	2·75	1·66
Lard	"	1·52	1·11	0·72	1·56	1·14	0·74	1·69	1·24	0·80
Milk	"	29·85	28·27	29·19	29·64	28·07	28·99	31·17	29·52	30·49
Butter	"	8·45	7·73	8·56	8·22	7·52	8·33	8·95	8·18	9·06
Eggs	"	9·35	8·64	8·76	9·03	8·35	8·47	9·46	8·75	8·87
Total Dairy Produce	"	61·10	55·43	56·85	60·06	54·50	55·86	63·14	57·33	58·75

From *Monthly Digest of Statistics* (based on National Food Survey)

* Specification of groups of households: Group A: low-income pensioners (as Appendix Table A3). Group B: middle-income, 1972 £30 and under £53 p.w. 1973 £34 and under £60 p.w. Group C: high-income, 1972 £53 p.w. and over 1973 £60 p.w. and over.

The comparison which might seem the most rewarding, and the one pursued here by way of illustration, is that between the high-income group C and the pensioner group A. In fact, the middle-income group B may be more interesting since a close reading of the value matrices (as done later in **4.7**) shows that this is the group paying the lowest prices and with the smallest consumption per head. But to proceed with the illustration, write price and quantity index numbers from the value matrices:

**INDEX NUMBERS, HIGH-INCOME GROUP C,
PENSIONER GROUP A = 100**

| | First quarter 1972 Weights of group | | First quarter 1973 Weights of group | |
	A	C	A	C
Dairy produce				
Unit values (prices)	103·9	101·8	103·3	103·3
Consumption (quantities)	103·3	101·2	93·0	93·0

The price index which can be described as of Laspeyres form is that with group A quantities as weights:

$$P_{ac}(q_a) = \frac{\sum p_c q_a}{\sum p_a q_a}100 = \frac{65 \cdot 10}{62 \cdot 68}100 = 103 \cdot 9 \text{ in } 1972$$

$$\text{and } = \frac{63 \cdot 14}{61 \cdot 10}100 = 103 \cdot 3 \text{ in } 1973$$

while the corresponding Paasche form has group C weights:

$$P_{ac}(q_c) = \frac{\sum p_c q_c}{\sum p_a q_c}100 = \frac{65 \cdot 89}{64 \cdot 75}100 = 101 \cdot 8 \text{ in } 1972$$

$$\text{and } = \frac{58 \cdot 75}{56 \cdot 85}100 = 103 \cdot 3 \text{ in } 1973$$

There is a fair spread between the Laspeyres and Paasche forms in 1972 but they are so close in 1973 that they agree within one decimal place.

What is clear in each of the two periods is that the high-income families tend to pay higher prices for butter, margarine and other dairy produce than do the pensioners. The difference is quantified; it is of the order of 3 %. It is less clear what can be concluded about relative levels of real consumption per head. High-income families are generally larger than those of pensioners; though they spend more per family, this is not necessarily so per head. The difference between money expenditures per head is shown by the ratios:

$$V_{ac} = \frac{\sum p_c q_c}{\sum p_a q_a} 100 = \frac{65 \cdot 89}{62 \cdot 68} 100 = 105 \cdot 1 \text{ in } 1972$$

$$\text{and} = \frac{58 \cdot 75}{61 \cdot 10} 100 = 96 \cdot 2 \text{ in } 1973$$

The high-income families appear, perhaps only by the accident of the particular data collections, to spend more on dairy produce per head in one period and less in the other, than do pensioners. The differences are carried through to the quantity index numbers measuring real consumption per head: about 3% one way in 1972 and 7% the other way in 1973. There is no evidence here of a continuing difference in spending per head on dairy produce.

3.7 Aggregative Index Numbers: External Trade

The block of data in Appendix B relates to the Gross Domestic Product (GDP) and its components as given for the U.K. in the annual publication on *National Income and Expenditure* (Central Statistical Office) usually described for short as the *Blue Book*. In addition, runs of quarterly data are published in *Economic Trends* and particularly long runs are shown in each October issue of this monthly journal.

The most convenient starting point in the analysis of GDP is by categories of expenditure at current prices (Appendix Table B2). Such broad aggregates are built up from a mass of data; they are the end-product of estimation in very fine detail. To illustrate, take two of the entries written in Table B2 as the difference: exports *less* imports of goods and services. The underlying data on external trade in merchandise – the goods as opposed to the services in the aggregate – are the definitive estimates published in the *Annual Statement of the Overseas Trade of the U.K.* It is enough to illustrate with one particular section of trade, and Table B1 relates to imports and exports of fuels in Section 3 of the Standard International Trade Classification. British practice is now to collect (through H.M. Customs and Excise) and to publish (by the Department of Trade) all overseas trade statistics on the *general system* of recording in which imports comprise all goods brought in, whether for home use or for re-export, and exports similarly include re-exported merchandise. There is a certain lack of precision in dating the figures of imports and exports arising from the administrative drill adopted by Customs, and some of the trade recorded in one month may well have been in ships arriving or departing in earlier or later months. These 'rough edges' to the data are much less troublesome in annual as opposed to monthly data. As Table B1 shows, each item of trade is given by quantity in specified units and in a valuation which is c.i.f. (cost, insurance, freight) for imports and f.o.b. (free on board) for exports. Quantities are not available, and only values recorded, for some of the more heterogeneous items. It happens that Section 3 of S.I.T.C. is free of such items: where they arise it is necessary to make the adjustments described in Allen (1953).

Since overseas trade statistics are recorded only by quantity and value, they provide a leading example of the use of *unit values* as substitutes for prices. Unit values for imports and exports are subject to exactly the same limitations as in the National Food Survey data of Table 3.8; they reflect not only movements in prices but also changes in the mix of trade in the various groups of commodities comprised within one item. Table 3.15 shows the recorded quantities alongside the unit values got by division of values by quantities item by item. For example, the unit value of imports of motor spirit is £90,689,000 divided by the tonnage of 7,531,000, or £12·042 per ton in 1970; unit values in the two later years are similarly obtained. The increase to £13·561 in 1971 and to £14·218 in 1972 must reflect some price increases but also shifts in the proportions of the various grades and octane ratings of motor spirit imported. There is one case where such shifts affect the figures badly: imports of coal and coke. Sometimes (as in 1970) only special grades at high prices are imported; at other times (as in 1971 and 1972) a good deal of more ordinary coal is brought in for special reasons and the unit value falls. In 1970 the unit value was above £12 per ton, falling to around £10 per ton in the following two years. The occasional appearance of such freak figures is one of the penalties for using unit values as surrogates for prices.

Index numbers of unit value (price) and of volume (quantity) are derived in both Laspeyres and Paasche forms from the data of Table 3.15 by means of the calculations of Table 3.16, as summarised in the 3×3 value matrices of Table 3.17. The direct valuations such as $\sum p_0 q_0$ appear in the leading diagonals of the matrices and simply reproduce the recorded values. The cross-valuations such as $\sum p_0 q_1$ are in the off-diagonal slots in the matrices and these are

QUANTITIES AND UNIT VALUES, EXTERNAL TRADE IN FUELS, 1970–72

Items: S.I.T.C.	Section 3	Quantities ('000 tons per year)			Unit values (£ per ton)		
		1970 q_0 (1)	1971 q_1 (2)	1972 q_2 (3)	1970 p_0 (4)	1971 p_1 (5)	1972 p_2 (6)
Imports							
321	Coal and coke	83·6	4,199	5,022	12·129	9·449	10·127
	Briquettes	143·1	397·9	417·9	16·744	19·236	20·105
331	Crude petroleum	99,170	105,633	102,665	6·9266	8·8012	8·9028
	Partly refined petroleum	2,179	2,006	2,682	11·440	12·981	12·312
332	Motor spirit	7,531	6,842	5,561	12·042	13·561	14·218
	Kerosene, etc.	1,130	1,504	1,475	13·521	14·495	14·344
	Gas oils, etc.	1,876	2,161	2,000	10·366	12·284	12·130
	Fuel oils	8,817	8,044	9,490	7·1457	7·7245	6·985
	Lubricating oils	520·4	499·3	530·2	29·418	31·152	31·290
	Other products	394·0	424·2	650·8	22·937	23·395	17·880
341	Gas	917·7	857·0	855·1	16·664	16·875	17·042
351	Electric energy*	639·0	97·1	469·5	2·5665	3·6972	3·6890
Exports							
321	Coal and coke	4,340	3,256	2,097	6·3864	6·3077	7·2241
	Briquettes	127·5	133·5	123·2	10·675	13·266	15·008
331	Crude petroleum	1,083·9	1,424·5	2,893·3	7·3355	6·9280	7·1323
	Partly refined petroleum	250·0	321·3	376·5	7·3880	8·2291	8·6560
332	Motor spirit	1,473	1,830	2,042	12·805	12·752	13·742
	Kerosene, etc.	1,123	1,188	1,172	11·856	14·471	13·596
	Gas oils, etc.	5,546	6,043	5,956	9·208	11·428	11·434
	Fuel oils	7,813	6,103	5,471	5·8925	6·6104	6·5304
	Lubricating oils	675·4	726·4	732·5	48·576	51·525	50·033
	Other products	217·2	428·7	399·1	20·230	25·094	27·306
341	Gas	88·4	121·9	133·2	16·199	12·412	17·477
351	Electric energy*	5·9	0·8	4·7	0·68	2·5	0·43

From Appendix Table B1

* Quantities: 000 MWh; Unit values: £ per MWh.

TABLE 3.16

VALUES OF EXTERNAL TRADE IN FUELS, 1970–72 (£m)

Items: S.I.T.C. Imports	Section 3	Products (4) ×			Products (5) ×			Products (6) ×		
		(1) p_0q_0	(2) p_0q_1	(3) p_0q_2	(1) p_1q_0	(2) p_1q_1	(3) p_1q_2	(1) p_2q_0	(2) p_2q_1	(3) p_2q_2
321	Coal and coke	1·0	50·9	60·9	0·8	39·7	47·5	0·8	42·5	50·9
	Briquettes	2·4	6·7	7·0	2·8	7·6	8·0	2·9	8·0	8·4
331	Crude petroleum	686·9	731·7	711·1	872·8	929·7	903·6	882·9	940·4	914·0
	Partly refined petroleum	24·9	22·95	30·7	28·3	26·0	34·8	26·8	24·7	33·0
332	Motor spirit	90·7	82·4	67·0	102·1	92·8	75·4	107·1	97·3	79·1
	Kerosene, etc.	15·3	20·3	19·9	16·4	21·8	21·4	16·2	21·6	21·15
	Gas oils, etc.	19·4	22·3	20·7	23·0	26·5	24·6	22·8	26·2	24·25
	Fuel oils	63·0	57·5	67·8	68·1	62·1	73·3	61·6	56·2	66·3
	Lubricating oils	15·3	14·7	15·6	16·2	15·6	16·5	16·3	15·6	16·6
	Other products	9·0	9·7	14·9	9·2	9·9	15·2	7·0	7·6	11·6
341	Gas	15·3	14·3	14·2	15·5	14·5	14·4	15·6	14·6	14·6
351	Electric energy	1·6	0·25	1·2	2·4	0·4	1·7	2·4	0·4	1·7
	Total Imports	944·8	1033·7	1031·0	1157·6	1246·6	1236·4	1162·4	1255·1	1241·6

Exports

321	Coal and coke	27·7	20·8	13·4	27·4	20·5	13·2	31·4	23·5	15·
	Briquettes	1·4	1·4	1·3	1·7	1·8	1·6	1·9	2·0	1·85
331	Crude petroleum	8·0	10·4	21·2	7·5	9·9	20·0	7·7	10·2	20·6
	Partly refined petroleum	1·8	2·4	2·8	2·1	2·6	3·1	2·2	2·8	3·3
332	Motor spirit	18·9	23·4	26·1	20·3	25·2	28·1	20·2	25·1	28·1
	Kerosene, etc.	13·3	14·1	13·9	16·2	17·2	17·0	15·3	16·2	15·9
	Gas oils, etc.	51·1	55·6	54·8	63·4	69·1	68·1	63·4	69·1	68·1
	Fuel oils	46·0	36·0	32·2	51·6	40·3	36·2	51·0	39·9	35·7
	Lubricating oils	32·8	35·3	35·6	34·8	37·4	37·7	33·8	36·3	36·65
	Other products	4·4	8·7	8·1	5·4	10·8	10·0	5·9	11·7	10·9
341	Gas	1·4	2·0	2·2	1·1	1·5	1·7	1·5	2·1	2·3
351	Electric energy	*	*	*	*	*	*	*	*	*
	Total Exports	206·8	210·1	211·6	231·5	236·3	236·7	234·3	238·9	238·6

From Table 3.15

* Less than £0·05 mn.

computed for index-number purposes. Imports of fuels are dominated by one large item subject to unusual price/quantity changes. Imports of the item, crude petroleum, increased in 1971 despite sharp price rises and then fell back in 1972. Similarly, though re-exports of crude petroleum are not large, they were increasing and

TABLE 3.17

VALUE MATRICES, EXTERNAL TRADE IN FUELS, 1970–2

Values (£mn) at unit values of:		Imports Quantities of:			Exports Quantities of:		
		1970	1971	1972	1970	1971	1972
Total trade	1970	944·8	1033·7	1031·0	206·8	210·1	211·6
	1971	1157·6	1246·6	1236·4	231·5	236·3	236·7
	1972	1162·4	1255·1	1241·6	234·3	238·9	238·6
Total excl.	1970	257·9	302·0	319·9	198·8	199·7	190·4
crude petroleum	1971	284·8	316·9	332·8	224·0	226·4	216·7
	1972	279·5	314·7	327·6	226·6	228·7	218·0

From Table 3.16

at fluctuating prices between 1970 and 1972. Subsequent years show even more erratic changes following the oil crisis of 1973. For these reasons the value matrices are given in Table 3.17 with and without crude petroleum.

Table 3.18 sets out the index numbers derived from the value matrices, again with and without crude petroleum. The interpretation proceeds more easily with crude excluded. Take exports,

TABLE 3.18

INDEX NUMBERS, EXTERNAL TRADE IN FUELS, 1970–72

Index Numbers (1970 = 100)		Unit-value (price) index Base-weighted	Current-weighted	Volume index Base-weighted	Current-weighted
Total imports	1971	122·5	120·6	109·4	107·7
	1972	123·0	120·4	109·1	106·8
Total imports excl.	1971	110·4	104·9	117·1	111·3
crude petroleum	1972	108·4	102·4	124·0	117·2
Total exports	1971	111·9	112·5	101·6	102·1
	1972	113·3	112·8	102·3	101·8
Total exports excl.	1971	112·7	113·4	100·5	101·1
crude petroleum	1972	114·0	114·5	95·8	96·2

From Table 3.17

first, as showing Laspeyres and Paasche index numbers so close that a definite split of the value change into price and volume components can be written. The value of exports increased from £198·8 mn in 1970 by 13·9% to £226·4 mn in 1971 but only by 9·7% to £218·0 mn in 1972. The index numbers of Table 3.18 show how the value increase in 1971 breaks into price and volume components: $1·14 = 1·13 \times 1·01$, as ratios to two decimal places. The 14% increase in value is almost all due to price increases, with only a small residual increase of 1% in volume. Similarly, in 1972, the value increase of $9\frac{3}{4}\%$ from 1970 is more than accounted for by prices ($14\frac{1}{4}\%$ increase) and volume fell off by 4%.

The small rise of 1% in real exports from 1970 to 1971 and the subsequent fall by about 5% from 1971 to 1972 are measured by index numbers appropriately weighted by the distribution of exports by value. The data also give, by addition over the items, the total tonnage of exports of fuels (including gas and excluding only electric energy). A different picture emerges:

1970: 22·7 mn tons;   1971: 21·6 mn tons;   1972: 21·4 mn tons

These figures answer a different question: what are the changes in the tonnage shipped from year to year? And the answers are numerically different: a fall of 5% in shipping tonnage from 1970 to 1971 when exports in real terms increased and an almost unchanged tonnage while real exports fell by some 5% from 1971 to 1972. Clearly the proportion of bulky items amongst exports of fuels was changing over the period.

Finally for imports of fuels, excluding crude petroleum, there are considerable shifts in the pattern of trade, and in the prices obtaining, with the result that the Laspeyres and Paasche index numbers are not at all close. It is the Laspeyres index which is the greater, in line with the analysis of **2.7** and confirming the tendency of importers to switch purchases away from items which rise most in price. It follows that it is not possible to give a split of the value change which is at all precise. Only broad indications can be offered for movements in real imports and in import prices. It is clear, however, that there was a sharp increase in prices from 1970 to 1971 and a modest fall subsequently to 1972. Equally clear is the substantial rise in real imports of fuels (excluding crude), by some 15% from 1970 to 1971 and by another 5% in the following year. This is a convenient summary of the position as it was before the interruption of oil supplies and the large increases in prices which followed the Arab–Israeli war in October 1973.

In the national accounts of the U.K., it is the practice to compute only one of the two sets of cross-valuations of the kind carried out in Table 3.16. It is the set of valuations of current trade at constant (base-year) prices which is obtained, giving a volume index in Laspeyres (base-weighted) form. The price index is then got by dividing the value change by the Laspeyres volume index, i.e. it is an implied index of Paasche form. As a result the 'heat' is taken off the use of unit values as substitutes for prices, and the constructions – though strictly involving unit values rather than price quotations – are officially described as 'price indices' as in the 1973 *Blue Book*, Table 16.

The results of Tables 3.17 and 3.18 can be rearranged to conform with official practice. Take exports as an illustration:

EXPORTS OF FUELS

	1970	1971	1972
		£mn	
(1) Value: at current prices	206·8	236·3	238·6
(2) at constant (1970) prices	206·8	210·1	211·6
		1970 = 100	
(3) Volume: Laspeyres index	100	101·6	102·3
(4) Price: implied Paasche index	100	112·5	112·8

Row (1) is the leading diagonal and row (2) is the first row of the relevant value matrix (Table 3.17). Row (3) scales row (2) to 1970 as 100. Row (4) is the implied index got by dividing corresponding entries in rows (1) and (2). This is the standard layout followed below in presenting the components of real GDP.

The aggregates written for fuels as one commodity group can be extended to all merchandise, the so-called 'visible' trade. They are on an *overseas trade statistics basis*, exactly as recorded by Customs on the traditional c.i.f./f.o.b. valuations. To bring them into line with the economic concepts of national income accounting, we need to convert them to a *balance of payments basis* by reduction of imports to the same (f.o.b.) values as exports and by making a range of coverage adjustments. Each month the Department of Trade converts the current-value aggregates of imports and exports from an overseas trade statistics to a balance of payments basis and proceeds to compute volume and unit-value index numbers on both bases. The volume index numbers are still of Laspeyres form, giving an implied (Paasche) index for unit values. In addition, the Department computes a Laspeyres version of the unit-value index, using a selection of fairly homogeneous commodity items weighted with the base-year pattern of trade. The official description says that 'as far as possible only those headings which cover a sufficiently homogeneous group of commodities for their unit values to move in much the same way as true prices are used in the calculation' (*Monthly Digest of Statistics*, Supplement, January 1974). Of the total value of trade (in 1961) this unit-value index covers 78% of imports and 62% of exports (*Economic Trends*, September 1963).

The index numbers of Table 3.19 are of Laspeyres form both for volume and for unit values, base-weighted in each case on the 1961 pattern of trade. Those on a balance of payments basis are available only from 1969 but they can be compared with the older runs on the overseas trade statistics basis over the four years 1969–72. The runs are much the same for unit values but the volume index is rather lower on the balance of payments basis. Table 3.19 also shows

TABLE 3.19

LASPEYRES INDEX NUMBERS,
EXTERNAL TRADE IN MERCHANDISE, 1969–72

Index Numbers (1961 = 100)		Overseas trade statistics basis		Balance of payments basis		
		Unit value	Volume	Value	Unit value	Volume
Imports	1969	126	149	178	126	146
	1970	132	156	195	131	155
	1971	136	162	210	134	160
	1972	143	177	243	143	177
Exports	1969	127	150	182	127	149
	1970	136	155	203	136	154
	1971	147	164	226	148	160
	1972	157	166	235	157	159

From *Monthly Digest of Statistics*

current-value aggregates (in percentage of 1961) as given in the *Blue Books* on the balance of payments basis. The two Laspeyres forms, one for unit values and one for volume, do not match in splitting value changes into price and quantity components. Indeed their product overstates the value change by a wide margin. The matching Paasche price index, implied by the Laspeyres volume index on the balance of payments basis, is got by dividing this volume index into the value change. It is shown below in comparison with the unit value index of Table 3.19, i.e. the Laspeyres form calculated from the selection of items.

PRICE (UNIT-VALUE) INDEX NUMBERS, BALANCE OF PAYMENTS BASIS

1961 =100	Implied Paasche index			Selective Laspeyres index		
	Imports	Exports	Terms of trade*	Imports	Exports	Terms of trade*
1969	122	122	100	126	127	101
1970	126	132	105	131	136	104
1971	131	141	108	134	148	110
1972	137	148	108	143	157	110

* Ratio of export to import prices (1961 = 100).

A Laspeyres index may well run higher than a corresponding Paasche form, at least for prices paid for imports, but the differences here are quite large. There is a suspicion that the selective index is biased, with the prices represented in the index and those excluded having rather different movements. Certainly, as seen in **3.4**, a selective index cannot be relied upon. Hence, for prices of imports and exports separately, the selective index runs give no more than a broad indication of movements. But, as often happens with biased series, the ratio between them performs better. The table above shows two runs of the *terms of trade*, the ratio of export to import prices, and their movements are seen to be quite close. The period saw a particularly 'favourable' change in the terms of merchandise trading; export prices increased faster than import prices, by some 8 to 10%. It was, in fact, a period sandwiched between two declines in the terms of trade, one after the 1967 devaluation of sterling and the other at the time of the downward float of the £ in 1972 and 1973.

A further adjustment is needed before imports and exports can be incorporated in the national accounts: the extension to goods and services by the addition of the 'invisibles'. A variety of sources is used to get trade in services at current and at constant prices, sources which can give less systematic and less accurate estimates than those for merchandise. As broad aggregates, however, the valuations are reasonably good; see Central Statistical Office (1968), pp. 468–70. They are shown in Table 3.20 in the standard layout already specified. The data are from the 1973 *Blue Book*, the first to take 1970 as the base for constant-price valuations. The last row of the table shows the terms of trade, now for goods and services together and expressed on 1970 as 100. On this wider coverage, the terms of trade still show a 'favourable' movement around 1970–71, but it is by no means as definite as for merchandise alone.

TABLE 3.20

IMPORTS AND EXPORTS OF GOODS AND SERVICES, 1963–72

	1963	1970	1971	1972
Imports		£*mn*		
(1) Value: at current prices	5,946	10,872	11,857	13,440
(2) at constant (1970) prices	7,761	10,872	11,398	12,556
		1970 = 100		
(3) Volume: Laspeyres index	71·4	100	104·8	115·5
(4) Price: implied Paasche index	76·6	100	104·0	107·0
Exports		£*mn*		
(1) Value: at current prices	5,809	11,255	12,632	13,331
(2) at constant (1970) prices	7,649	11,255	12,057	12,432
		1970 = 100		
(3) Volume: Laspeyres index	68·0	100	107·1	110·5
(4) Price: implied Paasche index	75·9	100	104·8	107·2
Terms of trade in goods and services				
Ratio of export to import prices	99·1	100	100·7	100·2

From Appendix Tables B2 and B3

Rows (1) and (2) of Table 3.20 are straight from the *Blue Book;* they measure changes in total trade in money and in real terms. Hence, to trace real imports or exports over time, it is enough to use row (2) as it stands. There is no need, except for convenience, to go to the volume index of row (3). Rows (2) and (3) contain precisely the same information; it is a matter of choice whether to have real changes in 1970 values, as in row (2), or in percentage of 1970 as in row (3). The increase in real exports from 1971 to 1972, for example, is shown equally well by a rise from £12,057 mn to £12,432 mn in 1970 £'s as by a movement in the volume index from 107·1 to 110·5% of 1970. The increase is one of some 3% in each case. The *Blue Book* is content for the most part to leave components of real GDP in the form of constant-price aggregates.

Though the main object of the calculation is to get national income in real terms, the implied price index drops out at once for use (e.g.) is estimating changes in the terms of trade. This price index is most quickly written by dividing the entry in row (1) by the corresponding entry in row (2). It is then seen to be a ratio of value aggregates from current trade, i.e. of current-weighted (Paasche) form. Alternatively, it comes by first expressing the entries in row (1) as percentages of

the 1970 figure and then dividing each by the corresponding volume
index of row (3). The emphasis here is on the basic property of the
implied index; together with the volume index it accounts, exactly
and by definition, for changes in recorded values.

3.8 Aggregative Index Numbers: Gross Domestic Product

As an economic-theoretic concept, the aggregate of GDP at current
prices is reached by three routes with an equivalent end-result; by
summing incomes, expenditures and outputs respectively. This is
clear from the circular flow of income: from income earned to
income spent (demand), activating output (supply) and so, to
complete the circle, generating income paid to the factors of production. In the *ex post* terms of the national accounts, here are
three aggregates quite different in their make-up: incomes by
various types; expenditures in various categories; net outputs in
various industrial sectors. But, when added up, the totals are
identically equal in concept and differing statistically only by reason
of residual errors in estimation; see Beckerman (1968).

Of the three methods of independent estimation of GDP possible
in practice, the *Blue Book* uses only two separate (and largely
independent) valuations for the U.K. One is based on a great range
of data on expenditures; the other uses statistics of incomes and
earnings derived for the most part from the tax-gathering activities
of Inland Revenue. Each valuation is subject to errors and omissions,
never to be completely avoided in practice. The *Blue Book* opts to
show only one residual-error term and to throw it into the income
rather than the expenditure aggregate; see Central Statistical Office
(1968).

Appendix Table B2 gives summary figures of the valuation
of GDP by categories of expenditure. The value aggregates are
appropriately in current *market prices* inclusive of indirect taxes and
net of subsidies. It is a simple matter to deduct indirect taxes (net of
subsidies) to obtain GDP at *factor cost* and this is done in Table B2.
The other approach provides a two-way split of GDP by various
categories of income (wages, salaries, and so on) and by net output
in the different industries. This is made possible by the fact that, in
Inland Revenue data, incomes are classified both by type of earner
and by industry in which generated. Summation of incomes and of
net outputs necessarily gives the same aggregate GDP since only

one block of data is used. This aggregate is, however, different from that built up from expenditures and the difference is shown in the *Blue Books* by a single *residual error;* see Table B2. British practice is to take GDP based on expenditure as the main estimate and to add a residual-error term to the alternative estimate based on incomes and net outputs to give the same GDP aggregate.

The expenditure aggregation is pursued here and the alternative approach in the next section. The *Blue Book* shows GDP at market prices disaggregated into quite considerable detail on expenditures but lumped together in Table B2 in four main categories: consumers' expenditure, current expenditure of public authorities, gross domestic capital formation and the external trade balance. The estimates are generally on a transactions basis (accruals rather than cash flows) and come commodity by commodity from many sources. For consumers' expenditure, for example, the sources are classified by the Central Statistical Office (1968) on the basis of 1966 data: 16% information on supplies; 34% figures of sales; 26% from such surveys as the NFS; and 24% miscellaneous.

In computing expenditures at constant market prices, the 1973 *Blue Book* uses 1970 prices, and valuations from 1971 onwards are a mixture of quantities revalued item by item at 1970 prices and of deflation of current values by price index numbers for various groups of items. As suggested in **3.5**, the intention here is to incorporate quality changes into real GDP, i.e. into the volume rather than the price index. The deflation of values is often the safer method since attention can be concentrated on getting pure price quotations for the deflator index. The two methods are used about equally in accounting for upwards of 80% of real consumers' expenditure and most of the balance consists of the use of a quantity index in projecting base (1970) values. The constant-price valuations of other expenditure categories depend heavily on deflation by some type of price index.

Such constant-price valuations are not accurate for more than a few years. It becomes first difficult and then impossible to match this year's quantities with prices from a year in the past or to obtain running price quotations on a fixed specification for a price deflator. The base needs to be changed every few years, to rebase real GDP on a new set of weights. British practice is to change base at about five-yearly intervals, and data on three successive bases (1958, 1963, 1970) are shown in Table B3.

The question is raised: at the change of base (e.g.) in the 1973 *Blue Book* from 1963 to 1970, is it useful to carry back the new constant-price valuations to the previous base year or earlier and, if so, how? If this is done, then backward and forward index numbers of Laspeyres and Paasche forms can be calculated and compared. The official computations do, in fact, carry the new constant-price aggregates back to the previous base year on a reasonably accurate method. The old GDP series in real terms are disaggregated into fairly fine components and reweighted with the new weights. The matter is examined further in Chapter 4.

GDP based on expenditures at current and constant market prices, and consumers' expenditure separately as the main component, are shown in standard layout in Table 3.21 on three successive bases. Similar tables for other GDP components can be constructed from Tables B2 and B3 and in more detail from the original tabulations in the *Blue Books*.

Real expenditure is to be traced by following the constant-price valuations of row (2), or alternatively the index numbers of row (3), with a jump back and forth at each change of base. One advantage, mentioned in **1.6**, of the constant-price valuations over the index numbers is that the components of real expenditure simply add to total real GDP in the same way as money expenditures do. Table B3 is arranged in this way. As a result, row (2) for consumers' expenditure in Table 3.21 is a proper part of row (2) for total GDP. So, it is possible to write consumers' expenditure directly as a proportion of total GDP both in money and in real terms:

CONSUMERS' EXPENDITURE IN
% OF TOTAL GDP

	1963	1970	1971	1972
In money (current prices)	66·3	62·4	62·1	63·7
In real terms (1970 prices)	65·4	62·4	62·5	64·7

Consumers took a smaller proportion of the total cake in 1970–71 than they did in 1963. The proportion increased in 1972 in money terms and rather faster in real terms, consumer prices rising less than other prices. To get such results from the volume index of row (3) requires the weighting process carried out (e.g.) in **3.2.**

The fact that consumer prices increased more slowly than prices generally can be checked from row (4) of Table 3.21. For consumers'

TABLE 3.21

GDP AT MARKET PRICES, BASED ON EXPENDITURE, 1958–72

	Blue Book, 1968 £mn		Blue Book, 1972 £mn				Blue Book, 1973 £mn			
	1958	1963	1958	1963	1970	1971	1963	1970	1971	1972
Consumers' Expenditure										
(1) Value: at current prices	15,362	20,195	15,296	20,130	31,216	34,504	20,118	31,404	34,838	39,263
(2) at constant prices	15,362	18,375	17,008	20,130	23,413	24,032	27,416	31,404	32,211	34,115
	1958=100		*1963=100*				*1970=100*			
(3) Volume: Laspeyres index	100	119·6	84·5	100	116·3	119·4	87·3	100	102·6	108·6
(4) Price: implied Paasche index	100	109·9	89·9	100	133·3	143·6	73·4	100	108·2	115·1
Total GDP										
(1) Value: at current prices	22,758	30,257	22,829	30,348	50,175	55,520	30,336	50,362	56,072	61,630
(2) at constant prices	22,758	27,146	25,662	30,348	36,899	37,478	41,936	50,362	51,562	52,747
	1958=100		*1963=100*				*1970=100*			
(3) Volume: Laspeyres index	100	119·3	84·6	100	121·6	123·5	83·3	100	102·4	104·7
(4) Price: implied Paasche index	100	111·5	89·0	100	136·0	148·1	72·3	100	108·7	116·8

From Appendix Tables B2 and B3

expenditure this row gives the *consumer price index*,* computed in Paasche form for the whole range of consumers' goods and services and obtainable in great detail from the *Blue Books*. It is the perfect match to the Laspeyres volume index representing changes in *real consumption* and given by row (3) of Table 3.21. We have now stacked up an interesting comparison between this Paasche price index, with its wide coverage and matching volume index, and the retail price index discussed at the beginning of this chapter, with its narrower coverage and its chain Laspeyres form. The story is taken up in Chapter 6.

The index numbers of Table 3.21 serve to illustrate the results of **2.5** on backward and forward forms. Adapt the shorthand $\sum$ notation in obvious ways to write index numbers based on 1970 and use the rows of Table 3.21 for GDP or any one of its components:

Year t: Laspeyres volume index $\dfrac{\sum p_{70}q_t}{\sum p_{70}q_{70}} = \dfrac{\text{year } t \text{ entry, row (2)}}{\text{year 1970 entry, row (2)}}$

Paasche price index $\dfrac{\sum p_t q_t}{\sum p_{70}q_t} = \dfrac{\text{year } t \text{ entry, row (1)}}{\text{year } t \text{ entry, row (2)}}$

which multiply to the value change, $\sum p_t q_t$ divided by $\sum p_{70}q_{70}$ These forms can be run backwards ($t<70$) as well as forwards ($t>70$), and they can be varied by changes of subscript to other base years. So:

VOLUME INDEX (REAL CONSUMPTION)

Index form	Comparison 1958–63	Comparison 1963–70
	1963	*1970*
(a) Forward Laspeyres	$\dfrac{\sum p_{58}q_{63}}{\sum p_{58}q_{58}} = 119\cdot6\%$ of 1958	$\dfrac{\sum p_{63}q_{70}}{\sum p_{63}q_{63}} = 116\cdot3\%$ of 1963
	1958	*1963*
(b) Backward Laspeyres	$\dfrac{\sum p_{63}q_{58}}{\sum p_{63}q_{63}} = 84\cdot5\%$ of 1963	$\dfrac{\sum p_{70}q_{63}}{\sum p_{70}q_{70}} = 87\cdot3\%$ of 1970
and reciprocal:	*1963*	*1970*
Forward Paasche	$\dfrac{\sum p_{63}q_{63}}{\sum p_{63}q_{58}} = 118\cdot3\%$ of 1958	$\dfrac{\sum p_{70}q_{70}}{\sum p_{70}q_{63}} = 114\cdot5\%$ of 1963

Here, at (b), the Laspeyres index of Table 3.21 is run back from the new to the old base year and its reciprocal is recognised as the

---

* Renamed the *consumers' expenditure deflator* by the Central Statistical Office in 1974; see Press Release on 'The Internal Purchasing Power of the Pound' (April 1974). The index is more easily recognised by its original name and this will continue to be used in the present text.

forward Paasche index from the old to the new base year. The forward Paasche is then directly comparable with the forward Laspeyres form (a). The Laspeyres index exceeds the Paasche, as expected from **2.7**; a small excess in the period 1958–63 and a larger one in 1963–70. Similar results are obtained for the consumer price index of Table 3.21. This jobbing back and forth between successive bases is a very useful device (e.g.) for the development of the splicing techniques of Chapter 4.

3.9 Three Measures of Real GDP

Aggregate GDP based on expenditure is given so far in terms of market prices. The other two GDP aggregates, summing incomes and net outputs respectively, are obtained from different data (from Inland Revenue) and are essentially at factor cost. To bring the aggregates into their conceptual equivalence, adjust the expenditure aggregate from market prices to factor cost by deduction of net indirect taxes, and add the residual-error term to the income/net output estimates.

So much for the aggregates at current prices. To compute the constant-price aggregates which correspond is a threefold exercise. Real GDP as expenditure has already been tackled (**3.8**). Two more stages remain, to get real GDP from the income side first and then to work with output data. British practice is to deal with real GDP as income, not by taking each separate item of income in turn, but by a short-cut method from the estimates already made of real GDP as expenditure. The method is displayed in Table 3.22 with 1972 data. Column (1) is simply the adjustment of current values already described. Column (2) shows, first, the adjustment of real GDP as expenditure at constant (1970) prices (Table 3.21) to factor cost. The implied price index at factor cost then emerges by division of the figures in columns (1) and (2). In 1972 it is 120·6% of 1970 as compared with 116·8% for market prices. It is the basic price index of the national accounts and described officially as *home costs per unit of output*. Note that, despite its label, it is got from expenditure data (though at factor cost). Next, real GDP based on income is *defined* by deflating money GDP as income by the basic price index (home costs per unit of output) on the *assumption* that this index applies equally to total income as to total expenditure. So the calculation is completed in Table 3.22 for 1972. It is clear that, by definition, the

TABLE 3.22
GDP AT FACTOR COST,
BASED ON EXPENDITURE AND ON INCOME, 1972

	GDP 1972 (£mn) At current prices (1)	At 1970 prices (2)	Implied Price Index 1972 (1970 = 100) (1)/(2)
GDP based on expenditure at market prices	61,630	52,747	116·8
less Indirect taxes (net)	−8,146	−8,403	96·9
GDP based on expenditure at factor cost	53,484	44,344	120·6
Residual error	345	286*	120·6
GDP based on income at factor cost	53,139	44,058*	120·6

From Appendix Tables B2 and B3

* Calculated on assumption that the implied price index is the same as for GDP based on expenditure, i.e. col. (1) divided by 1·206.

difference between real GDP as expenditure and as income is just the residual error deflated by the basic price index. This is very rough and ready, as admitted when the official description says that real GDP as income is 'obtained by deflating the income estimate of GDP at current prices by the price index implied by the current and constant-price estimates based on expenditure data' (1973 *Blue Book*, p. 96).

Table 3.23 sets out the two versions of real GDP now defined in standard layout and for selected years on three successive bases. Each version appears as constant-price valuations in row (2) and as index numbers in row (3). There is, by definition, only one price index, that of home costs per unit of output in row (4). The main conclusion is that, because of a fluctuating residual error, the income version of real GDP is sometimes higher (1963, 1970) and sometimes lower (1971, 1972) than real GDP as expenditure.

The remaining stage, the estimation of real GDP as output, is a quite separate exercise. A process of reducing net output, item by item and industry by industry, to constant-price terms proves in practice to be too difficult and uncertain. A different attack on the problem is needed and it is ready to hand: to use an equivalent base-weighted index of volume instead of a constant-price aggregate. The index is an average of quantity relatives obtained from the

TABLE 3.23

GDP AT FACTOR COST, BASED ON EXPENDITURE AND ON INCOME, 1958–72

GDP based on:	Blue Book, 1968		Blue Book, 1972				Blue Book, 1973			
	1958	1963	1958	1963	1970	1971	1963	1970	1971	1972
	£mn		£mn				£mn			
Expenditure										
(1) Value: at current prices	20,103	26,769	20,186	26,881	42,606	47,746	26,878	42,788	48,159	55,484
(2) at constant prices	20,103	23,824	22,793	26,881	32,493	32,896	35,454	42,788	43,668	44,344
	1958=100		1963=100				1970=100			
(3) Volume: Laspeyres index	100	118·5	84·8	100	120·9	122·4	82·9	100	102·1	103·6
(4) Price: implied Paasche index	100	112·4	88·6	100	131·1	145·1	75·8	100	110·3	120·6
Income										
(1) Value: at current prices	19,789	26,741	19,821	26,825	42,606	47,256	26,847	42,845	47,512	53,139
(2) at constant prices*	19,789	23,799	22,381	26,825	32,493	32,558	35,410	42,845	43,081	44,058
	1958=100		1963=100				1970=100			
(3) Volume: Laspeyres index	100	120·3	83·4	100	121·1	121·4	82·7	100	100·6	102·8
(4) Price: implied Paasche index	100	112·4	88·6	100	131·1	145·1	75·8	100	110·3	120·6

From Appendix Tables B2 and B3

* Implied, row (1) divided by row (4), the latter assumed the same as the corresponding row on the expenditure basis.

variation over time of quantitative estimates of net output industry by industry, weighted by the distribution of net output by value over the different industries in the base year (1970 in the 1973 *Blue Book*). There is no difficulty whatever about the weights; they are the components of GDP as output at current prices. The whole problem is to specify and then to obtain running estimates of the quantity relatives, a problem to which there is no tidy solution. British practice is summarised here with reference to the condensed version of the *Blue Book* data given in Appendix Table B4.

A prime difficulty is that, if duplication is to be avoided, all quantities should be net outputs, whereas such quantitative data are rarely available in practice. The solution to the practical problem turns on success in designing an industrial/commodity classification in sufficiently fine detail to provide acceptable substitute indicators for net output changes. The problem has been much discussed by (among others) Carter, Reddaway and Stone (1948), Reddaway (1950) and Central Statistical Office (1968).

The core of the computation is the official *index of industrial production* which measures changes in real output in an important segment of industry: mining, manufacturing, construction and utilities. The index is published monthly in its own right. It is a base-weighted index of quantity relatives obtained from substitute indicators, generally either gross output by quantity or output by value deflated by an appropriate price index. The index before the change to 1970 as base is described in Central Statistical Office (1970), and some illustrations of successive changes of base are given in Chapter 6.

The 1970 weight of the index of real GDP as output is distributed as to 44% to the segment of the industrial production index and 56% to the remaining segment of agriculture, transport, distribution and the range of services. The substitute indicators used in this second segment are many and various. The best is that used for agriculture; it is net output on the 'double deflation' method of estimating the difference between gross output and input each at (separate) constant prices. Other indicators are similar to those used in the industrial production index and still others are just inputs of materials (or even employment) as second-best attempts. As long as the poorer indicators remain, and they are being progressively discarded at successive rebasings of the index, total GDP as real output will fail to reflect all changes in productivity.

Table B4 separates off the components of the industrial production index, given to one decimal place, from the remaining sectors where the indices are rounded to the nearest whole percentage point to represent the fact that they are less accurate. The table, however, combines four groups of services separately shown in the basic data, and combined indices here are given to one decimal place.

There are two particular points to note. One is that the index of real GDP has one item with a *negative weight*, a feature which is certainly not ruled out by the weighted-average formula but which is rare in practice. It arises because net interest paid to companies providing financial services appears both in the net outputs of the industries using the services and in the net output of the services sector. The item with negative weighting removes this duplication. The other point is that, being an index rather than a constant-price aggregate, real GDP as output in total is not the sum of the constituent parts. To combine several constituents or to remove one or more from the total requires the weighting process already illustrated in **3.2**. As an example, obtain the output index in 1972 (1970 = 100) for all industry except public administration and services, and by two routes. One is by adding the appropriate groups and the other by subtraction from the total. Use the group index numbers of Table B4:

OUTPUT INDEX, 1972 (1970 = 100)

Groups	1970 weight	Index	Product
Industrial production	439	101·8	44690
Agriculture	30	108	3240
Transport, etc.	84	105	8820
Distribution	104	106	11024
Financial services	−31	116	−3596
Sum	626		64178
Total GDP as output	1000	103·9	103900
less			
Public administration	67	102	6834
Services	307	106·9	32818
Difference	626		64248

Divide the sum and the difference each by the net weight of 626, and both calculations give the 1972 index of all output, except public administration and services, as $102\frac{1}{2}\%$ of 1970. This is to be compared with the 1972 all-items index of 104%.

The three measures of real GDP are brought together in Table 3.24. They are all Laspeyres index numbers and on three successive bases (1958, 1963 and 1970). The output measure is calculated

TABLE 3.24

THREE MEASURES OF REAL GDP, 1958–72

Index Numbers		Real GDP based on: Expenditure	Income	Output	Average estimate
1958 = 100	1958	100	100	100	100
	1963	118·5	120·3	117·4	118·7
1963 = 100	1958	84·8	83·4	85·2	84·5
	1963	100	100	100	100
	1970	120·9	121·1	121·8	121·3
	1971	122·4	121·4	123·9	122·6
1970 = 100	1963	82·9	82·7	82·1	82·6
	1970	100	100	100	100
	1971	102·1	100·6	101·4	101·4
	1972	103·6	102·8	103·9	103·4

From Table 3.23 for expenditure and income measures; Appendix Table B4 supplemented by *Blue Book*, 1968 and 1972 for output measure

directly as a base-weighted index. The other two measures are essentially the comparisons of constant-price aggregates; they are also to be regarded as the sums of expenditures or incomes in money (current-price) terms but deflated by one and the same price index: home costs per unit of output. These two measures differ only because of fluctuation in the residual-error term.

No one measure of real GDP ever diverges seriously from the others. Equally, they are seldom so close together that the change in real GDP can be given an unambiguous (if rounded) figure. An average of the three measures is used officially as a composite estimate. The average shown in Table 3.24 is the simple arithmetic mean.

APPENDIX: SOURCE MATERIAL

A. Retail Prices and Consumption

TABLE A1

GENERAL RETAIL PRICE INDEX

Groups and subgroups	Weights, January (per 1000)			Index numbers (January 1962=100)					
	1971	1972	1973	1971 Jan.	1972 Jan.	1972 July	1973 Jan.	1973 July	1974 Jan.
Bread, etc.	37	36	33	156	169	174	179	190	225
Meat and bacon	65	64	73	155	172	188	216	240	270
Fish	8	9	8	157	190	195	220	244	319
Butter, etc.	11	14	10	128	177	161	147	148	168
Milk, cheese, eggs	37	39	36	141	162	150	165	176	202
Tea, etc.	14	13	12	123	126	128	131	129	131
Sugar, etc.	23	23	21	161	177	176	178	168	188
Fruit	13	13	14	117	133	141	157	186	188
Vegetables	25	24	25	156	167	190	188	222	224
Other food	17	16	16	143	153	159	163	161	176
All food	250	251	248	147·0	163·9	169·2	180·4	194·6	216·7
Alcoholic drink	65	66	73	151·3	154·1	159·3	163·3	164·3	166·0
Tobacco	59	53	49	138·6	138·4	138·4	141·6	141·0	142·2
Housing	119	121	126	164·2	178·8	190·6	203·8	213·7	225·1
Fuel and light	60	60	58	152·6	168·2	172·8	178·3	175·3	188·6
Durables	61	58	58	132·3	138·1	140·7	144·2	149·7	158·3
Clothing	87	89	89	128·4	136·7	141·1	146·8	154·6	166·6
Transport	136	139	135	141·2	151·8	156·7	159·4	165·5	175·0
Miscellaneous goods	65	65	65	151·2	166·2	167·5	169·8	173·6	182·2
Services	54	52	53	160·8	174·7	180·0	189·6	204·8	212·8
Meals out	44	46	46	153·1	172·9	181·8	190·2	214·9	229·5
All items	1,000	1,000	1,000	147·0	159·0	164·2	171·3	179·7	191·8

From Department of Employment *Gazette*

TABLE A2

RETAIL FOOD PRICES: AVERAGE PRICE QUOTATIONS (d per unit)

Subgroup	Item	Unit	1968 Jan.	1971 Jan.	1972 Jan.	1972 July	1973 Jan.	1973 July	1974 Jan.
Butter, etc.	Butter, N.Z.	lb	40·3	43·9	71·5	62·4	54·5	50·4	51·1
	Danish	,,	47·8	51·6	76·3	68·4	60·2	56·6	58·8
	Margarine, standard	½ lb	11·0	14·1	14·9	14·6	14·6	15·6	18·7
	Lower-priced	,,	8·3	11·7	13·2	12·5	12·5	13·2	16·3
	Lard	lb	16·1	22·1	22·8	21·1	21·4	24·0	35·0
Milk, cheese, eggs	Milk, ordinary	pint	10·0	12·0	13·2	12·0	13·2	13·2	13·2
	Cheese, Cheddar	lb	43·0	48·9	69·8	75·4	76·6	77·3	80·4
	Eggs, large	doz	51·9	62·4	57·1	45·4	54·2	75·8	117·1
	standard	,,	46·5	55·3	49·0	38·4	48·5	68·2	111·6
	medium	,,	41·4	48·9	42·7	33·4	43·9	63·8	101·5
Fruit	Apples, cooking	lb	18·4	11·5	15·6	21·4	26·4	33·6	21·6
	dessert	,,	22·1	20·2	23·3	24·0	30·0	34·6	26·9
	Pears, dessert	,,	22·1	19·1	22·8	25·2	31·2	36·7	30·7
	Oranges	,,	15·0	16·4	18·7	18·5	20·9	21·4	24·5
	Bananas	,,	16·0	17·6	20·4	20·6	21·4	26·9	26·9
Vegetables	Potatoes, white	,,	3·8	4·0	4·3	5·5*	5·3	6·2*	5·8
	red	,,	4·5	4·8	5·3	7·0*	6·2	7·0*	7·0
	Tomatoes	,,	30·7	44·7	42·5	36·0	46·6	44·4	53·5
	Mushrooms	¼ lb	14·5	16·0	17·3	16·3	17·3	17·0	20·2
	Cabbage, greens	lb	8·8	9·0	10·1	11·5	11·3	12·2	16·8
	hearted	,,	6·6	7·8	8·6	11·3	9·4	12·2	13·9
	Cauliflower	,,	18·6	23·3	25·2	21·6	23·0	19·9	30·7
	Carrots	,,	6·8	7·2	7·9	15·8	9·4	19·4	11·0
	Onions	,,	8·2	10·2	9·6	14·4	14·2	18·7	15·1

From Department of Employment *Gazette*.
Prices converted from new pence (from 1972)

* August, no price quotations in July

TABLE A3
FOOD CONSUMPTION AND EXPENDITURE:
LOW-INCOME PENSIONER FAMILIES

Subgroup	Item	Unit	Consumption,* first quarter (Units per head per week)			Expenditure,* first quarter (d per head per week)		
			1968	1972	1973	1968	1972	1973
Butter, etc.	Butter	oz	7·21	5·79	6·23	NA	NA	20·98
	Margarine	,,	3·09	4·10	3·76	NA	NA	7·56
	Lard, etc.	,,	2·74	2·98	2·66	NA	NA	3·65
	Total, Butter, etc.	,,	13·04	12·87	12·65	27·10	40·85	32·29
Milk, cheese, eggs	Milk	pint	5·31	5·11	5·47	53·55	70·85	71·64
	Cheese	oz	3·71	3·86	3·98	10·75	17·83	20·28
	Eggs	each	4·62	4·49	4·62	18·86	20·90	22·44
Fruit	Fresh	oz	16·64	16·85	16·16	16·51	19·54	22·39
	Other	,,	4·92	5·93	5·16	7·00	10·18	9·65
Vegetables	Potatoes	,,	43·99	42·49	48·08	10·77	10·39	14·78
	Other	,,	34·72	35·62	39·32	28·67	37·51	40·63

From *Monthly Digest of Statistics* (based on National Food Survey). Pensioner families with weekly income below £11·50 (1968), £17 (1972), £19·50 (1973)

* Consumption: purchase, free foods and net withdrawal from store (certain home-produced foods). Expenditure: purchases only; converted from new pence (1972 and 1973).

B. Gross Domestic Product from Expenditure and Output Data

TABLE B1

EXTERNAL TRADE, MERCHANDISE: FUELS

S.I.T.C.	Item	Quantities, '000 tons			Values, £000		
		1970	1971	1972	1970	1971	1972
Section 3							
Imports	(c.i.f.)						
321	Coal and coke	83·6	4,199	5,022	1,014	39,677	50,856
	Briquettes	143·1	397·9	417·9	2,396	7,654	8,402
331	Crude petroleum	99,170	105,633	102,665	686,912	929,696	914,005
	Petroleum, partly refined	2,179	2,006	2,682	24,927	26,040	33,020
332	Motor spirit	7,531	6,842	5,561	90,689	92,784	79,067
	Kerosene, etc.	1,130	1,504	1,475	15,279	21,800	21,157
	Gas oils, etc.	1,876	2,161	2,000	19,390	26,545	24,259
	Fuel oils	8,817	8,044	9,490	63,004	62,136	66,288
	Lubricating oils	520·4	499·3	530·2	15,309	15,554	16,590
	Other products	394·0	424·2	650·8	9,037	9,924	11,636
341	Gas	917·7	857·0	855·1	15,293	14,462	14,573
351	Electric energy*	639·0	97·1	469·5	1,640	359	1,732
	Total, Section 3				944,889	1,246,631	1,241,585

Exports	(f.o.b.)					
321	Coal and coke	4,340	3,256	2,097	27,717	20,538	15,149
	Briquettes	127·5	133·5	123·2	1,361	1,771	1,849
331	Crude petroleum	1,083·9	1,424·5	2,893·3	7,951	9,869	20,636
	Petroleum, partly refined	250·0	321·3	376·5	1,847	2,644	3,259
332	Motor spirit	1,473	1,830	2,042	18,862	25,167	28,062
	Kerosene, etc.	1,123	1,188	1,172	13,314	17,191	15,934
	Gas oils, etc.	5,546	6,043	5,956	51,067	69,058	68,103
	Fuel oils	7,813	6,103	5,471	46,038	40,343	35,728
	Lubricating oils	675·4	726·4	732·5	32,808	37,428	36,649
	Other products	217·2	428·7	399·1	4,394	10,758	10,898
341	Gas	88·4	121·9	133·2	1,432	1,513	2,328
351	Electric energy*	5·9	0·8	4·7	4	2	2
	Total, Section 3				206,795	236,282	238,597

From *Annual Statement of the Overseas Trade of the U.K.* (vol. 1)

* Quantities: 000 MWh.

Table B2
GDP BASED ON EXPENDITURE AND ON INCOME

Goods and services at current prices, £mn	Blue Book, 1968			Blue Book, 1972				Blue Book, 1973		
	1958	1963	1958	1963	1970	1971	1963	1970	1971	1972
Current expenditure:										
Consumers	15,362	20,195	15,296	20,130	31,216	34,504	20,118	31,404	34,838	39,263
Public authorities	3,672	5,080	3,742	5,170	9,022	10,278	5,176	9,095	10,339	11,702
Gross domestic capital formation*	3,603	5,118	3,670	5,185	9,544	9,954	5,179	9,480	10,120	10,774
External trade:										
Exports	4,707	5,814	4,707	5,809	11,240	12,593	5,809	11,255	12,632	13,331
less Imports	−4,586	−5,950	−4,586	−5,946	−10,847	−11,809	−5,946	−10,872	−11,857	−13,440
GDP at market prices	22,758	30,257	22,829	30,348	50,175	55,520	30,336	50,362	56,072	61,630
less Indirect taxes (net)†	−2,655	−3,488	−2,643	−3,467	−7,569	−7,774	−3,458	−7,574	−7,913	−8,146
GDP at factor cost:										
based on expenditure‡	20,103	26,769	20,186	26,881	42,606	47,746	26,878	42,788	48,159	53,484
based on income§	19,789	26,741	19,821	26,825	42,606	47,256	26,847	42,845	47,512	53,139
Difference: residual error	314	28	365	56	—	490	31	−57	647	345

From *Blue Book*, 1968, 1972 and 1973

* Fixed capital and value of physical increase in stocks and work in progress.
† Taxes on expenditure *less* subsidies.
‡ GDP at market prices (total of expenditure categories) adjusted to factor cost by deduction of indirect taxes (net).
§ Total of incomes (separately estimated) with allowance for stock appreciation.

TABLE B3
REAL GDP BASED ON EXPENDITURE

Goods and services at constant prices, £mn	At 1958 prices		At 1963 prices				At 1970 prices			
	1958	1963	1958	1963	1970	1971	1963	1970	1971	1972
Current expenditure:										
Consumers	15,362	18,375	17,008	20,130	23,413	24,032	27,416	31,404	32,211	34,115
Public authorities	3,672	4,153	4,563	5,170	5,878	6,082	7,984	9,095	9,430	9,786
Gross domestic capital formation	3,603	4,788	3,933	5,185	7,345	7,062	6,648	9,480	9,262	8,970
External trade:										
Exports	4,707	5,573	4,911	5,809	8,621	9,046	7,649	11,255	12,057	12,432
less Imports	−4,586	−5,743	−4,753	−5,946	−8,358	−8,744	−7,761	−10,872	−11,398	−12,556
GDP at market prices	22,758	27,146	25,662	30,348	36,899	37,478	41,936	50,362	51,562	52,747
less Indirect taxes (net)	−2,655	−3,322	−2,869	−3,467	−4,406	−4,582	−6,482	−7,574	−7,894	−8,403
GDP at factor cost	20,103	23,824	22,793	26,881	32,493	32,896	35,454	42,788	43,668	44,344

From *Blue Book*, 1968, 1972 and 1973

TABLE B4

REAL GDP BASED ON OUTPUT

At constant (1970) factor cost	Weights 1970	Index numbers (1970 = 100)			
		1963	1970	1971	1972
Industrial production:					
Mining	16	126·7	100	99·7	84·0
Manufacturing	327	77·9	100	99·7	101·2
Construction	64	82·6	100	102·8	105·2
Gas, water, electricity	32	71·3	100	103·9	111·1
Total industrial production	439	79·7	100	100·5	101·8
Other output:					
Agriculture	30	86	100	106	108
Transport and communication	84	78	100	100	105
Distribution	104	87	100	101	106
Public administration	67	96	100	101	102
Services*	307	80·8	100	103·1	106·9
Adjustment for financial services†	− 31	71	100	108	116
GDP at factor cost	1,000	82·1	100	101·4	103·9

From *Blue Book*, 1973

* Insurance, banking, professional and scientific services, ownership of dwellings and miscellaneous; four series combined into one with relevant weights.

† See *Blue Book*, p. 98.

4 Runs of Index Numbers

4.1 Introduction

The term 'run' suggests something taking place over time. Runs of index numbers are indeed almost always temporal comparisons, the case considered here. The analysis applies, however, to spatial or inter-group comparisons with only minor modifications. Take a run of index numbers at annual intervals, prices or quantities in a *current year* t being compared with those in some *reference-base year* 0. When the run is given more frequently, e.g. monthly or quarterly, the additional problem of seasonal variations arises and this is considered later (**4.8**). The index can in general run backwards as well as forwards and the current year is to be written: $t = \ldots -2, -1, 0, 1, 2, \ldots$. In a special but quite usual case, the run commences with the base year and comparisons are forward from year 0 to year t where $t = 0, 1, 2, \ldots$.

The range of possibilities is more extensive than in Chapter 2. The simplest case has an index of one of the standard types in a run of separate *binary comparisons* between each year t and the base year 0. This usually means a run of a Laspeyres or a Paasche index but others are possible, e.g. a run of Fisher Ideal index numbers. The case is not only the simplest but also the natural procedure when a particular index is to be computed and published regularly over time. Apart from routine revisions, an index once published remains unchanged, and all that normally happens is that the next index (for the following month, quarter or year) is computed and added to the run. It is difficult to see what other system could be adopted by a statistical agency in a programme of regular publication of series of index numbers.

There are, however, serious limitations from an economic point of view. In a run of binary comparisons the index for year t depends *only* on prices/quantities of year t (and the fixed base year); the course of prices/quantities *between* years 0 and t is completely ignored. Yet economic common sense would suggest that (e.g.) a consumer price index in year t would be influenced by prices before year t as well as those achieved in that year. Further, from the statistical angle, the run of binary comparisons is inefficient in that it does not make full use of all the data as they unfold over time. The question of using back data on a continuing basis is taken up in Chapter 5 and the analysis there leads to more efficient runs, to the Divisia Integral Index and its practical realisation as a chain index.

The simple binary system can be contrasted with a system at the other end of the spectrum. The question put is: given price/quantity data in each year in a closed period $t = 0, 1, 2, \ldots k$, what price and quantity index runs over the whole period are the 'best fit' in some specified sense? The answer is not just a chain index. The index in year t in a best-fitting run depends on all the data from year 0 to year k, i.e. on prices/quantities in years before t, in year t and in years after t. The run does not evolve year by year; it is fitted at one swoop and each index is influenced by later as much as by earlier years. Such a run has no place in the regular publishing programme of a statistical agency. Where it comes into its own is in econometric studies of macro-economic behaviour in specified periods. The problem is taken up in Chapter 7.

A final note here: the need for binary comparisons does not arise for a run of spatial or inter-group index numbers. Such a run is computed at one and the same time and there is no reason why it is not got as a 'fit' to the whole complex of price/quantity data. Even so, it is often sensible to adopt a sequential approach. A price index over a spectrum of countries, for example, may be best obtained by running through a selected series of 'neighbourly' countries from (say) Sweden to Germany and Austria and so on before finishing with India or Japan.

4.2 Runs of Laspeyres Index Numbers

There is little difficulty in writing the formula for a run of a Laspeyres index on the basis of the analysis of **1.6** and **2.2**. A set of weights is selected and kept fixed as the **weights base** of the run. If a change is made to different weights, then a different run is defined; the Laspeyres index has been rebased and reweighted. On the other hand, the **reference base** as the year written as 100 in the run is completely at choice. A Laspeyres run is just as easily read backwards as forwards and presents no obstacle to a switch of reference base from one year to an earlier or to a later one. The run can be written on year $t = \ldots -2, -1, 0, 1, 2, \ldots$ with year 0 as the weights base, and the reference base can then be switched from year 0 in either direction. It is, therefore, convenient to start with what is a special case, i.e. a run of the Laspeyres price index in which year 0 is both the weights and the reference base:

$$P_{0t}(q_0) = \frac{\sum p_t q_0}{\sum p_0 q_0} \quad \text{for } t = \ldots -2, -1, 0, 1, 2, \ldots \quad (1)$$

and the corresponding quantity run by interchange of the p's and q's.

The Laspeyres price run (1) measures the **changing cost of the fixed budget** q_0 taken from the weights base (year 0) as the prices change from the reference base (also year 0) to the current year t. The run may be forward $(t > 0)$ or backward $(t < 0)$ through time. This 'changing-cost' property remains valid under any switch of reference base. Switch the reference base from year 0 to year 1:

$$P_{1t}(q_0) = \frac{\sum p_t q_0}{\sum p_1 q_0} \quad \text{for } t = \ldots -2, -1, 0, 1, 2, \ldots \quad (2)$$

which is no more than a rescaling of (1) on division through by the index for year 1:

$$P_{1t}(q_0) = \frac{P_{0t}(q_0)}{P_{01}(q_0)} \quad \text{for } t = \ldots -2, -1, 0, 1, 2, \ldots \quad (3)$$

It is easily checked that (1), (2) and (3) are algebraically consistent. With weights base fixed at year 0, the original run (1) on year 0 as reference base is rescaled in (3) to year 1 as reference base and the 'changing-cost' property (2) still holds.

The general expression for the Laspeyres run of index numbers with weights base at year 0 gives a comparison between any two years r and s:

$$P_{rs}(q_0) = \frac{\sum p_s q_0}{\sum p_r q_0} = \frac{P_{0s}(q_0)}{P_{0r}(q_0)}$$

From this it follows that interchange of r and s implies taking the reciprocal:

$$P_{sr}(q_0) = 1/P_{rs}(q_0)$$

This is the result that a comparison backwards from year s to year r is the reciprocal of the comparison forwards from year r to year s.

The weighted-average form of the Laspeyres run is:

$$P_{0t}(q_0) = \frac{1}{\sum w_0} \sum w_0 \frac{p_t}{p_0} \quad \text{where } w_0 = p_0 q_0 \tag{4}$$

in the special case where the weights and reference bases coincide. More generally, when the reference base differs from the weights base:

$$P_{1t}(q_0) = \frac{1}{\sum w_1} \sum w_1 \frac{p_t}{p_1} \quad \text{where } w_1 = p_1 q_0 \tag{5}$$

It is only in the special case (4) that the weights are the actual values of the selected budget. More generally, in (5), the weights are the values of the fixed budget (q_0) repriced at the prices of the reference base (p_1). To summarise:

The run of a Laspeyres price index with fixed weights base at year 0 measures the changing cost of the fixed budget (q_0) over time. The reference base can be any year and switched from one year to another by re-scaling the run. Each index in the run is a weighted average of price relatives on the reference base, weights being given by the cost of q_0 at the prices of the reference base.

An exactly similar summary can be written for a Laspeyres quantity index.

The simplicity of the Laspeyres run, both in its properties and in ease of computation, makes it the most popular case in practice. Numerous examples can be quoted from official index numbers but one suffices for illustration: the Laspeyres run of real consumption at constant market prices. The construction of the index has already been displayed in Table 3.21, and Table 4.1 now sets out three runs on successive weights bases (1958, 1963, 1970). To illustrate the ease of switch of reference base, take the run from 1958 to 1968 on weights base 1963 and switch the reference base first backwards to 1958 and then forward to 1968:

INDEX OF REAL CONSUMPTION,
1963 WEIGHTS BASE

Reference base	1958	1959	1960	1961	1962	1963
Original: 1963	84·5	88·2	91·6	93·8	95·8	100
Switched: 1958	100	104·4	108·4	111·0	113·4	118·3
1968	75·0	78·3	81·3	83·2	85·0	88·7

Reference base	1964	1965	1966	1967	1968
Original: 1963	103·5	105·3	107·4	109·9	112·7
Switched: 1958	122·5	124·6	127·1	130·1	133·4
1968	91·8	93·4	95·3	97·5	100

TABLE 4.1

CONSUMERS' EXPENDITURE AT MARKET PRICES,
1948, 1953 AND 1958–72

Year	Consumption at current prices*		Real consumption Laspeyres index of volume			Consumer price index implied Paasche index†		
	£m	1958 =100	1958 =100	1963 =100	1970 =100	1958 =100	1963 =100	1970 =100
1948	8,552	55·9	81·6			68·5		
1953	11,402	74·5	87·6			85·1		
1958	15,296	*100*	*100*	84·5		*100*	90·0	
1959	16,117	105·4	104·7	88·2		100·7	90·9	
1960	16,933	110·7	108·9	91·6		101·6	91·9	
1961	17,835	116·6	111·5	93·8		104·6	94·5	
1962	18,923	123·7	114·0	95·8		108·5	98·2	
1963	20,118	131·5	119·6	*100*	87·3	110·0	*100*	73·4
1964	21,488	140·5	124·2	103·5	90·0	113·1	103·2	76·0
1965	22,878	149·6	126·4	105·3	91·4	118·3	108·0	79·7
1966	24,251	158·5	129·0	107·4	93·2	122·9	112·2	82·9
1967	25,455	166·4	131·6	109·9	95·0	126·5	115·2	85·3
1968	27,335	178·7		112·7	97·3		120·6	89·5
1969	28,968	189·4		113·3	97·6		127·1	94·5
1970	31,404	205·3		116·3	*100*		134·2	*100*
1971	34,838	227·8		119·4	102·6		145·1	108·2
1972	39,263	256·7			108·6			115·1

From *Blue Book*, 1968, 1972 and 1973

* Comparable run of values from 1973 *Blue Book*.
† Given run of values divided by each run of Laspeyres index numbers of volume; these adjusted runs are slightly different from those published (on 1958 and on 1963) in the *Blue Book*, 1968 and 1972.

The first switch is made by dividing through by the original 1958 index (84·5) and the second by division by the original 1968 index (112·7). That these eleven-year runs are simply rescaled versions of each other is evident in Fig. 4.1, drawn on ratio scales; the three graphs are exactly parallel, indicating the same percentage movements whatever reference base is taken.

Table 4.2 shows for later use the similar Laspeyres runs for real GDP based on expenditure, both at constant market prices and at constant factor cost. A shorter time span and only two successive weights bases (1963, 1970) are taken here.

Tables 4.1 and 4.2 illuminate a small piece of recent economic history: the changes in real consumption in comparison with real GDP in total. The first of these aggregates is a component of the second but differential movements are to be expected. The increases in the two runs are almost identical from 1958 to 1963 but then real

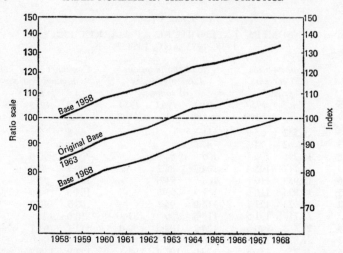

F_{IG}. 4.1 Index of real consumption

consumption rises more slowly than the rest of real GDP, i.e. personal consumption becomes a smaller slice of the whole real GDP cake. What is perhaps less expected is that the increase in real GDP is different, though only slightly so, when measured at market

T_{ABLE} 4.2

GDP BASED ON EXPENDITURE, 1958 AND 1963–72

Year	Real GDP as Expenditure Laspeyres Volume Index Numbers				All Prices in GDP Implied Paasche Index Numbers			
	At market prices		At factor cost		Market prices		Factor cost*	
	1963 =100	1970 =100	1963 =100	1970 =100	1963 =100	1970 =100	1963 =100	1970 =100
1958	84·6		84·8		87·9		88·6	
1963	100	83·3	100	82·9	100	72·4	100	75·8
1964	105·6	88·0	105·4	87·7	103·0	74·7	102·6	78·8
1965	108·0	89·9	108·1	89·9	108·1	78·5	106·8	81·0
1966	110·4	91·7	110·4	91·7	112·8	82·1	110·4	84·3
1967	112·8	93·8	112·7	93·8	116·3	84·7	114·4	86·8
1968	116·8	97·1	116·4	97·3	120·8	88·3	117·7	89·5
1969	118·9	98·2	118·6	98·5	127·0	93·3	121·8	92·9
1970	121·6	100	120·9	100	136·0	100	131·1	100
1971	123·5	102·4	122·4	102·1	148·1	108·2	145·1	110·3
1972		104·7		103·6		116·8		120·6

From *Blue Book*, 1972 and 1973

* The *Blue Books* described these price index numbers at factor cost as 'home costs per unit of output'.

prices than at factor cost. This is because the weighting of the quantity index is dependent on whether the value weights are at the market prices or at the factor costs of the base year.

4.3 Runs of Paasche Index Numbers

The development of **1.6** and **2.3** establishes the Paasche index as a derivative form and one which requires careful handling. Corresponding price and quantity index numbers generally need to be considered together. For expository purposes here a Paasche price index is taken in relation to a Laspeyres quantity index but all results are easily adapted to the case where the matching index numbers are Paasche for quantity and Laspeyres for price.

A Paasche price index has two very convenient features in the two-situation case: it is **current-weighted** with the budget of the current situation and it is the **implied price index** to match the Laspeyres index of quantity in accounting for value changes. Difficulties arise in any attempt to write a run of Paasche index numbers. The two features can in fact be retained *only* if the reference base is kept fixed and *only* for comparisons between the current year and the reference base. If the Paasche run is to have, as it should, the facility of a reference base which can be switched at will, then one or other of the two features must be sacrificed. Which should it be? The balance of advantage is found to lie in the discard of the current-weighted property and the retention of the implied index feature. All this needs to be established formally.

Start again with the special case where year 0 is the combined weights and reference base for the quantity index of Laspeyres form:

$$Q_{0t}(p_0) = \frac{\sum p_0 q_t}{\sum p_0 q_0} \quad \text{for } t = \ldots -2, \ -1, 0, 1, 2, \ldots \tag{1}$$

and the corresponding Paasche price index:

$$P_{0t}(q_t) = \frac{\sum p_t q_t}{\sum p_0 q_t} \quad \text{for } t = \ldots -2, \ -1, 0, 1, 2, \ldots \tag{2}$$

Here (1) and (2) multiply to the value change and (2) can be written:

$$P_{0t}(q_t) = \frac{V_{0t}}{Q_{0t}(p_0)} \quad \text{where } V_{0t} = \frac{\sum p_t q_t}{\sum p_0 q_0} \tag{3}$$

As long as the combined base year 0 is retained, $P_{0t}(q_t)$ is a Paasche run with the double feature represented by (2) and (3).

The retention of the fixed reference base is a serious limitation. Each comparison $P_{0t}(q_t)$ of year t with year 0 stands on its own; there can be neither a direct nor an indirect comparison between two years t_1 and t_2 where $t_1 \neq t_2 \neq 0$. This is because the index has quantities of year t_1 as weights when $t = t_1$ and *different* weights, quantities from year t_2, when $t = t_2$. It is an easy matter to devise examples where all prices rise from one year to another and yet the index $P_{0t}(q_t)$ does not show a rise.

To see what happens when the reference base is shifted from year 0 to year 1, with weights base unchanged, first write (1):

$$Q_{1t}(p_0) = \frac{\sum p_0 q_t}{\sum p_0 q_1} = \frac{Q_{0t}(p_0)}{Q_{01}(p_0)} \tag{4}$$

as in **4.2**. Next keep the current-weighted property (2) of the Paasche form and write:

$$P_{1t}(q_t) = \frac{\sum p_t q_t}{\sum p_1 q_t} \tag{5}$$

Finally, as a different switch, keep the deflated-value property (3):

$$P'_{1t}(q_t) = \frac{V_{1t}}{Q_{1t}(p_0)} = \frac{\sum p_t q_t}{\sum p_0 q_t} \times \frac{\sum p_0 q_1}{\sum p_1 q_1} \tag{6}$$

Forms (5) and (6) are not equal, except by accident, and a choice has to be made between them in selecting the rule for switching reference base. The switch (5) loses contact altogether with the weights base year 0; indeed the corresponding quantity index has ceased to be the run $Q_{1t}(p_0)$ and has become the quite different run $Q_{1t}(p_1)$. On the other hand, if (6) is the switching rule, there is a matching pair:

$$Q_{1t}(p_0) = \frac{Q_{0t}(p_0)}{Q_{01}(p_0)} \quad \text{and} \quad P'_{1t}(q_t) = \frac{P_{0t}(q_t)}{P_{01}(q_1)} \tag{7}$$

The quantity index run of (7) is just (4); the price index run comes from (2) and the switching rule (6).

The results (7) are so useful that they must decide the issue; they state that the runs $Q_{1t}(p_0)$ and $P'_{1t}(q_t)$ on year 1 as reference base are simply rescalings of the original runs $Q_{0t}(p_0)$ and $P_{0t}(q_t)$ on year 0 as reference (and weights) base. The choice of the switching rule for the Paasche run settles on $P'_{1t}(q_t)$; it has the deflated-value property (6) and the rescaling facility (7). What is lost is the current-weighted interpretation (5) and hence any simple expression of the Paasche index in weighted-average form. This is not such a great loss since, even in the two-situation case of **2.4,** the weighted-average form is very awkward for the Paasche index. To summarise:

The run of a Paasche price index, to correspond to a Laspeyres quantity index fixed-weighted on year 0, is got by deflating the value change by the Laspeyres quantity index year by year. The reference base can be any year and switched by rescaling the run. The Paasche price index measures the changing cost of the current budget if and only if the reference base is year 0.

Exactly similar results obtain for matching runs of Paasche quantity and Laspeyres price index numbers.

Tables 4.1 and 4.2 show the Paasche price index runs implied by the Laspeyres runs for real consumption and real GDP. The runs are on successive weights bases which are also the reference bases. The *consumer price index* of Table 4.1 is given in three runs on weights bases in 1958, 1963 and 1970; in each run the index measures the changing cost of the current budget. For example, the 1972 index at 115·1% of 1970 shows that the 1972 consumer budget cost 15·1% more in that year than it would have done in 1970. Reference bases can be changed, by rescaling the runs to other years as 100, but the 'changing-cost' interpretation is then lost. The 1972 index on (e.g.) 1963 as 100 is 115·1/73·4 or 156·8% of 1963. This does *not* imply that the cost of the 1972 budget was 56·8% more in 1972 than it would have been in 1963; this is a calculation not performed in the computation of the index run. What always holds, however the reference base is changed, is the relation between the Paasche consumer price index and the Laspeyres volume index of real consumption; they multiply to the change in consumers' expenditure at current prices.

Table 4.2 gives similar index runs for total GDP based on expenditure, and in two disguises: at factor costs and at market prices. Of the two runs of price index numbers in implied (Paasche) form, that at factor costs is described officially as *home costs per unit of output.* The relation of this run to the other index run, at market prices, reflects the changing incidence of indirect taxes net of subsidies. The market-prices index generally rose faster than the index of factor costs in the 1960s, a result of increasing indirect taxation. The position was reversed in 1970–1.

In the long run the consumer price index tends to conform fairly closely to the market-prices index for all GDP. There can be considerable divergences, however, over short periods. Tables 4.1 and 4.2 show that, more often than not in the 1960s and early 1970s, consumer prices rose more slowly than prices generally.

4.4 Runs Read Backwards and Forwards

Runs of index numbers, both of Laspeyres and of Paasche form, are defined here so that comparisons can be made between any years, backwards as well as forwards, and on any reference base. For example, a run may be given in the original computations backwards from a combined weights and reference base, as in Tables 4.1 and 4.2. The same run can be read forwards by simply shifting the reference base back to an earlier year. Similarly a shift of reference base ahead permits an index originally running forwards to be read backwards.

The basic result for a binary comparison is established in **2.5**: the reciprocal of the forward Laspeyres index from year 0 to year 1 is the backward Paasche index from year 1 to year 0, and conversely. An illustration was given at the end of **3.8**. The result is now developed for expository purposes in terms of a Laspeyres run base-weighted on year 0 and given for years $t = \ldots -2, -1, 0, 1, 2, \ldots$ All results apply equally to a Paasche run defined with the switching rule of **4.3**.

There is a serious limitation on the application of the basic result to runs of index numbers. One of the two years compared must be the weights base of the index and the other year, once selected, must be used as the year to which the reference base is switched in order to reverse the comparison. So, given a weights base and a selected reference base, the backward/forward comparison involving an index and its reciprocal is frozen on just these two years. The result *never* applies to a comparison not involving the weights base and it *only* applies to a year different from that first selected by starting afresh and shifting to the newly selected year as reference base; see Fowler (1974).

Look forward in a given Laspeyres run from the base year 0 to a year t $(t > 0)$. Then take the reciprocal and interpret as a Paasche index back from year t as a reference base to year 0. It is in this way that the forward Laspeyres run provides a sequence of backward comparisons, each a one-off Paasche index on its own reference base.

A sequence of one-off forward Paasche comparisons arises in the same way from a backward Laspeyres run.

Ample illustration is found in the runs of Laspeyres index numbers of real consumption and real GDP of Tables 4.1 and 4.2. For example, a run base-weighted on 1963 can be read back to 1958 or ahead to 1970; appropriate shifts backwards or forwards can then be made in the reference base to reverse the direction of comparison. So, shifting the base forward to 1968 gives:

Index	Real consump- tion	Real GDP Market prices	Factor cost
(i) Forward Laspeyres 1968 (1963 = 100)	112·7	116·8	116·4
(ii) Reciprocal 1963 (1968 = 100)	88·7	85·6	85·9

Row (i) is straight from Tables 4.1 and 4.2. Each of (ii) is then interpreted as a one-off Paasche index backwards from the new reference base of 1968 to the weights base of 1963. A whole sequence of such backward Paasche index numbers can be written, from each year after 1963 back to 1963. The forward Laspeyres index numbers (e.g. of real consumption) are all comparable one with another; from 1963 to 1964, then to 1965, and so on. The reciprocals are one-off index numbers (of real consumption) of Paasche form from 1964 back to 1963, then separately from 1965 to 1963, and so on. They all run back to 1963 and to no other year. To get a Paasche index back to (say) 1964 from a later year is an impossible exercise given only a 1963-based Laspeyres run; it requires a Laspeyres run based on 1964.

The parallel Laspeyres runs of quantity index numbers base-weighted first on 1963 and then on 1970 yield a comparison of the Laspeyres and Paasche forms of the index in 1970 (1963 = 100) by a use of the reciprocal result already illustrated in **3.8**. Here:

Index	Real consump- tion	Real GDP Market prices	Factor cost
(i) Backward Laspeyres 1963 (1970 = 100)	87·3	83·3	82·9
(ii) Reciprocal:			
Forward Paasche 1970 (1963 = 100)	114·5	120·0	120·6
(iii) Forward Laspeyres 1970 (1963 = 100)	116·3	121·6	120·9

Here (i) and (iii) come from runs base-weighted on 1963 and on 1970 in Tables 4.1 and 4.2; each entry in (ii) is the reciprocal of the corresponding entry in (i). The result used is that the 1970-based column of

Laspeyres index numbers in Table 4.1 or 4.2 provides in reciprocal a sequence of one-off Paasche index numbers from 1963, then from 1964, and so on, each to the weights-base year 1970. The one index that happens to link with the 1963-based column, and the only one to do so, is that from 1963 to 1970. Hence, rows (ii) and (iii) are precisely comparable and, as expected from the analysis of **2.7**, the Laspeyres form exceeds the Paasche in each case.

The exercise can be repeated for the matching index numbers of prices to round off the story and to show the basic result on reciprocals in its application to Paasche runs:

		Consumer price index	All GDP prices Market prices	Factor cost
Index				
(i) Backward Paasche	1963 (1970 = 100)	73·4	72·4	75·8
(ii) Reciprocal:				
Forward Laspeyres	1970 (1963 = 100)	136·2	138·1	131·9
(iii) Forward Paasche	1970 (1963 = 100)	134·2	136·0	131·1

Though the results add little to what has already been obtained, these implied (Paasche) index numbers are interesting, each a deflator of the value change giving the Laspeyres index numbers of quantity of the previous tabulation. Again, as must be, the Laspeyres forms given in this price index table are all greater than the Paasche forms which correspond.

4.5 Splicing in Practice

The calculations made on the index numbers of Table 4.1 have an immediate use in the process of splicing runs of index numbers on successive bases, here 1958, 1963 and 1970. Each run is carried back to the base year of the previous run, an overlap more than ample for splicing. The problem is illustrated by alternative splicings of the Laspeyres runs of real consumption shown in Table 4.3 and by alternative splicings of the matching Paasche runs of consumer prices shown in Table 4.4. It is considered from three angles; first, the *need* for splicing; second, the *cost* in terms of the various techniques of splicing used; finally, the *price* to be paid in the compromises and approximations involved in splicing.

As seen in **1.5**, the need for splicing arises simply from the fact that any index run constructed on what must be a rigid formula gets more difficult and eventually quite impossible to realise in practice as time

TABLE 4.3

REAL CONSUMPTION AT MARKET PRICES, 1948, 1953 AND 1958–72

| | 1958 series | *Run obtained by splicing on:* | | | | Fisher ideal links |
| | | | 1963 series | | 1970 series | |
Year	1958 =100 (1)	1963 =100 (2)	Switched to 1958=100 (3)	1970 =100 (4)	Switched to 1958=100 (5)	1958 =100 (6)
1948	81·6	69·0	81·6	60·2	81·6	81·6
1953	87·6	74·0	87·6	64·6	87·6	87·6
1958	100	84·5	100	73·8	100	100
1959	104·7	88·2	104·4	77·0	104·4	104·6
1960	108·9	91·6	108·4	80·0	108·4	108·6
1961	111·5	93·8	111·0	81·9	111·0	111·1
1962	114·0	95·8	113·4	83·6	113·4	113·6
1963	119·6	100	118·3	87·3	118·3	119·0
1964	123·8	103·5	122·5	90·0	122·0	122·9
1965	125·9	105·3	124·6	91·4	123·8	124·9
1966	128·5	107·4	127·1	93·2	126·3	127·3
1967	131·4	109·9	130·1	95·0	128·7	130·1
1968	134·8	112·7	133·4	97·3	131·8	133·3
1969	135·5	113·3	134·1	97·6	132·2	134·0
1970	139·1	116·3	137·6	100	135·5	137·3
1971	142·7	119·3	141·2	102·6	139·0	140·9
1972	151·1	126·3	149·5	108·6	147·2	149·1

From Table 4.1

TABLE 4.4

CONSUMER PRICE INDEX, 1948, 1953 AND 1958–72

| | 1958 series | *Run obtained by splicing on:* | | | | Fisher Ideal links |
| | | | 1963 series | | 1970 series | |
Year	1958 =100 (1)	1963 =100 (2)	Switched to 1958=100 (3)	1970 =100 (4)	Switched to 1958=100 (5)	1958 =100 (6)
1948	68·5	61·65	68·5	45·25	68·5	68·5
1953	85·1	76·6	85·1	56·2	85·1	85·1
1958	100	90·0	100	66·1	100	100
1959	100·7	90·9	101·0	66·7	101·0	100·7
1960	101·6	91·9	102·1	67·45	102·1	101·7
1961	104·6	94·5	105·0	69·4	105·0	104·9
1962	108·5	98·2	109·1	72·1	109·1	109·0
1963	110·0	100	111·1	73·4	111·1	110·55
1964	113·5	103·2	114·7	76·0	115·0	114·2
1965	118·8	108·0	120·0	79·7	120·6	119·6
1966	123·4	112·2	124·7	82·9	125·5	124·4
1967	126·7	115·2	128·0	85·3	129·1	127·8
1968	132·7	120·6	134·0	89·5	135·5	134·0
1969	139·8	127·1	141·2	94·5	143·1	141·4
1970	147·6	134·2	149·1	100	151·4	149·5
1971	159·7	145·2	161·3	108·2	163·8	161·7
1972	169·9	154·5	171·7	115·1	174·2	172·0

From Table 4.1

goes on. The usual type of formula includes a cross-valuation of quantities of one year at prices of another, requiring completely comparable data on prices and quantities over the span of years. Every item in the index must have a quantity and a matching price quotation on a specification which is detailed, explicit and unchanging. All this must be defeated sooner or later by the operation of economic change in demand or supply and by innovation and technical progress. Goods and services change in many ways; old items disappear and new items take their place. The cross-valuation on which an index depends soon becomes approximate and finally has to be given up.

As an illustration, consider the Laspeyres index measuring real consumption and dependent on the valuation of current goods and services at the fixed prices of some base year. Among the items so to be valued are durable goods of all shapes and sizes. It is not possible precisely, and difficult approximately, to name a base-year price for (e.g.) this year's TV set. Model changes are frequent: one model is not easily compared with the next either technically or in terms of consumer preferences. The cross-valuation can be kept going as a reasonable approximation for some time but eventually something happens to make it collapse, as when a really new product such as colour TV hits the market. It is perhaps less clear that much the same thing can happen to many consumables; breakfast cereals and women's shoes are just two of many items liable to technical innovation or changing fashion. It is hardly possible to name a single item which remains unchanged over decades, still less centuries; even our daily bread would be unrecognisable to the Victorians, let alone to the Tudors.

A first reaction is to give up any attempt to calculate index numbers of real consumption or consumer prices valid for more than a few years. Indeed most fixed-weighted forms are primarily regarded by their constructors as short-run indicators. Yet the question which an index is required to answer is valid, useful and meaningful not only for this year as compared with last but also over scores or indeed hundreds of years. What is the standard of living, or the value of money, in 1974 in comparison with 1964, or with 1914, or with 1850? This is a sensible question and it calls for a sensible answer in terms of an index of real consumption or of consumer prices. There is even some sense in asking the question for a comparison with 1066 or 1485. So what sensible answer is there? There can be no question of valuing present purchases of breakfast cereals, TV sets and so forth at prices of remote years in the past. Something might be done by sticking to a few staples such as flour and bread, but only a very rough indicator of general price/quantity changes would emerge. Clearly the best that can be done is to have successive runs of index numbers, each computed on a strict formula as long as possible and given up before it splutters out. Long-run comparisons are then to be made by splicing methods.

The justification for splicing in purely statistical or economic-theoretic terms is seen (in **1.5**) to be far from convincing. Yet the need is so pressing that splicing must be accepted as a rough and ready job and on its own terms. Each index run in a succession of runs must be viewed as an approximation to changes in a non-measurable concept, such as the general price level, remaining valid over long periods. A sequence of Laspeyres runs of real consumption may be strictly interpreted as changing expenditure at (say) 1958 prices for the first run, at 1963 prices for the second, and so on. But then each run dies in its tracks and splicing has no meaning. The splicing process only makes sense if each run can be taken as some approximation to changes in the broad and non-measurable concept of a standard of living.

Once this position is accepted, it follows that the splicing job can be done in more than one way. It is necessary to make statistical estimations and to choose between statistical estimators. Alternative splicings become available to the extent that successive runs overlap; the question is which run provides the splice in the overlap. The three 'straight' splicings in Table 4.3 or 4.4 differ according to which run is taken in the overlaps of 1958–63 and 1963–70. There is another possibility: to use a compromise index formula in an overlap and the compromise which suggests itself is the Fisher Ideal form, as used in the last splicings in Tables 4.3 and 4.4. The following detailed account of splicing techniques refers to columns as numbered in these tables. The figures quoted are for real consumption (Table 4.3); explanations apply equally to the consumer price index (Table 4.4).

The three 'straight' splicings are respectively on the 1958 run, on the 1963 run and on the 1970 run, the selected run being given the longest period of validity in the splicing. Column (1) splices on the 1958 run, allowed to continue as long as convenient: this is up to 1963 when its value is 119·6% of 1958. The 1963 run with each entry multiplied by 1·196 continues to 1970 when the index is 1·196 × 116·3 = 139·1 % of 1958. The final leg is the 1970 run, each entry being multiplied by 1·391. In other words, the method of generating the splicing on 1958 is to proceed down the 1958 run of Table 4.1 until 119·6 is reached in 1963, to continue with the rescaled 1963 run (each times 1·196) until 139·1 is reached in 1970, and finally to complete with the rescaled 1970 run (each times 1·391).

The same kind of splicing is carried out with the 1963 run as the base one, and with 1963 as 100, in column (2). The 1963 run is taken as spanning the period from 1958 to 1970. Rescaled versions of the 1958 run and of the 1970 run are used before 1958 and after 1970; the rescaling factors are respectively 0·845 and 1·163, from the 1963-based index in 1958 and in 1970. Column (3) switches the run for convenience to the reference base 1958. A third splicing is shown in column (4) on the 1970 base and switched to 1958 in column (5). The basic run here is that of 1970, taken back as far as 1963 before the 1963 run is spliced on back to 1958 and the 1958 run before that date.

A more elaborate calculation is required for the Fisher Ideal splicing of column (6). The main elements are the Fisherian links, first for the period 1958–63 and then for 1963–70, as calculated from the data of Table 4.1:

Index	Link: 1958–63		Link: 1963–70	
	1958	1963	1963	1970
Forward Laspeyres (1)	100	119·6	100	116·3
Backward Laspeyres	84·5	100	87·3	100
Forward Paasche (2)	100	118·35	100	114·55
Fisher Ideal: GM of (1) and (2)	100	119·0	100	115·4

The two links are finally spliced together to give the three basing points in the Fisher Ideal splicing.

1958: 100;   1963: 119·0   1970: 1·19 × 115·4 = 137·3

The completion of the spliced run of column (6) is a matter of interpolation between the basing points and of extrapolation outside them. The latter raises no problems; extrapolation before 1958 uses the 1958 run and that after 1970 uses the 1970 run. There is, however, a choice on the method of interpolation. For the 1958–63 period, this can be by means either of the 1958 run or of the 1963 run, both available over the whole period. On a fairly standard practice, interpolation is by the base series, i.e. the 1958 run from 1958 to 1963 and similarly the 1963 run for 1963–70. So, in year t between 1958 and 1963, let the increase from 1958 be $x\%$ on the 1958 run and write:

$$100 + \frac{19 \cdot 0}{19 \cdot 6} x \qquad \% \text{ of } 1958$$

as the interpolated index. This is just the arithmetic process of reducing the index figure of 119·6 achieved in 1963 on the 1958 run to the required basing point of 119·0 of the Fisher Ideal link.

The spliced runs of Table 4.3, and equally of Table 4.4, only differ *between* the basing points of 1958 and 1970. The 1958 run is the only one available before 1958, and only the 1970 run after 1970, and each of the spliced runs faithfully reproduces them. Between 1958 and 1970 on the spliced runs for real consumption (Table 4.3, with 1958 as 100), the 1958 splicing is consistently highest and the 1970 splicing the lowest. The Fisherian splicing fulfils expectations by falling neatly in the middle. The positions on the spliced runs for the consumer price index (Table 4.4) are the mirror image and this is to be expected. The price index is of implied Paasche form; the 1958 splicing runs lowest, the 1970 splicing highest and the Fisherian splicing again falls into place in between. There is enough consistency in the whole set of spliced runs to provide the broad conclusion: the standard of living (real consumption) rose by 49% and the consumer price level by 72% between 1958 and 1972.

The price to be paid for splicing is considerable but under most conditions it is acceptable. It can be specified under two heads. The first price is the loss of the familiar properties of an aggregative index in passing from a single to a spliced run. A single Laspeyres run of real consumption, for example, is to be interpreted as expenditure at constant prices; a spliced run cannot be so interpreted and indeed involves valuations at several sets of prices in succession. What may be more serious is that, whereas a Paasche run of price index numbers is implied by the corresponding Laspeyres run of quantity index numbers, this is no longer true of spliced runs. Matching pairs of spliced runs fail to multiply to the value change. The discrepancy should not, however, be exaggerated; it is usually quite small in practice, as is found in the illustration on p. 162. The spliced price and quantity runs here may not multiply *exactly* to the value change but they do so *approximately* and quite closely.

The second price to be paid for the facility of splicing is that the components of an aggregate, each got by a separate splicing, no

Index (1958 = 100)	*1958 series*	*1963 series*	*1970 series*	*Fisher Ideal links*
1968		Value: 178·7% of 1958		
Real consumption	134·8	133·4	131·8	133·3
Consumer prices	132·7	134·0	135·5	134·0
Product	178·9	178·8	178·6	178·6
1970		Value: 205·3% of 1958		
Real consumption	139·1	137·6	135·5	137·3
Consumer prices	147·6	149·1	151·4	149·5
Product	205·3	205·2	205·1	205·3
1972		Value: 256·7% of 1958		
Real consumption	151·1	149·5	147·2	149·1
Consumer prices	169·9	171·7	174·2	172·0
Product	256·7	256·7	256·4	256·5

Runs spliced on:

From Tables 4.3 and 4.4

longer add to the total aggregate obtained by splicing. Addition here means either straight summation of constant-price (or constant-quantity) valuations or the equivalent weighted combination of component index numbers. As an illustration which makes direct use of *Blue Book* data, take real consumption as one component of real GDP as expenditure, and add the other components as specified in Chapter 3, Appendix Tables B2 and B3. The 1970-based run of real consumption is shown in Table 4.1 back only to 1963, and similarly the 1963-based run goes back only to 1958. This omission is *not* because the *Blue Books* stop short in this way in their published backward runs. It is rather because the earlier entries are calculated on such a different basis that they are not comparable with the later ones. The run of real consumption based on 1970 is computed in full detail of repricing at 1970 prices after 1970 and in a reasonably approximate form back to 1963 (see **3.8**). No attempt is made, however, to revalue at 1970 prices in years before 1963; instead, the previous 1963-run is spliced on in precisely the way described here. The splicing is done separately for each component and for total GDP. Consequently, in the years before 1963, total GDP is not the sum of its components, all estimated (by splicing) at 1970 prices. The following data taken from the 1973 *Blue Book* illustrate this result for the years 1956, 1958 and 1960, in comparison with 1963 as the first year of repricing directly with 1970 prices:

Real GDP £mn at 1970 market prices	Estimated by splicing on the 1963 run*			Valued at 1970 prices
	1956	1958	1960	1963
Current expenditure:				
Consumers	22,122	23,178	25,136	27,416
Public authorities	7,327	7,046	7,352	7,984
Gross domestic capital formation	4,916	5,050	6,518	6,648
Exports less imports	422	263	− 385	− 112
Discrepancy	− 93	− 55	+ 41	—
GDP at 1970 market prices	34,694	35,482	38,662	41,936

* Run of constant (1963) price valuations spliced in 1963 onto run of direct valuations at 1970 prices.

There is a difference between total GDP and the sum of its components as long as the constant-price valuations are obtained by the splicing method. There is no difference (by definition) in the run of direct valuations at 1970 prices from 1963 onwards. The discrepancy arising from splicing is fairly substantial and it can be in either direction. It is a feature of the splicing process which cannot be ignored though it must be accepted.

4.6 The Value Matrix

The matrix of direct and cross-valuations, from which all aggregative index numbers are computed, is written in **1.6** in the conventional form with prices constant across rows and quantities constant down columns. In shorthand, write:

$$V = [\sum p_r q_s] \quad \text{for } r, s = 0, 1, 2, 3, \ldots$$

in the case where all runs start from year 0 and continue indefinitely. The general entry shown in the square brackets in the matrix is the valuation of year s quantities at year r prices.

There is a vast amount of information stored in V. The complete matrix, even when it is stopped after a given period of years, is calculated in practice only for special purposes, e.g. in an econometric study of a specific period or in such experimental work as Fowler (1970) on the index of retail prices. The leading diagonal is the run of actual recorded values and from it is derived:

$$V_{rs} = \frac{\sum p_s q_s}{\sum p_r q_r} \quad \text{value change from year } r \text{ to year } s$$

As a regular and continuing matter, however, off-diagonal entries are computed only as needed in the runs of index numbers to be obtained.

The analysis of **1.6** can be recapitulated and developed. Index runs base-weighted on year 0 need only the entries in the first column (for prices) and in the first row (for quantities) of V, all divided by the first entry in the leading diagonal. In year t:

First-column entry:

$$\sum p_t q_0 \qquad \text{and} \qquad \text{Laspeyres price index: } P_{0t}(q_0) = \frac{\sum p_t q_0}{\sum p_0 q_0}$$

First-row entry:

$$\sum p_0 q_t \qquad \text{and} \qquad \text{Laspeyres quantity index: } Q_{0t}(p_0) = \frac{\sum p_0 q_t}{\sum p_0 q_0}$$

The corresponding Paasche runs are derivative and use the leading diagonal entry for year t as well as entries in the first row or column:

$$\text{Paasche price index:} \qquad P_{0t}(q_t) = \frac{V_{0t}}{Q_{0t}(p_0)} = \frac{\sum p_t q_t}{\sum p_0 q_t}$$

$$\text{Paasche quantity index:} \qquad Q_{0t}(p_t) = \frac{V_{0t}}{P_{0t}(q_0)} = \frac{\sum p_t q_0}{\sum p_t q_t}$$

As long as year 0 remains the weights base, the index runs can be switched to any reference base and the cross-valuations still come only from the first row or column of V. For example, the Laspeyres price run on year r as reference base is:

$$P_{rt}(q_0) = \frac{P_{0t}(q_0)}{P_{0r}(q_0)} = \frac{\sum p_t q_0}{\sum p_r q_0} \qquad r \text{ given and } t = 0, 1, 2, 3, \ldots$$

Other rows or columns of V are needed only when the index runs are rebased on the selection of (say) year s as a new weights base $(s \neq 0)$. These runs are different and derived from entries in the $(s+1)$th row and the $(s+1)$th column of V in place of the first row and column.

The computational consequence is simple. To get both price and quantity index runs in both Laspeyres and Paasche forms, entries need be added to V year by year only in the leading diagonal *plus* the $(s+1)$th row and column, where year s is the weights base. Even less is needed if only one matching pair of runs is computed. If the pair is the Laspeyres run for quantity and the Paasche run for price, as in the

British national accounts, then continuing entries in V are needed only in the leading diagonal *plus* the $(s+1)$th row.

This economical way of getting year by year a single split of value changes into price and quantity components is illustrated by the value matrix of Table 4.5 for consumers' expenditure in the years

TABLE 4.5

CONSUMERS' EXPENDITURE AT MARKET PRICES:
VALUE MATRIX (£ billions)

Prices in year:	1958	Quantities in year 1963	1970	1971	1972
1958	15·4	18·4	NA	NA	NA
1963	17·0	20·1	23·4	24·0	NA
1970	NA	27·4	31·4	32·2	34·1
1971	NA	NA	NA	34·8	NA
1972	NA	NA	NA	NA	39·3

From Chapter 3 Appendix Tables B2 and 3

1958, 1963 and 1970–2. The current runs of index numbers of real consumption and consumer prices are based on 1970 and the matrix is extended year by year by adding entries only in the leading diagonal and in the 1970 row. More is needed only when a change is made in the weights base and the required entries then drop from one row to another. Changes in weights base were made in 1958, 1963 and 1970 so that the matrix of Table 4.5 has extra entries for these years, making it possible for both pairs of matching index numbers (and not just the regular single pair) to be calculated between them.

4.7 Relation between Laspeyres and Paasche Runs

The statistical-theoretic result (5) of **2.7** relates the Paasche to the Laspeyres form in any one year. It can be illustrated in its application to index runs and the way prepared for a consideration of the question of the 'drift' of an index of Laspeyres or Paasche form away from the true index as time goes on.

The evidence so far is that the Laspeyres and Paasche forms differ little in the short run but that where significant differences occur, not overlaid by observational errors, they tend to conform to expectations as analysed in **2.7**. Tables 3.12 and 3.18 provide illustrations. In a demand-dominated market such as that for imports and for consumer goods, the Laspeyres price index is generally the larger of the two. In the less usual situation of markets dominated by suppliers, the Paasche index tends to be the higher, e.g. for export prices as in Table 3.18. The same Paasche/Laspeyres relation holds for the quantity index as for the corresponding price index.

Comparisons between Laspeyres and Paasche forms can be made in Table 4.1 for real consumption and consumer prices, if only for years which are successive weights bases. The two forms are quite close and the Laspeyres is the greater of the two both from 1958 to 1963 and again from 1963 to 1970. The Fisherian links are here found to be convenient figures falling in the narrow range set by the Laspeyres and Paasche forms. The question remains whether the gap between the two forms tends to open up by a gradual drift apart as the time span of the comparison increases. If so, the further question is whether the Fisher Ideal index is a closer approximation to the true index than either the Laspeyres or the Paasche index by itself. A little light is thrown on these questions by the longer runs of Tables 4.3 and 4.4. The three original runs of real consumption, here spliced together, are of base-weighted (Laspeyres) form. It makes sense that the 1958-splicing runs the highest of the three in Table 4.3 over the period from 1958 to 1970 and that the 1970-splicing should be the lowest. For the splicing which makes most use of the 1958 original run is more heavily 'base-weighted' than the splicing which emphasises the original run based on 1970.

A possible compromise here is to take the intermediate splicing mainly dependent on the Laspeyres run of real consumption based on 1963. Before 1963 this splicing is of backward Laspeyres, and so of forward Paasche, type and so runs low. After 1963 it is of forward Laspeyres type and so runs high. The compromise is of a 'blow-hot-blow-cold' nature and there is little to be said for it. As Fowler (1974) notes, it is no help to have an index which first diverges in one direction and then in the other.

A better job at a compromise is likely to be the spliced run of real consumption constructed from Fisher Ideal links. At least the links split the difference between the Laspeyres and the Paasche forms at each successive basing year. The same is true of the spliced runs of the index of consumer prices (Table 4.4). The relation between the runs is in the opposite direction, since the original runs are of Paasche form, but the splicing constructed from Fisher Ideal links again splits the difference between them.

In the usual notation for Laspeyres and Paasche runs base-weighted on year 0, the result (5) of **2.7** can be written:

$$\frac{P_{0t}(q_t)}{P_{0t}(q_0)} = \frac{Q_{0t}(p_t)}{Q_{0t}(p_0)} = 1 + \rho_{0t}$$

where the *discrepancy* $\quad \rho_{0t} = r \, \dfrac{\sigma_p}{P_{0t}(q_0)} \, \dfrac{\sigma_q}{Q_{0t}(p_0)}$ (1)

The expression for ρ_{0t} involves the weighted correlation coefficient and variances of price/quantity relatives in year t on year 0 as base. It is an economical procedure to supplement a given Laspeyres run by calculating the discrepancy ρ_{0t} each year from the basic data. The entry for year t in a Paasche run is then $(1 + \rho_{0t})$ times the Laspeyres index of year t. So, given P_{0t} and Q_{0t} as the Laspeyres price and quantity runs respectively on the base year 0:

Year	1	2	...	t	...
Discrepancy	ρ_{01}	ρ_{02}	...	ρ_{0t}	...
Price index run:					
Laspeyres	P_{01}	P_{02}	...	P_{0t}	...
Paasche	$P_{01}(1+\rho_{01})$	$P_{02}(1+\rho_{02})$	...	$P_{0t}(1+\rho_{0t})$	...
Quantity index run:					
Laspeyres	Q_{01}	Q_{02}	...	Q_{0t}	...
Paasche	$Q_{01}(1+\rho_{01})$	$Q_{02}(1+\rho_{02})$	...	$Q_{0t}(1+\rho_{0t})$	...
Change in value:					
V_{0t}	$P_{01}Q_{01}(1+\rho_{01})$	$P_{02}Q_{02}(1+\rho_{02})$	...	$P_{0t}Q_{0t}(1+\rho_{0t})$	...

The economical nature of this formulation is seen in the fact that the row for V_{0t} automatically includes both splits of the value change:

$$P_{0t} \times Q_{0t}(1+\rho_{0t}) \quad \text{and} \quad P_{0t}(1+\rho_{0t}) \times Q_{0t}$$

Laspeyres   Paasche   Paasche   Laspeyres

The formulation concentrates attention on the discrepancy ρ_{0t} given by (1), with sign determined by the correlation coefficient r and magnitude jointly by this coefficient and the spread of price and quantity relatives. Usually: $r < 0$ and so: $\rho_{0t} < 0$. From the long-run point of view, however, the questions are whether ρ_{0t} keeps the same sign and whether it starts small and then grows more or less slowly.

Once the weights base is fixed at year 0, the value matrix V can be divided through by the leading element $(\sum p_0 q_0)$ and expressed in terms of Laspeyres index runs together with ρ_{0t}:

$$D = \begin{bmatrix} 1 & Q_{01} & Q_{02} & \cdots \\ P_{01} & P_{01}Q_{01}(1+\rho_{01}) & \cdots & \cdots \\ P_{02} & \cdots & P_{02}Q_{02}(1+\rho_{02}) & \cdots \\ \cdots & \cdots & \cdots & \cdots \end{bmatrix} \tag{2}$$

where the only entries written explicitly are in the leading diagonal (value changes) and in the first row and column (Laspeyres index runs). The other off-diagonal entries are cross-valuations usually not computed. If the weights base is changed from year 0 to year r, then the row and column needed in (2) shift to the $(r+1)$th. The simplest procedure is to move this row and column up into the first slot in D and so keep the form (2).

To illustrate, take the consumption of dairy produce by three income groups as given in Table 3.14. This example demonstrates that an index run need not be a run through time. Unlike the temporal case, there is here no fixed order and the groups are arranged in Table 3.14 for convenience only: A, low-income pensioners; B, middle-income families; C, high-income families. The analysis of **3.6** suggests a different order from the point of view of consumption of dairy produce per head: B, C, A. The value matrices in the two quarters considered are shown below with the groups arranged in this new order and with entries in p per head per week (expenditure on dairy produce).

| | First quarter 1972 Quantities consumed by: | | | First quarter 1973 Quantities consumed by: | | |
	B	C	A	B	C	A
Unit values:						
Group B	57·66	61·31	60·50	54·50	55·86	60·06
C	62·04	65·89	65·10	57·33	58·75	63·14
A	59·75	64·75	62·68	55·43	56·85	61·10

With group B as base, the matrices D are:

First Quarter 1972

$$\begin{bmatrix} 1 & 1\cdot063 & 1\cdot049 \\ 1\cdot076 & 1\cdot143 & \cdots \\ 1\cdot036 & \cdots & 1\cdot087 \end{bmatrix}$$

First Quarter 1973

$$\begin{bmatrix} 1 & 1\cdot025 & 1\cdot102 \\ 1\cdot052 & 1\cdot078 & \cdots \\ 1\cdot017 & \cdots & 1\cdot121 \end{bmatrix}$$

Here the discrepancies are not significantly different from zero; for example, in the first quarter, 1972:

$$1 + \rho_{bc} = \frac{V_{bc}}{P_{bc}Q_{bc}} = \frac{1\cdot143}{1\cdot076 \times 1\cdot063} = 1\cdot000 \quad \text{to three decimal places}$$

It follows that the Laspeyres and Paasche forms are approximately equal and their common values can be read off the matrices D:

INDEX NUMBERS, GROUP B=100

Group	First quarter	Price Unit values	Quantity Real consumption
C	1972	107·6	106·3
	1973	105·2	102·5
A	1972	103·6	104·9
	1973	101·7	110·2

So, both low-income pensioners (A) and high-income families (C) pay higher prices and have a higher real consumption of dairy produce per head than middle-income families (B). This is not surprising since middle-income families tend to be larger and, in particular, to have more children. It is more surprising that the difference is so large, of the order of 5% for real consumption per head.

4.8 Monthly or Quarterly Runs: Seasonal Variation

There is no difficulty in accommodating the analysis to monthly or quarterly instead of annual runs of index numbers. Several examples have already been cited. The index of retail prices of Table 3.1 is a monthly run, as are the index numbers of unit values and volume of merchandise trade quoted (as annual averages) in Table 3.19. The retail price index for pensioners and any index based on the National Food Survey are quarterly runs, as are all aggregates or index numbers obtained from the national income accounts published at quarterly intervals in *Economic Trends*. The October issue each year of this monthly journal gives long runs of quarterly figures for all the main components of GDP. Nevertheless it is worth pursuing briefly the particular features of an index run as a time series at more frequent intervals than annually and to consider especially the question of estimating and eliminating seasonal variation.

A monthly quantity series, whether in physical units, in constant price values, or in index form, has a time dimension in that it depends on the number of days in the month. The same is true of a quarterly series even if it is obtained as an average over the months of the quarter. Seasonal factors also operate from the demand and from the supply side: weather, fashion and holidays to name only a few. It is important to isolate at least the regular seasonal influences.

The position is simpler for monthly or quarterly price series since the time dimension is lacking. A price quotation or a unit value is either a spot figure or an average over a period. The index of retail prices, for example, uses prices collected at a spot date, the Tuesday nearest the fifteenth of each month. Import and export prices are unit values averaged over the month of the statistical return. There is also less scope for the operation of seasonal factors; for example, holidays have little effect on prices. Apart from some special cases, e.g. prices of fruits and vegetables, there is unlikely to be any reason to adjust a price series for seasonal factors.

Various models of time series, whether or not in index-number form, can be constructed and applied to the estimation of seasonal factors. The quarterly case can be used for illustration: the series X_t for quarters $t = 0, 1, 2, 3, \ldots$. An additional subscript is needed to indicate which quarter of the year t happens to be: $i = 1, 2, 3, 4$. A model then splits X_t into three components: trend T_t, seasonal factors S_{it} depending on i as well as t, and finally a random or residual term ϵ_t. In the short-run problem of seasonality, the trend sweeps in variations which turn out to be cyclical in the longer run. A simple form may be adopted for the seasonal element:

$$S_{it} = \alpha_i T_t + \beta_i$$

where α_i and β_i represent each a set of four constants taken over the quarters of the year. On this formulation, seasonal variation has a constant amplitude (β_i) over time, or an amplitude ($\alpha_i T_t$) which is proportional to trend, or a combination of the two. Hence:

$$X_t = (1 + \alpha_i)T_t + \beta_i + \epsilon_t \tag{1}$$

is a rather general model with two particular cases:

$$X_t = T_t + \beta_i + \epsilon_t \tag{2}$$

and $$X_t = (1 + \alpha_i)T_t + \epsilon_t \tag{3}$$

where (2) with $\alpha_i = 0$ can be called an *additive model* and (3) with $\beta_i = 0$ a *multiplicative model* from the way in which the seasonal factors enter. In (2), the spread of the seasonal factors over the four quarters is constant from year to year; in (3), it grows or declines as a fixed proportion of the trend. In the first case, the data are to give estimates of $\beta_1, \beta_2, \beta_3, \beta_4$ for the seasonal pattern; in the other case it is the fixed percentages $100\alpha_1, 100\alpha_2, 100\alpha_3, 100\alpha_4$ which are to be estimated.

There are three stages in the estimation of seasonal adjustment: estimation of trend T_t; estimation of α_i and/or β_i in the model (1); elimination of seasonal factors to give:

$$\frac{X_t - \beta_i}{1 + \alpha_i} \quad \text{for } t = 0, 1, 2, 3, \ldots \quad \text{and} \quad i = 1, 2, 3, 4$$

as the seasonally adjusted series. This can be quite complicated in practice, e.g. when trend is found on a two-stage process of estimation and when α_i and β_i are estimated by regression techniques; see Brown, Cowley and Durbin (1971), Durbin and Murphy (1975).

TABLE 4.6

CONSUMERS' EXPENDITURE AT MARKET PRICES:
ALCOHOLIC DRINK, QUARTERLY 1967–73

Year	Quarter	£mn at current prices (1)	Beer £mn at 1970 prices Implied price index* (2)	Un-adjusted (3)	Season-ally adjusted (4)	Wines, spirits, etc. £mn at 1970 prices Un-adjusted (5)	Season-ally adjusted (6)
1967	3	287	85·4	336	304	195	210
	4	253	85·2	297	295	313	212
1968	1	231	85·9	269	309	164	242
	2	269	86·2	312	308	180	202
	3	292	86·4	338	305	199	212
	4	275	87·0	316	313	341	228
1969	1	251	90·9	276	318	144	212
	2	294	90·7	324	322	179	203
	3	339	91·4	371	335	195	211
	4	317	93·8	338	334	331	223
1970	1	280	98·9	283	326	148	222
	2	334	99·4	336	335	199	225
	3	380	99·7	381	344	229	262
	4	361	101·7	355	350	380	247
1971	1	325	105·5	308	355	167	248
	2	385	108·1	356	354	228	260
	3	422	108·2	390	352	251	270
	4	394	107·9	365	358	407	275
1972	1	350	110·4	317	365	201	298
	2	419	112·9	371	369	269	302
	3	447	114·3	391	353	284	302
	4	434	115·7	375	367	453	305
1973	1	365	115·9	315	363	239	353
	2	446	116·1	384	382	350	393

From *Economic Trends*, October, 1973

* All columns from source except (2) which is derived from (1) divided by (3) and has 1970 = 100.

Take a simple case for illustration: model (2) with trend found either as a four-quarter centred moving average or by linear regression. Two particular components of consumers' expenditure (beer; wines, spirits, etc.) are used, each with a marked seasonal pattern. Table 4.6 gives a run of data over six years by quarters in real terms at constant (1970) prices. In addition, to provide a check on possible seasonal factors in prices, Table 4.6 gives a run of prices of beer. These are unit values but beer is a group homogeneous enough to make them good approximations to prices. The official series for real consumption (but not prices) are given in the table both unadjusted and adjusted for seasonal factors; the seasonal adjustment is by the sophisticated methods described in Central Statistical Office (1968), pp. 53–7. A comparison can be made here with the results obtained from the simple additive model.

The quantity and price runs for beer have trends sufficiently close to straight lines to make it possible to estimate the seasonal variation by a *linear-trend method*. All that is required of the linear trend is its slope, i.e. the average increase in the series per quarter. Once this is estimated, the correction for trend can be left until the end. Apart from the trend, model (2) has only the pair of terms $(\beta_i + \epsilon_t)$ and β_i can be estimated by taking each quarter of the year (β_i constant) in turn and by eliminating the random ϵ_t by averaging over the years. The estimates here for beer prices and quantities use the five complete years 1968–72. The slopes of the linear trends estimated by least squares, are 1·71 points per quarter for prices (1970 = 100) and £4·1 mn per quarter for the quantity series at 1970 prices. The means of the two series are respectively 99·75 and 338·6 over the five years. The trends within the year and around the overall means are:

| | | Quarterly | \multicolumn{4}{c}{Trend in quarters:} | | | |
Beer	Mean	increase	1	2	3	4
Prices, 1970 = 100	99·75	1·71	97·2	98·9	100·6	102·3
Consumption, £mn at 1970 prices	338·6	4·1	332·45	336·55	340·65	344·75

These are stored for use at the end. Arrange the given series in columns for the quarters of the year and average down the columns. The last row gives estimates of the four constants β_1, β_2, β_3 and β_4; they add to zero and represent the pattern of a seasonal variation.

Beer prices have a small seasonal variation; they are perhaps a little high early in the year and a little low later, but the differences

Beer	Prices (1970=100)				Real consumption (£mn)			
	Q.1	Q.2	Q.3	Q.4	Q.1	Q.2	Q.3	Q.4
1968	85·9	86·2	86·4	87·0	269	312	338	316
1969	90·9	90·7	91·4	93·8	276	324	371	338
1970	98·9	99·4	99·7	101·7	283	336	381	355
1971	105·5	108·1	108·2	107·9	308	356	390	365
1972	110·4	112·9	114·3	115·7	317	371	391	375
Sum	491·6	497·3	500·0	506·1	1,453	1,699	1,871	1,749
Mean	98·3	99·5	100·0	101·2	290·6	339·8	374·2	349·8
Trend	97·2	98·9	100·6	102·3	332·45	336·55	340·65	344·75
Difference	+ 1·1	+ 0·6	− 0·6	− 1·1	− 42	+ 3	+ 34	+ 5

are not significant. It is possible to ignore the seasonal influences, the situation expected for prices. The position is quite different for beer consumption; there is a marked seasonal pattern with consumption high in the summer and low in the winter. This is the expected variation and it is now quantified: first-quarter consumption is below trend on average by £42mn or well over 10% and the other quarters have above-trend consumption, significantly so only in the third quarter (by £34mn). A seasonally-adjusted series on model (2) is: $X_t - \beta_i = T_t + \epsilon_t$. Adjust real consumption of beer by subtraction of the seasonal pattern and compare with the official series adjusted by more sophisticated techniques:

REAL CONSUMPTION OF BEER, SEASONALLY ADJUSTED, £mn AT 1970 PRICES

Year	Quarter	Linear method	Official series	Year	Quarter	Linear method	Official series
1967	3	302	304	1970	3	347	344
	4	292	295		4	350	350
1968	1	311	309	1971	1	350	355
	2	309	308		2	353	354
	3	304	305		3	356	352
	4	311	313		4	360	358
1969	1	318	318	1972	1	359	365
	2	321	322		2	368	369
	3	337	335		3	357	353
	4	333	334		4	370	367
1970	1	325	326	1973	1	357	363
	2	333	335		2	381	382

The differences are not large, about $1\frac{1}{2}$%. Certainly, in this run with a clear linear trend, the simple linear method is quite adequate.

A more general, but still quite simple, computation of seasonal variation is by a *moving-average method*. The scheme is the same except that the first stage is to estimate the trend T_t as a four-quarter centred moving average. It can then be eliminated at once by writing deviations from trend: $X_t - T_t = \beta_i + \epsilon_t$. The estimation of β_i by averaging over each quarter of the year separately proceeds as before. A four-quarter moving average centred on quarter t requires the use of two successive averages:

$$(X_{t-2} + X_{t-1} + X_t + X_{t+1}) \quad \text{and} \quad (X_{t-1} + X_t + X_{t+1} + X_{t+2})$$

These are centred respectively half-way between X_{t-1} and X_t and half-way between X_t and X_{t+1}. A simple average of the two is then centred as required on X_t. The formula is:

$$T_t = \tfrac{1}{8}(X_{t-2} + 2X_{t-1} + 2X_t + 2X_{t+1} + X_{t+2}) \tag{4}$$

an average of five successive quarters, the outside quarters being given half the weight of the three inside ones.

As illustrations take real consumption, first of beer as before, and then of the other alcoholic-drink group. The trend in each case is to be obtained by the use of (4) from the data of Table 4.6. The deviations from trend then follow by subtraction of trend from the original figures:

		Beer £mn at 1970 prices			Wines, spirits, etc. £mn at 1970 prices		
Year	Quarter	X_t	T_t	X_t-T_t	X_t	T_t	$X_t - T_t$
1968	1	269	303·8	− 34·8	164	213·5	− 49·5
	2	312	306·4	+ 5·6	180	217·5	− 37·5
	3	338	309·6	+ 28·4	199	218·5	− 19·5
	4	316	312·0	+ 4·0	341	215·9	+ 125·1
1969	1	276	317·6	− 41·6	144	215·2	− 71·2
	2	324	324·5	− 0·5	179	213·5	− 34·5
	3	371	328·1	+ 42·9	195	212·8	− 17·8
	4	338	330·5	+ 7·5	331	215·8	+ 115·2
1970	1	283	333·2	− 50·2	148	222·5	− 74·5
	2	336	336·6	− 0·6	199	232·9	− 33·9
	3	381	341·9	+ 39·1	229	241·4	− 12·4
	4	355	347·5	+ 7·5	380	247·4	+ 132·6
1971	1	308	351·1	− 43·1	167	253·8	− 86·8
	2	356	353·5	+ 2·5	228	259·9	− 31·9
	3	390	355·9	+ 34·1	251	267·5	− 16·5
	4	365	358·9	+ 6·1	407	276·9	+ 130·1
1972	1	317	360·9	− 43·9	201	286·1	− 85·1
	2	371	362·2	+ 8·8	269	296·0	− 27·0
	3	391	363·2	+ 27·8	284	306·5	− 22·5
	4	375	364·6	+ 10·4	453	321·4	+ 131·6

The remaining job is the derivation of a slightly improved estimate of seasonal variation for beer consumption, allowing for some small

divergence of trend from linearity, and of a first estimate of the
seasonal pattern for consumption of wines, spirits, etc. about what
is seen to be a very non-linear trend. The procedure is similar to that
already carried out:

Deviations from trend	Beer £mn at 1970 prices				Wines, spirits, etc. £mn at 1970 prices			
	Q.1	Q.2	Q.3	Q.4	Q.1	Q.2	Q.3	Q.4
1968	− 34·8	+ 5·6	+ 28·4	+ 4·0	− 49·5	− 37·5	− 19·5	+ 125·1
1969	− 41·6	− 0·5	+ 42·9	+ 7·5	− 71·2	− 34·5	− 17·8	+ 115·2
1970	− 50·2	− 0·6	+ 39·1	+ 7·5	− 74·5	− 33·9	− 12·4	+ 132·6
1971	− 43·1	+ 2·5	+ 34·1	+ 6·1	− 86·8	− 31·9	− 16·5	+ 130·1
1972	− 43·9	+ 8·8	+ 27·8	+ 10·4	− 85·1	− 27·0	− 22·5	+ 131·6
Sum	− 213·6	+ 15·8	+ 172·3	+ 35·5	− 367·1	− 164·8	− 88·7	+ 634·6
Mean	− 42·7	+ 3·2	+ 34·5	+ 7·1	− 73·4	− 33·0	− 17·7	+ 126·9
Seasonal variation*	− 43	+ 2½	+ 34	+ 6½	− 74	− 34	− 18	+ 126

* Means adjusted to add to zero and rounded off.

The results are clear enough for beer consumption in real terms.
The trend is confirmed as quite close to a straight line. Consequently
the estimate of the seasonal pattern by this more general method is
little different from that obtained by the linear-trend method. The
trend in consumption of the other group (wines, spirits, etc.) is far
from linear; after wavering up and down for two years, it takes off
on what seems to be an exponential growth in 1970–2. It appears
from the arrangement of the deviations from trend in columns of
quarters that the largest deviations (in opposite directions) are in the
first and fourth quarters and that they tend to increase over time.
The deviations in the other two quarters are both smaller and more
nearly constant. This suggests that the additive model (2) suits the
two middle quarters but that the multiplicative model (3) may be
better for the other quarters. The best results are likely to be obtained
by using the combined model (1) for the whole series. The additive
model adopted here must be expected to give estimates of seasonal
variation which are rough and ready.

All this is confirmed by a comparison of the estimates of the
seasonal pattern on the additive model and the simple moving-
average method with the more elaborate estimates obtained for the
official series as quoted after seasonal adjustment in Table 4.6. The
simple method gives a seasonal pattern of constant profile over time.
Real consumption of wines and spirits is heavily concentrated in the
last quarter; it is much lower in other quarters and especially low in

the quarter after Christmas. The official estimates of seasonal variation are to be deduced by subtracting column (6) from column (5) in
Table 4.6. They show inevitably the same general pattern but with an
increasing amplitude as the trend rises over time. The upward
seasonal deviation in the fourth quarter (in £mn at 1970 prices) rises
from 101 in 1967 to 148 in 1972; the downward variation of the first
quarter grows from 78 in 1968 to 114 in 1973. Smaller changes occur
in the other quarters.

One last point can be made. Total expenditure on alcoholic drink
(the sum of the two groups of Table 4.6) can be handled quite separately to provide an estimate of seasonal variation in the total, and
hence to give a total series adjusted for season. This would be an
inefficient exercise since the two components of the total behave in
such different ways; beer consumption peaks in the summer and
wines and spirits at Christmas. It is clearly better to adjust each of
the component series separately and then to add the results. The
seasonally adjusted series of real consumption of alcoholic drink in
total is the sum of columns (4) and (6) in Table 4.6.

5 Chain Index Numbers

5.1 Economic-theoretic Approach

The runs of index numbers of Chapter 4 are subject to the limitation that each is simply a sequence of *binary comparisons* between the current year *t* and the base year 0. There is no reference whatever to the course of prices/quantities in between. Something better than this must be sought, something more in line with economic common sense and making more efficient use of all the data. The suggestion which now comes up for consideration is that, in the practical job of calculating and publishing an index year by year, use can be made of all the price/quantity information from the base year up to and including the current year. Such an index provides a *rolling comparison* of year *t* back to year 0 using all the data as *cumulated* to the current year. This concept leads to the *Divisia Integral Index* in theory and to the *chain index* as its practical realisation. It is not to be confused with the more extreme exercise, to be pursued in Chapter 7, of estimating all index numbers in a given period from all the data of the period. The present job is to make the current index depend on back data; the wider problem has an index dependent both on back data and on data to come within the overall period.

The same concept can be approached from another direction. Runs of Laspeyres or Paasche index numbers tend to break down after a time and the practical response in Chapter 4 to this difficulty is to take only short runs spliced together into longer runs. This is often achieved, e.g. in British national income data, by changing the base at intervals of about five years. Done systematically such a splicing is (e.g.) a five-yearly chain of a Laspeyres or Paasche index. The question is: why not accelerate and go for annual chaining? There is no reason why not and, indeed, the retail price index of **3.2** above is just such an annual chain.

On an economic-theoretic approach, the analysis proceeds in terms of the constant-utility price index (**2.8**) and makes use of the consumer's preference map (Fig. 2.1). A similar analysis can be made using the constant-resources price deflator (**2.9** and Fig. 2.2). The limitation of the binary comparison of two separated years 0 and 1 is seen in the fact that there are alternative ways of getting from point q_0 to point q_1, across the preference map of Fig. 2.1, one involving the constant-utility price index at the constant level u_0 and the other the index at the level u_1. Neither makes any use of the actual path along which the consumer proceeds from q_0 to q_1. This is so even if the preference map remains fixed; the difficulty is compounded if the move is through time across a shifting preference map. The corresponding index of real consumption is that implied by the constant-utility price index on the assumption that the preference map is unchanged; it is one indicator of ordinal utility, increasing with the utility level as expenditure rises at constant prices along an Engel curve. Take a shifting preference map, however, and the single ordinal-utility concept disappears; the real-consumption index is then just the match of whatever is the price index.

The way out of the difficulty is that suggested at the end of **2.8** above, to follow the mathematician in replacing finite changes 'in the limit' by differential (infinitesimal) movements. Take dp for a differential price change from p and let the quantity change for which the consumer opts be dq from q. The relation between dp and dq is a *differential equation* for the consumer's path across his preference map as prices change. The actual path is to be found by *integrating* the differential equation. What remains, then, is to analyse (uniquely) a value change into price and quantity components, or into substitution and income effects, and to integrate separately for price and quantity index numbers as explicit functions of time. Once achieved, as in **5.2** below, it takes the heat off the need to assume an unchanged preference map. Each differential change is on a momentarily frozen preference map and integration can proceed whether or not the map shifts over time.

5.2 Statistical-theoretic Approach: Divisia Integral Index

Against this economic background, the analysis proceeds in mathematical/statistical terms in arriving at a definition of a price or quantity index varying continuously over time. The development follows Divisia (1925) as further elaborated by Roy (1927); it is based on the circular and factor-reversal tests of Irving Fisher (1922). Start from the assumption that the continuous price index $P(t)$ and quantity index $Q(t)$ always satisfy:

$$V(t) = P(t) \times Q(t) \qquad \text{for all } t \tag{1}$$

the factor-reversal condition on the value change $V(t)$ given continuously over time. The circular test is different; it imposes a requirement on $P(t)$ and $Q(t)$ separately. Let P_{0t} be a particular form adopted for $P(t)$ with base year 0. The circular-test condition:

$$P_{0t} = P_{0s} \times P_{st} \qquad \text{for any } s \ (0 < s < t)$$

gives: $\quad P_{0t} = P_{01} \times P_{12} \times P_{23} \times \ldots \times P_{(t-1)t}$

and so embodies the concept of chaining. Stuval (1957) observes that an aggregative index does not pass the test because of:

the fact that the volume structure and the price structure of an aggregate change over the course of time. One could hardly expect this to be built into the index numbers of volume and price. After all any aggregate involves a certain amount of loss of information. ... In terms of statistical movements this means that instead of Laspeyres indices with unchanging weights one would need Laspeyres indices of volume and price the weights of which refer for each current year to the year preceding it.

This is the point to be followed up here.

Prices and quantities of n commodities $(i = 1, 2, 3, \ldots n)$ aggregate to a current-price value:

$$p_i(t), \quad q_i(t) \qquad \text{giving} \quad V(t) = \sum_{i=1}^{n} p_i(t) q_i(t)$$

For differential changes:

$$dV(t) = \sum_{i=1}^{n} q_i(t) dp_i(t) + \sum_{i=1}^{n} p_i(t) dq_i(t) \tag{2}$$

and from (1):

$$dV(t) = Q(t) dP(t) + P(t) dQ(t) \tag{3}$$

To separate the price/quantity effects in (2) and (3), note that proportional changes are appropriate to the index-number problem and use a logarithmic transform. Divide (2) by $V(t)$:

$$\frac{dV(t)}{V(t)} = \frac{\sum_{i=1}^{n} q_i(t) dp_i(t)}{\sum_{i=1}^{n} p_i(t) q_i(t)} + \frac{\sum_{i=1}^{n} p_i(t) dq_i(t)}{\sum_{i=1}^{n} p_i(t) q_i(t)} \tag{4}$$

and divide (3) by $V(t) = P(t)Q(t)$:

$$\frac{dV(t)}{V(t)} = \frac{dP(t)}{P(t)} + \frac{dQ(t)}{Q(t)} \quad \text{i.e. } d\{\ln V(t)\} = d\{\ln P(t)\} + d\{\ln Q(t)\} \tag{5}$$

in terms of natural logarithms (ln) to base e. The *definitions* of $P(t)$ and $Q(t)$ are laid down so that the separate components of (4) and (5) agree; they are given as *differential equations*:

$$d\{\ln P(t)\} = \frac{dP(t)}{P(t)} = \frac{\sum\limits_{i=1}^{n} q_i(t)dp_i(t)}{\sum\limits_{i=1}^{n} p_i(t)q_i(t)} \quad \text{and}$$

$$d\{\ln Q(t)\} = \frac{dQ(t)}{Q(t)} = \frac{\sum\limits_{i=1}^{n} p_i(t)dq_i(t)}{\sum\limits_{i=1}^{n} p_i(t)q_i(t)} \tag{6}$$

Given the courses of $p_i(t)$ and $q_i(t)$ over time ($i = 1, 2, 3, \ldots n$) it remains to integrate (6). Write:

$$\phi(t)dt = \frac{\sum\limits_{i=1}^{n} q_i(t)dp_i(t)}{\sum\limits_{i=1}^{n} p_i(t)q_i(t)} \quad \text{and} \quad f(t) = \int_0^t \phi(\tau)d\tau \tag{7}$$

The function $f(t)$ of (7) is given by the course of commodity prices/quantities cumulatively from the base year 0 to the current year t. The first differential equation of (6) integrates:

$$d\{\ln P(t)\} = \phi(t)dt \quad \text{giving} \quad \ln P(t) - \ln P_0 = \int_0^t \phi(\tau)d\tau = f(t)$$

Hence $\quad P(t) = P_0 e^{f(t)} \quad$ where $P_0 = 100$ in base year 0 $\tag{8}$

A result corresponding to (8) is obtained for $Q(t)$.

The continuous index $P(t)$ or $Q(t)$ so defined and expressed by (8) is the **Divisia Integral Index.** It is a theoretical construct designed to maintain the constraint (1) continuously over time; it requires continuous price/quantity data for all commodities. It remains to find a practical approximation which is applicable to the discrete time intervals to which actual index numbers relate and which satisfies the circular test.

5.3 Chain Index with Annual Links

Take the price index for expository purposes, defined by (6) integrating to (8) of **5.2**; the result for the quantity index is precisely similar. Moreover, when the price index is found, the implied quantity index drops out at once from the constraint (1) of **5.2** above.

As an initial gambit, take a year as the practical interval of time and aim to approximate the continuous index $P(t)$ by an annual run of the price index. The point is re-examined later (**5.6**). Adapt the notation to the usual form by writing p_t and q_t as price and quantity of a typical item in year t, dropping explicit reference to the subscript i. Replace $P(t)$ and $Q(t)$ by P_t and Q_t. Finally, get the required approximation by substituting the *forward difference* Δ from year t to year $(t+1)$ for the differential d:

$$\Delta p_t = p_{t+1} - p_t \quad \text{for } dp(t) \qquad \text{and} \qquad \Delta P_t = P_{t+1} - P_t \quad \text{for } dP(t)$$

and similarly for quantities. The Divisia Integral form of $P(t)$ given by (6) of **5.2** transforms to:

$$\frac{\Delta P_t}{P_t} = \frac{\sum q_t \Delta p_t}{\sum p_t q_t} \quad \text{i.e.} \quad \frac{P_{t+1} - P_t}{P_t} = \frac{\sum q_t (p_{t+1} - p_t)}{\sum p_t q_t}$$

giving the ratio of the annual price index numbers in years t and $(t+1)$:

$$\frac{P_{t+1}}{P_t} = \frac{\sum p_{t+1} q_t}{\sum p_t q_t} = P_{t(t+1)}(q_t) \qquad \text{Laspeyres} \qquad (1)$$

The result is both important and very simple: the annual realisation of the continuous Divisia index has a Laspeyres form, base-weighted on year t, as the link in the chain from t to $(t+1)$. Repeated use of (1), starting from an arbitrary P_0 in year 0, gives the chain:

$$\frac{P_t}{P_0} = \frac{P_1}{P_0} \times \frac{P_2}{P_1} \times \frac{P_3}{P_2} \times \ldots \times \frac{P_t}{P_{t-1}} = P_{01}(q_0) \times P_{12}(q_1) \times P_{23}(q_2) \times \ldots$$
$$\times P_{(t-1)t}(q_{t-1})$$

Take year 0 as base ($P_0 = 100$) to give the **Chain Laspeyres Index**:

$$P_t = 100 \, P_{01}(q_0) \quad P_{12}(q_1) \quad P_{23}(q_2) \ldots P_{(t-1)t}(q_{t-1}) \qquad (2)$$

and a precisely similar chain for quantities.

A similar chain of Paasche links is obtained by using *backward differences*:

$$\Delta p_t = p_t - p_{t-1} \quad \text{for } dp(t) \qquad \text{and} \qquad \Delta P_t = P_t - P_{t-1} \quad \text{for } dP(t)$$

in (6) of **5.2**, simplifying as before and chaining from $P_0 = 100$ in the base year. The result is the **Chain Paasche Index** of prices on base year 0 as 100:

$$P'_t = 100 \, P_{01}(q_1) \quad P_{12}(q_2) \quad P_{23}(q_3) \ldots P_{(t-1)t}(q_t) \qquad (3)$$

and a similar form for quantities. Either (2) or (3) is the required discrete approximation to the continuous Divisia form; it satisfies the circular test as suggested by Stuval (1957).

The interpretation of the chain form (2) makes a good deal of sense. The index in year t comprises a sequence of t separate links, each representing the changing cost of a fixed budget. The budget is fixed at the beginning of each year and is changed from year to year. As with any splicing of index numbers, the run of the chain index is built up on a shifting base. It has, however, the very great advantage that the base is brought constantly up to date, that the calculation can be continued automatically as long as budget data are available. The chain is never broken. The Paasche chain (3) only differs in that each link uses a budget fixed at the end of the year.

The annual chain formula (2) or (3) can be extended to apply to an index computed more frequently than once a year, e.g. monthly. The time t in the formula is then the current month, but the sequence 0, 1, 2, ... $(t-1)$ still represents the run of years before t. All the links are year-to-year until the last link is reached when the comparison is only up to the current month. There is a certain amount of choice here. The links (except the last) may be the average of one year to that of the next, or they may be (e.g.) from one January to the next.

Write Q_t and Q'_t for the chain index numbers of quantity similar to (2) and (3). It follows at once that the value change from year 0 to year t is made up:

$$V_{0t} = P_t \times Q'_t = P'_t \times Q_t$$

since each link has this property of the Laspeyres and Paasche forms. Hence, the chain Paasche index for prices is that implied by the Laspeyres index for quantities (and conversely) in the usual sense of accounting for value changes.

The base year 0 is arbitrary in the chain index (2) or (3); it can be shifted at choice to any year r without altering the links in any way. All that is done is to lop off the first r links so that:

$$100 \, P_{r(r+1)}(q_r) \times P_{(r+1)(r+2)}(q_{r+1}) \times \ldots \times P_{(t-1)t}(q_{t-1})$$

is the chain Laspeyres index for prices in year t on year r as 100 $(r < t)$. All changes in the index are completely unaffected both in the short run within a year and in the longer (spliced) run over the years.

5.4 Chaining in Practice

The leading example of a chain Laspeyres index in Britain is the retail price index calculated since January 1962 by the Department of Employment. It is published monthly and weights are changed in each successive January. The link which runs from January 1973 to January 1974, for example, shows the changing cost of the fixed budget of January 1973, and the next link from January 1974 to January 1975 then shows the changing cost of the new budget fixed in January 1974.

Since the reference base of an index so calculated is quite arbitrary, it can be changed whenever it is thought to be convenient to do so. The chain index was introduced from January 1962 and this was the obvious choice of a reference base. A decision was taken later to shift the reference base forward to January 1974. This change was purely formal, a matter of convenience; the month-by-month changes in the index are precisely the same on the old (January 1962) reference base and on the new one of January 1974.

Short of some catastrophic upheaval, the retail price index can continue indefinitely, as the chain form is designed to do. It is self-adjusting each year for all changes in consumer preferences, for all quality changes and for all 'births' and 'deaths' of commodities, provided only that these things show up in the budgets fixed afresh each January. There is one rather incidental qualification to make on the up to dateness of the fixed budgets which arises because of time-lags in processing data from the *Family Expenditure Survey* from which the budgets are derived. Though the 1973 weights should be the relative expenditures on various items in a budget at January 1973, they are approximated in practice by taking the budget as given by the Survey averaged over the three years to mid-1972 and priced at the prices of January 1973. A similar approximation is made each January.

As an illustration of the operation of this chain index, some work begun in **3.2** can be completed. The exercise is to get the retail price index, chained back to January 1962, for all items, for the housing group alone and by difference for all items except housing. Whenever groups are to be combined or recombined, it is essential to make the calculations with each link of the chain index separately, e.g. by first dechaining a published index run and then by chaining again. The data for the exercise on this basis are set out in Table 5.1.

There are twelve annual links in the index from 1962 to 1974 so that twelve separate calculations of the exclusion of housing need to be made. Columns (4) and (5) of Table 5.1 give the annual links for all items and for housing obtained by dechaining the published run

TABLE 5.1

INDEX OF RETAIL PRICES, WITH AND WITHOUT HOUSING, 1962–74

Index at January:	Weights*			Index†		Products		Index: All excl. Housing $\frac{(6)-(7)}{(3)}$
	All items	Housing	All excl. Housing	All items	Housing	$(1) \times (4)$	$(2) \times (5)$	
	(1)	(2)	(3)	(4)	(5)	(6)	(7)	(8)
1963	1,000	102	898	102·70	105·50	102,700	10,761·0	102·38
1964	1,000	104	896	101·95	105·12	101,950	10,932·5	101·58
1965	1,000	107	893	104·58	104·69	104,580	11,201·8	104·57
1966	1,000	109	891	104·38	106·55	104,380	11,614·0	104·11
1967	1,000	113	887	103·67	106·14	103,670	11,993·8	103·36
1968	1,000	118	882	102·62	105·56	102,620	12,456·1	102·23
1969	1,000	121	879	106·17	103·68	106,170	12,545·3	106·51
1970	1,000	118	882	104·96	104·80	104,960	12,366·4	104·98
1971	1,000	119	881	108·49	109·03	108,490	12,974·6	108·42
1972	1,000	119	881	108·16	108·89	108,160	12,957·9	108·06
1973	1,000	121	879	107·74	113·98	107,740	13,791·6	106·88
1974	1,000	126	874	111·97	110·45	111,970	13,916·7	112·19

From Department of Employment *Gazette*

* Weights at previous January.
† Based on previous January as 100.

of January index numbers. The index for all items except housing is then obtained in the same annual-link form in column (8). All that remains is to rechain back to January 1962 by cumulation of column (8) and by a final rounding:

Date	Calculation	Rounded index
Jan. 1963	$1 \cdot 0238 \ 100 = 102 \cdot 38$	102·4
Jan. 1964	$1 \cdot 0238 \ 1 \cdot 0158 \ 100 = 103 \cdot 998$	104·0
Jan. 1965	$1 \cdot 0238 \ 1 \cdot 0158 \ 1 \cdot 0457 \ 100 = 108 \cdot 750$	108·8
...	... ...	...

The complete runs at each January date from 1962 to 1974 are then assembled in the table below, each of chain Laspeyres form on January 1962 as 100. The all-items and housing runs are as published; what is new is the run for all items except housing, as required. The calculations are confined here to the January index each year; the index for any other month (say March 1974) is to be got similarly by adding another link from January 1974 to March 1974.

January	All items	Housing	All items except housing
1962	100	100	100
1963	102·7	105·5	102·4
1964	104·7	110·9	104·0
1965	109·5	116·1	108·8
1966	114·3	123·7	113·2
1967	118·5	131·3	117·0
1968	121·6	138·6	119·6
1969	129·1	143·7	127·4
1970	135·5	150·6	133·8
1971	147·0	164·2	145·0
1972	159·0	178·8	156·7
1973	171·3	203·8	167·5
1974	191·8	225·1	187·9

The exclusion of housing makes a significant reduction in the rate of increase of the all-items index. This is the kind of calculation needed, for example, if the influence of inflation on pensioners is to be compared with that on the general run of 'index' households, as in 3.6. Since most pensioners have their rent and rates refunded or paid for them under social security rules, such a comparison is best done with housing excluded, and the official index of retail prices for pensioners is so published.

5.5 Runs of Index Numbers: Drifting

Several questions arise to which it is important to get some kind of answer. Does a chain index run tend to diverge over time from the corresponding direct index? If the direct Laspeyres index tends to run high, as is quite usual, does the chain Laspeyres index run even higher or does it tend to correct the movement of the direct index? Is there a different effect in the long run as opposed to a run over a few months? The general issue is whether index runs of various forms tend to *drift* apart from each other or from some 'true' index. This is an issue far from settled despite a considerable amount of investigation by Frisch (1936), Zarnowitz in Stigler (1961), Allen (1963) and others.

A statistical relation between chain and direct index numbers can be derived in a form similar to that between the Laspeyres and Paasche forms (2.7). Take price index numbers of Laspeyres form as illustration. Write the *chain Laspeyres index*:

$$P_t = P_{01}(q_0) \quad P_{12}(q_1) \ldots P_{(t-1)t}(q_{t-1}) \qquad \text{where } P_{rs}(q_r) = \frac{\sum p_s q_r}{\sum p_r q_r}$$

and the corresponding *direct Laspeyres index*:

$$P_{0t}(q_0) = \frac{\sum p_t q_0}{\sum p_0 q_0}$$

Express each as the product of similarly written links:

$$P_t = \frac{\sum p_1 q_0}{\sum p_0 q_0} \times \frac{\sum p_2 q_1}{\sum p_1 q_1} \times \ldots \times \frac{\sum p_t q_{t-1}}{\sum p_{t-1} q_{t-1}}$$

$$P_{0t}(q_0) = \frac{\sum p_1 q_0}{\sum p_0 q_0} \times \frac{\sum p_2 q_0}{\sum p_1 q_0} \times \ldots \times \frac{\sum p_t q_0}{\sum p_{t-1} q_0}$$

from which the *ratio of chain to direct index* follows:

$$\frac{P_t}{P_{0t}(q_0)} = \left(\frac{\sum p_2 q_1}{\sum p_1 q_1} \times \frac{\sum p_1 q_0}{\sum p_2 q_0} \right) \times \left(\frac{\sum p_3 q_2}{\sum p_2 q_2} \times \frac{\sum p_2 q_0}{\sum p_3 q_0} \right) \times \ldots$$
$$\times \left(\frac{\sum p_t q_{t-1}}{\sum p_{t-1} q_{t-1}} \times \frac{\sum p_{t-1} q_0}{\sum p_t q_0} \right)$$

Write D_r for the rth factor here and put $w = p_r q_0$ to get:

$$D_r = \sum w \sum w \frac{p_{r+1}}{p_r} \frac{q_r}{q_0} \Big/ \left(\sum w \frac{p_{r+1}}{p_r} \right) \left(\sum w \frac{q_r}{q_0} \right) \tag{1}$$

so that

$$\frac{P_t}{P_{0t}(q_0)} = D_1 \times D_2 \times \ldots \times D_{t-1} \qquad (t > 1) \qquad (2)$$

The factor D_r is easily reduced to a statistical expression in weighted means, variances and correlation coefficients. Take the variables

$$x = p_{r+1}/p_r \qquad \text{and} \qquad y = q_r/q_0$$

and weights $w = p_r q_0$ so that:

$$\bar{x} = \frac{1}{\sum w} \sum w \frac{p_{r+1}}{p_r}; \quad \bar{y} = \frac{1}{\sum w} \sum w \frac{q_r}{q_0}; \quad r_{xy}\sigma_x\sigma_y = \frac{1}{\sum w} \sum wxy - \bar{x}\bar{y}$$

Substitute in (1) and simplify:

$$D_r = \sum w \frac{\sum wxy}{(\sum wx)(\sum wy)} = \frac{\bar{x}\bar{y} + r_{xy}\sigma_x\sigma_y}{\bar{x}\bar{y}}$$

Hence: $D_r = 1 + r_{xy}\dfrac{\sigma_x}{\bar{x}}\dfrac{\sigma_y}{\bar{y}}$ where $x = \dfrac{p_{r+1}}{p_r}$ and $y = \dfrac{q_r}{q_0}$ $\qquad (3)$

The ratio of chain to direct index then follows from (2).

Light is now thrown on the question of the drift of the chain form from the direct Laspeyres index. P_t diverges upwards from $P_{0t}(q_0)$ if most D_r's are above unity. A drift this way arises when there tends to be a positive correlation between the immediate price change x and the past quantity change y on result (3). The drift is the other way if there tends to be a negative correlation between x and y.

Consider, first, the early years of the index runs. P_1 and $P_{01}(q_0)$ are the same and it is in the second year that a divergence occurs between P_2 and $P_{02}(q_0)$ with ratio D_1 dependent by (3) on the correlation between p_2/p_1 and q_1/q_0. This may go either way. An item showing an above-average quantity increase in year 1 may then have an above-average price change in year 2 if suppliers 'cash in' on a good market – or it may equally have a below-average price change in year 2 if demand needs to be stimulated to clear the higher supply. In the former case, $D_1 > 0$ and $P_2 > P_{02}(q_0)$; in the latter case $D_1 < 0$ and $P_2 < P_{02}(q_0)$. What empirical evidence there is suggests that the divergence can be in either direction but that it is generally small.

Consider, next, the possibility of drift in the long run. When year t is remote from the base year, the change in the ratio (2) from year $(t-1)$ to year t, given by D_{t-1}, depends by (3) on the correlation between the immediate price rise in year t (p_t/p_{t-1}) and the long-run change in quantity from the previous year back to the base (q_{t-1}/q_0). The former can be quite volatile but the latter tends to be stable for any particular item. The immediate price change tends to be a random variable in comparison with the slow trend change in quantity over a long period. The correlation coefficient and hence D_{t-1} tend to be random and there is no reason to expect that the chain Laspeyres drifts above the direct Laspeyres index nor, equally, that it tends to correct any propensity for the direct index to run high. Empirical evidence is needed and some is offered in **5.7**.

5.6 Chaining more Frequently than Annually

There is one immediate application of the formulae (2) and (3) of **5.5** above: to a review of the possibility of an index run chained more frequently than each year. In view of the demands made on the basic data there are clear practical objections to chaining an index monthly or quarterly. What is more important, however, is the conclusion reached below that such a chaining is to be avoided when there are strong seasonal influences at work.

Take the case of a quarterly chain Laspeyres index of prices, the run P_t over quarters $t = 0, 1, 2, 3, \ldots$, in comparison with the corresponding run $P_{0t}(q_0)$ of the direct Laspeyres index base-weighted on quarter $t = 0$. Write R_t for the ratio of P_t to $P_{0t}(q_0)$ so that by **5.5** above $R_1 = 1$ and for $t > 1$:

$$R_t = D_1 \times D_2 \times \ldots \times D_{t-1} \tag{1}$$

where $\quad D_{t-1} = 1 + r_{xy} \dfrac{\sigma_x}{\bar{x}} \dfrac{\sigma_y}{\bar{y}} \quad$ for $\quad x = \dfrac{p_t}{p_{t-1}} \quad$ and $\quad y = \dfrac{q_{t-1}}{q_0} \tag{2}$

Here D_{t-1} is the factor multiplying R_{t-1} to get R_t in (1). If $r_{xy} > 0$ and so $D_{t-1} > 1$, then the ratio R_t is greater than R_{t-1}. It is still possible for the chain index to be getting nearer the direct index (if $R_t < 1$) or for the two to be diverging from each other ($R_t > 1$). (A parallel conclusion follows if $r_{xy} < 0$.) The point about seasonal items is that there can be a *large* correlation r_{xy} between the change in supplies in the previous quarter ($y = q_{t-1}/q_0$) and the price change in the current quarter ($x = p_t/p_{t-1}$). The direction of the correlation can be either way but the case to look for is that of *positive* correlation. This situation arises when a seasonal rise in supplies in one quarter is followed by a price rise in the next quarter (as supplies decline). If this kind of thing is at all common among the items included in the index, then the ratio R_t tends to be erratic and the chain index is not stable in comparison with the direct index. The existence of items with seasonal price variations is a sign to avoid quarterly chaining of a price index and to depend either on a direct index with weights broadly based on one or more years, or on an annual chain index, even when the index is published more frequently than annually. The monthly retail price index is an example.

An actual if highly simplified instance serves to illustrate the problem. Vegetables are among the more seasonal of the items in the retail price index for food. The *National Food Survey* provides quarterly data in some but not overelaborate detail on consumption and expenditure on these and other foods and hence on unit values as substitute indicators for prices. Table 5.2 sets out data for three

TABLE 5.2
CONSUMPTION AND UNIT VALUES, VEGETABLES, QUARTERLY, 1972–3

	1972	1973			
	Q.4	Q.1	Q.2	Q.3	Q.4
Consumption					
(lbs per head per week)	q_0	q_1	q_2	q_3	q_4
Potatoes	3·056	3·085	2·524	2·585	3·288
Tomatoes	0·214	0·134	0·228	0·412	0·181
Fresh greens	0·833	0·721	0·720	0·984	0·692
Unit value					
(p per lb)	p_0	p_1	p_2	p_3	p_4
Potatoes	1·675	1·919	3·510	2·507	1·810
Tomatoes	11·495	21·57	23·90	11·24	15·41
Fresh greens	4·84	6·16	7·19	5·21	6·40
Expenditure					
(p per head per week)	p_0q_0	p_1q_1	p_2q_2	p_3q_3	p_4q_4
Potatoes	5·12	5·92	8·86	6·48	5·95
Tomatoes	2·46	2·89	5·45	4·63	2·79
Fresh greens	4·03	4·44	5·18	5·13	4·43
Total	11·61	13·25	19·49	16·24	13·17

From *Monthly Digest of Statistics* (based on National Food Survey)

categories of vegetables in a short run of quarters. A quarterly chain of Laspeyres index numbers of vegetable prices (unit values) can be calculated from the data and compared with the direct Laspeyres index based on the last quarter of 1972. The calculations giving the quarterly chain index are:

CROSS-VALUATIONS, p PER HEAD PER WEEK

	p_1q_0	p_2q_1	p_3q_2	p_4q_3
Potatoes	5·86	10·83	6·33	4·68
Tomatoes	4·62	3·20	2·56	6·35
Fresh greens	5·13	5·18	3·75	6·30
Total	15·61	19·21	12·64	17·33
Link in chain	1·3445	1·450	0·6485	1·067

The links for cumulating into the chain index, in the last row, are obtained by division by the actual values (expenditures) of the previous quarter as given in Table 5.2, e.g. 15·61/11·61 for the first link (1·3445). The comparable direct index comes by writing the changing cost of the fixed quantities of the last quarter of 1972:

CROSS-VALUATIONS, p PER HEAD PER WEEK

	p_1q_0	p_2q_0	p_3q_0	p_4q_0
Potatoes	5·86	10·73	7·66	5·53
Tomatoes	4·62	5·11	2·41	3·30
Fresh greens	5·13	5·99	4·34	5·33
Total	15·61	21·83	14·41	14·16

The actual index is got by dividing each of these totals by the base expenditure (11·61) from Table 5.2.

The results can be assembled and the ratios of chain to direct index numbers obtained:

CHAIN AND DIRECT LASPEYRES
PRICE INDEX NUMBERS, 1973

	4th Qtr. 1972=100	1st Qtr. ($t=1$)	2nd Qtr. ($t=2$)	3rd Qtr. ($t=3$)	4th Qtr. ($t=4$)
Chain index		134·45	194·95	126·4	134·9
Direct index		134·45	188·0	124·1	122·0
Ratio R_t		1·0	1·037	1·019	1·106
Factor D_{t-1}*		...	1·037	0·982	1·086

* Ratio of R_t to R_{t-1}, see formulae (1) and (2).

The conclusion is that quarterly chaining is not appropriate to seasonal vegetable prices, at least in such a simplified example as this one. The quarterly chain index varies more than the direct index simply because two of the three correlation coefficients r_{xy} of

(2) are large and positive, giving two out of the three factors D in excess of unity. The strongest correlation and the greatest deviation of D above unity occur in the last quarter of 1973 when the correlation coefficient r_{xy} is obtained from:

	Potatoes	Tomatoes	Fresh greens
$x = p_4/p_3$	0·722	1·371	1·228
$y = q_3/q_0$	0·846	1·925	1·181

Though there are only three items, the positive correlation is clear: $r_{xy} = 0·865$ on evaluation. Hence, for this quarter, $D_3 = 1·086$ and the ratio $R_4 = 1·106$.

The quarterly chain index also runs a good deal higher than the direct form. This lends some support to the contention that frequent chaining of seasonal prices can introduce a drift in the chain index; see Allen (1963), p. 288.

5.7 Chain and Direct Index Numbers Compared: Retail Prices

A comprehensive set of calculations of index numbers of chain and direct forms has been made by Fowler (1970, 1973, 1974). The work uses expenditure data for the group of 'index' households of the retail price index taken from the *Family Expenditure Survey* conducted by the Department of Employment. The index runs calculated are for retail prices and real consumption over the eleven years 1958–68; the price runs are examined here and those for real consumption in the following section.

At the level of disaggregation set by the 92 sections of the commodity classification in the retail price index, consumption per household is valued and cross-valued at the prices of each year over 1958–1968. Difficulties with seasonal items are avoided by taking the valuations in each quarter of the year separately and by pricing at the prices of the *same* quarter every year; yearly totals are then obtained by summing over the four quarters. The full value matrix of order 11×11 is reproduced in Fowler (1973), Appendix A. All the index numbers here and in **5.8** are run off this matrix.

Runs of the direct Laspeyres and of the direct Paasche price index are given in Table 5.3, both forwards from 1958, and backwards from 1968. The Laspeyres runs come respectively from the first (1958) column and the last (1968) column of the value matrix, giving

TABLE 5.3

RETAIL PRICES: SOME DIRECT INDEX NUMBERS, 1958–68

	Forward from 1958 = 100		Backward and forward around 1963 = 100		Backward from 1968 = 100	
Year	Laspeyres	Paasche	Laspeyres	Paasche	Laspeyres	Paasche
1958	100	100	92·2	89·5	78·2	73·7
1959	100·9	100·5	92·8	90·4	78·5	74·8
1960	101·7	101·1	93·1	91·8	78·5	76·1
1961	105·0	103·8	95·3	94·6	80·3	78·5
1962	109·3	107·9	98·4	98·1	82·8	81·3
1963	111·7	108·4	100	100	84·2	83·1
1964	115·6	112·4	103·2	102·9	86·2	85·6
1965	121·2	116·1	108·1	107·6	90·0	89·8
1966	126·1	120·8	112·1	111·7	93·3	93·3
1967	129·4	123·4	114·9	114·3	95·4	95·5
1968	135·6	127·9	120·4	118·7	100	100

From Fowler (1973), Appendix A (based on Family Expenditure Survey)

expenditures on a fixed budget; it is only necessary to divide through by the base expenditure in the leading diagonal. The Paasche runs are got by dividing the leading-diagonal entry each year by the corresponding entry in the 1958 or 1968 row. Of the four runs, the forward Laspeyres is seen to diverge upwards from the forward Paasche, as expected on the analysis of 2.7, and the fact that the backward Laspeyres is the reciprocal of the forward Paasche (and conversely) is checked within the usual errors of rounding. Between 1958 and 1968:

Type of index	Index, Table 5.3		% increase 1958–68
	1958	1968	
Forward Laspeyres	100	135·6	35·6
Backward Paasche	73·7	100	35·7
Backward Laspeyres	78·2	100	27·9
Forward Paasche	100	127·9	27·9

The value matrix also provides direct Laspeyres and Paasche runs on any other base and Table 5.3 shows them for the middle year 1963 as base. A mixed interpretation has to be given to such intermediate runs which go both backwards and forwards. The Laspeyres run base-weighted on 1963 is equivalent before 1963 to a forward Paasche index from each year t ahead to 1963 and it runs low (as expected of a Paasche form) in comparison with the forward Laspeyres form. On the other hand, as a 'straight' Laspeyres index after 1963, it tends to run high. The following comparisons illustrate:

Laspeyres runs	1958–63	% increase 1963–68	1958–68
1958-based	11·7	21·4	35·6
1963-based	8·5	20·4	30·6
1968-based	7·7	18·8	27·9

The 1963-based run is more like the 1968-based (forward Paasche) run before 1963 and more like the 1958-based (forward Laspeyres) run after 1963. There is little to recommend it, a conclusion reached on the runs of Table 4.3 or 4.4 spliced on the middle year (again 1963). Certainly it is to be hoped, and will in fact be found, that a much better compromise run for the whole period is provided by a chain index.

The year-to-year links of the chain index runs are calculated from the value matrix and set out in Table 5.4. The method of calculation

TABLE 5.4

RETAIL PRICES: CHAIN INDEX NUMBERS, 1958–68

t =	% changes, year (t-1) to year t Laspeyres link year (t-1) quantities	Paasche link year t quantities	Chain index numbers (1958 =100) Laspeyres	Paasche
1959	0·86	0·545	100·9	100·5
1960	0·86	0·58	101·7	101·1
1961	2·86	2·70	104·6	103·9
1962	3·725	3·64	108·5	107·6
1963	1·97	1·64	110·7	109·4
1964	3·215	2·95	114·2	112·6
1965	5·27	4·63	120·3	117·8
1966	3·83	3·79	124·9	122·3
1967	2·39	2·55	127·8	125·4
1968	4·71	4·79	133·9	131·4

From Fowler (1973), Appendix A (based on Family Expenditure Survey)

is shown by the following formulae for the links from year $(t-1)$ to year t:

Laspeyres link:

$$\frac{\sum p_t q_{t-1}}{\sum p_{t-1} q_{t-1}} = \frac{\text{entry immediately below diagonal, } q_{t-1} \text{ column}}{\text{diagonal entry, } q_{t-1} \text{ column}}$$

Paasche link:

$$\frac{\sum p_t q_t}{\sum p_{t-1} q_t} = \frac{\text{diagonal entry, } q_t \text{ column}}{\text{entry immediately above diagonal, } q_t \text{ column}}$$

These are shown in Table 5.4 as % changes (rather than as ratios) and they are easily chained together cumulatively to give the chain index runs of the table:

Chain Laspeyres: 1959 $100 \cdot 86 = 100 \cdot 9$
                    1960 $100 \cdot 86 \times 1 \cdot 0086 = 101 \cdot 7$
                    1961 $100 \cdot 86 \times 1 \cdot 0086 \times 1 \cdot 0286 = 104 \cdot 6$

and so on. The chain Paasche run is similarly derived.

Comparisons of chain and direct runs follow at once from Table 5.5 where all runs are expressed on 1958 as a convenient reference

TABLE 5.5

RETAIL PRICES: CHAIN AND
DIRECT INDEX NUMBERS COMPARED, 1958–68

1958 =100	Forward Laspeyres forms			Forward Paasche forms		
	1958-based	1968-based*	Chain	1958-based	1968-based†	Chain
1959	100·9	101·5	100·9	100·5	100·4	100·5
1960	101·7	103·3	101·7	101·1	100·4	101·1
1961	105·0	106·5	104·6	103·8	102·7	103·9
1962	109·3	110·3	108·5	107·9	105·9	107·6
1963	111·7	112·8	110·7	108·4	107·7	109·4
1964	115·6	116·1	114·2	112·4	110·2	112·6
1965	121·2	121·8	120·3	116·1	115·1	117·8
1966	126·1	126·6	124·9	120·8	119·3	122·3
1967	129·4	129·6	127·8	123·4	122·0	125·4
1968	135·6	135·7	133·9	127·9	127·9	131·4

From Tables 5.4 and 5.3

* Reciprocal of backward Paasche, comparing each year t with 1968 (year t weights).

† Reciprocal of backward Laspeyres, comparing each year t with 1968 (year 1968 weights).

base, except that the 1963-based runs are omitted for reasons already given. The forward Laspeyres section of the table compares the chain index both with the 'straight' 1958-based direct index and with the backward 1968-based (Paasche) run written in reciprocal form and interpreted as a forward Laspeyres index from each year t ahead to 1968. In any specific year, e.g. 1963, the two direct Laspeyres index numbers differ; the 1958-based index is an entry in a continuous run with 1958 weights and the 1968-based index is a one-off entry with 1963 weights (see **4.4**). The forward Paasche section of the table is similar. The conclusions are clear: either Laspeyres index runs high, either Paasche index runs low, and the two chains are not far apart and fall neatly in the middle. The two chain runs start off quite close together and later on 'drift' apart but by no more than some $2\frac{1}{2}$ percentage points in the whole period of eleven years.

A 'true' price index of constant-utility form *either* lies below the direct Laspeyres index *or* lies above the direct Paasche index, according to which utility level is taken; but it is not possible to be certain, though a safe bet in most practical situations, that it lies between the direct Laspeyres and Paasche forms (**2.8**). It is equally not certain but a good bet that the chain Laspeyres and Paasche runs are closer to the 'true' index than the direct runs. In any case, the chain runs are approximations to the Divisia form with its theoretical background as given in **5.2**. Either chain index run is a practicable proposition but the chain Laspeyres form is the easier of the two in computation. All the evidence supports the choice of the annual chain Laspeyres formula adopted for the Retail Price Index by the Department of Employment since 1962.

5.8 Chain and Direct Index Numbers Compared: Real Consumption

To each of the direct and chain index runs of retail prices given in Tables 5.3 and 5.4 there corresponds a run of quantity index numbers representing changes in real consumption, to be derived also from the value matrix of Fowler (1973). The quick derivation is by deflation of value changes by the selected price index. The two index runs for real consumption given the label FES in Table 5.6 are those implied by the direct and chain Paasche runs of price index numbers, both forward from 1958, obtained in Tables 5.3 and 5.4 from the Family Expenditure Survey data. They are to be interpreted as direct and chain Laspeyres runs, based on constant-price valuations of household expenditure either (direct index) over the whole period 1958–68 or (chain index) from one year to the next. These two particular runs are selected so that still another comparison can be made, that with the real consumption calculations for the whole range of consumers' expenditure in the national income accounts. Table 5.6 shows consumers' expenditure at constant (1958) market prices from the 1968 *Blue Book* and also the index run base-weighted on 1958 obtained by division through by the 1958 expenditure.

All the runs of Table 5.6 are consistent, perhaps surprisingly so in view of two differences between the National Income (NI) and Family Expenditure Survey (FES) data. The first difference is that the

TABLE 5.6

REAL CONSUMPTION: CHAIN AND
DIRECT INDEX NUMBERS COMPARED, 1958–68

	Expenditure at 1958 prices FES,		Index Numbers (1958 = 100) FES		
Year	NI aggregates £mn	£ per year per household	NI Direct Laspeyres	Direct Laspeyres	Chain Laspeyres
1958	15,362	783·0	100	100	100
1959	16,080	812·4	104·7	103·8	103·8
1960	16,735	845·1	108·9	107·9	107·9
1961	17,127	868·3	111·5	110·9	110·8
1962	17,517	852·8	114·0	108·9	109·1
1963	18,375	914·4	119·6	116·8	115·8
1964	19,082	890·1	124·2	113·7	113·5
1965	19,421	968·1	126·4	123·6	121·9
1966	19,811	953·2	129·0	121·7	120·3
1967	20,211	976·6	131·6	124·7	122·7
1968	...	1,009·3	...	128·9	125·5

From *Blue Book*, 1968, Table 4.1 and Fowler (1973) Appendix A

NI = National Income.
FES = Family Expenditure Survey.

NI index numbers are derived from *aggregate* data on expenditure which increases over time with the growth in population, whereas the FES data relate to *average* consumption per household. The population of the U.K. increased by 7% between 1958 and 1968, and the number of households by at least this percentage, enough to account for the excess, running at some 6% towards the end of the 1958–68 period, of the NI real-consumption index over that given by FES. The other difference is that the NI data cover all households whereas the FES data used by Fowler are restricted to 'index' households, i.e. excluding both pensioners and the higher-income groups. This difference is more difficult to quantify but it may go some way towards accounting for the many small discrepancies between the real-consumption runs. The NI run, for example, increases from year to year whereas the FES index has its ups and downs. This feature of the FES runs may arise from the restrictive coverage combined with the fact that the basic data are from the (only moderately large) samples used in the Family Expenditure Survey with consequential sampling errors which are not negligible.

As with the price runs, so with real consumption: the chain Laspeyres index is nearly the same as the direct FES index in the early years and then they drift apart. The chain index is the lower of the two, a divergence in the 'right' direction if the direct Laspeyres form (as expected) does run high. The conclusion again is that, as a practical measure of changes in real consumption, the chain Laspeyres index is as good or better than any of the other possibilities. In particular, it runs lower than the NI index even when the latter is adjusted to the basis of average expenditure per household. In this respect it may well be close to a 'true' index of real consumption per household. The chain Laspeyres index shows a growth in real consumption per household of around 25% between 1958 and 1968, as opposed to something nearer 29% on the direct FES index and to about the same figure from NI data when extended to 1968 and reduced to a pre-household basis.

6 Some Applications

6.1 Introduction

A range of illustrations of how to construct and use index numbers was given in Chapter 3. The purpose of the present chapter is different; it is to provide examples of index numbers in their application to real problems. No apology is needed on the selection of the problems which are almost entirely in the fields of economics and of economic aspects of social questions. The predominant use of index numbers is undoubtedly in applied economics and econometrics. A comparison of the contents of *Economic Trends* and of *Social Trends* confirms this; the former includes index numbers of all shapes and sizes, the latter scarcely refers to one at all.

The applications, therefore, are more than illustrations of methods. They aim, at least, to start up analyses leading to substantive conclusions. The first two assemble alternative runs of price index numbers on the course of prices in the middling run since about 1948 and in the longer run since mid-nineteenth century. One run is concerned with commodity price; others place the emphasis on prices paid by the consumer and hence on his standard of living. The longer the run considered the more it is necessary to rely on commodity rather than consumer prices; copper or cotton prices can be got from commodity markets over longer periods than retail prices of radios or refrigerators. Equally the standard of living can be considered for changes in the short or middling period but in the longer run it is the broader concept of the value of money which can be approximated by a commodity-price index. At the same time some rough indicators of wages and the cost of living can be carried back into the nineteenth century and shown alongside commodity prices. A broad survey of modern economic history depends on a look at such long series of price movements.

The next block of applications has to do with real income in one aspect or another. There are, first, two comparisons of real income across different income levels in this country and then across a range of different countries. Attention is next directed at the measurement over time of real GDP from annual and quarterly output data, to supplement estimates already made from the expenditure side. Of the three measures of real GDP (3.9), the output estimates are published first and so, for quick assessments of economic changes, it is important to know how consistent these first estimates are with the later and more elaborate computations from expenditure data. In this connection, a close eye must be kept on the main constituent of real GDP as output: the index of industrial production. This index, published monthly and carrying nearly half the weight in real GDP, is criticised on the score that it is subject to major revisions from time to time, a criticism which deserves close attention.

The two remaining applications seem much simpler at first sight but do raise considerable problems when viewed from a wide economic angle. One is on the measurement of changes over time in the labour force. This may seem an easy, indeed a trivial matter. Why not just follow the number of (e.g.) the unemployed as recorded officially with an occasional 'splice' as in 1.5 to allow for a change of coverage? On further reflection we must conclude that this won't do. Even on the broad social level numbers of unemployed are not sufficient indicators of the effect of unemployment; the distribution and duration of unemployment are equally relevant. From an economic angle, moreover, numbers are completely inadequate measures of labour input and it is here that index-number techniques must be called in aid.

The last application is the derivation of an indicator of the general level of stock-market prices. The well-known *Financial Times* index provides many observers with just what they need, a daily sensitive index of the mood of the market as reflected in the movements of quotations for leading industrial shares. Whether this is enough becomes doubtful when we turn to such problems as long-run portfolio management and the capitalisation of the shares quoted on the market.

6.2 Commodity Prices

Price quotations of some basic commodities on one type of market or another are available over long periods in the past and several attempts, more or less successful, have been made to throw them together in long-run index numbers of commodity prices. It is only

TABLE 6.1

COMMODITY PRICES, 1860–1972

Year	'Economist' index 1845–50 =100	'Statist' index* 1846–50 =100	Cost of Living† 1914 =100	Money Wages† 1914 =100	Year	'Economist' index 1845–50 =100	'Statist' index* 1846–50 =100	Cost of Living† 1914 =100	Money Wages† 1914 =100	Year	'Economist' index 1845–50 =100
1860	124	120	113	58	1900	99	91	91	94	1940	175
1861	128	119	..	..	1901	92	85	90	93	1941	193
1862	141	122	..	..	1902	90	83½	90	91	1942	201
1863	160	125	..	..	1903	94	83½	91	91	1943	207
1864	170	127	..	..	1904	98	85	92	89	1944	212
1865	152	122	..	..	1905	100	87	92	89	1945	216
1866	141	123½	114	66	1906	109	93	93	91	1946	230
1867	128	121	..	..	1907	114	97	95	96	1947	265
1868	124	120	..	..	1908	101	88	93	94	1948	293
1869	122	119	..	..	1909	103	90	94	94	1949	307
1870	122	116	110	66	1910	109	94	96	94	1950	453
1871	122	121	..	..	1911	115	97	97	95	1951	558
1872	135	132	..	..	1912	123	103	100	98	1952	450
1873	133	134	..	..	1913	122	103	102	99	1953	413
1874	128	123½	115	80	1914	123	103	100	100	1954	444
1875	124	116	..	..	1915	153	131	..	..	1955	435
1876	119	115	..	..	1916	196	165	..	..	1956	428
1877	120	114	110	77	1917	247	217	..	..	1957	421
1878	110	105	..	..	1918	269	232	..	..	1958	389
1879	107	100½	..	..	1919	302	249	..	..	1959	379

Year				
1880	113	106½	105	72
1881	106	103	103	72
1882	110	102	102	75
1883	102	99	102	75
1884	98	92	97	75
1885	93	87	91	73
1886	93	83½	89	72
1887	97	82	88	73
1888	99	85	88	75
1889	99	87	89	80
1890	102	87	89	83
1891	99	87	89	83
1892	96	82	90	83
1893	96	82	89	83
1894	90	76	85	83
1895	89	75	83	83
1896	89	74	83	83
1897	87	75	85	84
1898	87	77½	88	87
1899	92	82	86	89

Year				
1920	332	304	:	:
1921	222	188	:	:
1922	198	159	:	:
1923	198	156	:	:
1924	213	168	175	194
1925	204	165	175	196
1926	185	152½	172	195
1927	181	148	167	196
1928	177	145	166	194
1929	167	139	164	193
1930	140	117	157	191
1931	116	100¼	147	189
1932	112	97	143	185
1933	116	96	140	183
1934	120	99	141	183
1935	124	102	143	185
1936	135	108	147	190
1937	148	123½	154	:
1938	131	110	156	:
1939	135	:	:	:

Year	
1960	380
1961	369
1962	361
1963	409
1964	442
1965	447
1966	469
1967	444
1968	437
1969	475
1970	500
1971	486
1972	562

From *The Economist* and Mitchell (1962)

* Based on Sauerbeck (1886) and continued first by Sauerbeck and then by *the Statist*.
† Computed by Bowley (1937).

to be expected that such runs become less precise the further back they are taken. What is more surprising is that some kind of index run of commodity prices can be constructed from the Middle Ages to the present, to provide a sensible answer to the question of how much prices have risen over the past several hundred years. Mitchell (1962) gives the basic data and an account of long-run index numbers and Halsbury (1963) includes as Appendix 4, Graph II, a bold attempt at showing the course of prices since A.D. 800 on the base of 1451–75 as 100.

There is one long-run index of commodity prices still computed regularly week by week: the index of *The Economist* on the reference base of 1845–50 as 100. The original object of the index was to direct attention to the rise in prices following the gold discoveries of the 1840s and it has continued as a sensitive indicator of changes in the prices of basic foods and raw materials. At first a simple weighting of prices, mainly on British commodity markets, was used. Subsequently the weighting system became explicitly based on commodity trade of the main industrial countries and prices were drawn from both U.S. and British commodity markets. In the 1974 revision of the index, described in *The Economist* of 5 January and 2 March 1974, the current index is chained back to 1970 on an annual reweighting based on changing commodity trade.

The nearest competitor up to 1938 was the Sauerbeck/*Statist* index of prices, introduced by Sauerbeck (1886) and continued later by the *Statist*, on the reference base of 1867–77 as 100. After the 1939–45 war the index lost its importance and soon petered out. It had a rather wider coverage and a simpler construction than *The Economist* index, being an equi-weighted arithmetic mean of 45 price relatives, each obtained from one, two or three price quotations, and comprising both basic commodities and such processed items as butter, leather and refined petroleum. Both index numbers are shown in Table 6.1 and graphed on ratio scales in Fig. 6.1 to show percentage changes over the years. *The Economist* index is on its original base of 1845–50 and the long run is got by 'straight' splicing between dates when the index was reweighted. The *Statist* run is switched to 1846–50 as 100, and stopped in 1938.

The differences between the two runs are not great. *The Economist* index, being more influenced by U.S. commodity prices, shows a greater rise during the time of the War between the States. The *Statist* index falls below that of *The Economist* until the 1890s and

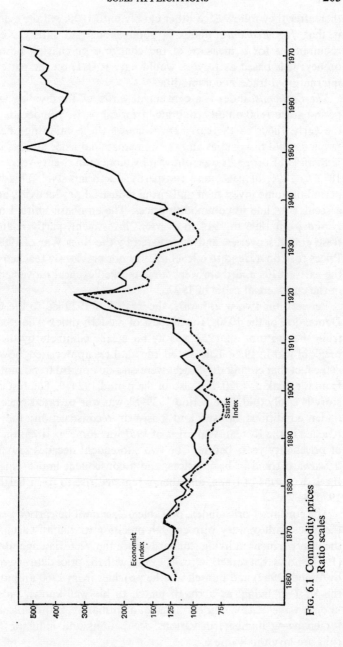

Fig. 6.1 Commodity prices
Ratio scales

thereafter they follow each other closely until 1938. All the evidence is that *The Economist* index is good enough to satisfy Keynes' requirement for a measure of the changing purchasing power of money; it is based as Keynes would have it (**1.1**) on the pattern of international trade in commodities.

The Economist index is a convenient yardstick for dividing up the period since 1860 on an economic-historical basis. The decade from the early 1860s to the early 1870s shows the continuing affect of previous gold discoveries and the immediate influence of wars in the U.S. and in Europe. It was followed by more than twenty years, from 1872 to 1896, of peace and prosperity, Victorian style. This was a period of home investment and rising industrial productivity, and of a secular decline in commodity prices. The emphasis shifted in the period from 1896 to 1914 to overseas investment, partly related to fresh gold discoveries, and punctuated by the Boer War of 1900–01. Prices rose on a trend to a level in 1914 not previously reached since the early 1870s and there were some marked cyclical movements as in the commercial crisis of 1907.

Between the two world wars, the 'crash' of 1929 led to the Great Depression of the 1930s, the deepest of modern times. The recovery from the 'bottom' of 1932 was by no means complete by the outbreak of war in 1939. This is well known. Less appreciated, however, is the fact that commodity prices were on a downward trend, not only from the peak of 1920, but also in the period 1924–9. The rest of the story is easily told. The period 1939–51 was one of rapid price rises under conditions of war and post-war reconstruction; the peak reached in the Korean War crisis of 1951 was some six times the level of prices fifty years before. The two subsequent decades saw first a downward trend in basic prices, and a consequent improvement in the U.K. terms of trade, and then a renewed rise to fresh heights in 1972–3.

The consumer price index, of Table 6.2, cannot be carried back to the nineteenth century with enough precision to quantify accurately the improvement in living standards since the Victorian age. Bowley (1937) shows that something can be done with the price data assembled by Wood (1909) and himself and he provides from 1860 an index of the 'cost of living' as a rough match to his well-known index of 'money wages' as average earnings for a normal week after allowance for changing numbers in various occupations and industries. The runs are given in Table 6.1.

To the extent that Bowley's cost-of-living index can be relied upon, the course of retail price is similar in trend, but less in variation about trend, to the path of commodity prices. Retail prices show the same decline in the long period of prosperity from the early 1870s to the mid-1890s and in the short period of economic calm before the storm of 1929. The reductions, however, were smaller: 28 % from the early 1870s to 1896 and only 6% from 1924 to 1929, as compared with 36 % and 22 % respectively for commodity prices. The ratio of money wages to the cost of living is to be described as 'real wages' only within the limits set by the 'numerous qualifications' mentioned by Bowley (1937). The following broad movements, however, are shown by the data:

	1860	1874	1896	1914	1924	1929	1936
Real wages, 1914=100	51	70	100	100	111	118	129

There is an upward secular trend in real wages, except between 1896 and 1914 when commodity prices were rising but real wages oscillated with no definite trend.

6.3 Consumer Prices versus Retail Prices

The question just raised can be pursued: what measure of price change is appropriate for the deflation of such aggregates as consumption and wages at current prices to show up movements in real terms? More baldly: how is the fall in the purchasing power of the £ to be measured? This is a problem of statistical estimation so that there is no cut-and-dried answer. Several possible estimators are on offer according to the purpose and varying with the period over which the deflator is required. In any case, the decision in the end is a matter of coming down in favour of the best or most efficient estimator on some criterion or other. Such a decision is needed, for example, when a cost-of-living clause is inserted in a contract or a sliding-scale for wages.

The present application aims at getting a general-purpose deflator for use in the middling run, specifically from 1948 to the early 1970s. Two different index runs are available as candidates for selection: the consumer price index of the national income accounts (or the consumers' expenditure deflator, to use its most recent label), and the retail price index of the Department of Employment. The index of retail price is strongest in short-run applications and it is, indeed, the only one available monthly. The consumer price index can be estimated quarterly but is essentially an annual construction and its strength lies in comparisons over a period of several years. As the general deflator sought, the retail price index is good in the short run since 1962 but over longer periods the consumer price index seems to have it. The reasons for the preferences are easily elaborated.

The base year of the consumer price index is changed fairly regularly, as it must be if the index is to continue, and currently at about five-yearly intervals. A critical point is how the index runs are to be chained to provide a run over longer periods. The index on a particular base is calculated forwards as a Paasche form, implied by the corresponding Laspeyres index of real consumption; but it is also carried back to the previous base year making it possible to get both a Laspeyres and a Paasche index in the link from one base to the next. There are objections (5.7) to a Laspeyres index which tends to run high, to a Paasche form running low and to a run based on a year in the middle as switching from divergence one way to divergence the other way. An answer is to split the difference by use of Fisher Ideal links and such a chaining is practicable for the consumer price index.

Table 4.4 above shows a spliced run of the consumer price index using Fisherian links between 1958, 1963 and 1970 bases. It remains to carry the splicing back to 1948 by providing two additional links, 1948–54 and 1954–8. The first three series in the post-war *Blue Books* are based successively on 1948, 1954 and 1958 and they suffice to give the required links:

		Link: 1948–54		Link: 1954–8	
		1948	1954	1954	1958
Forward Paasche	(1)	100	125·66	100	115·06
Backward Paasche with reciprocal:		79·34	100	87·80	100
Forward Laspeyres	(2)	100	126·04	100	113·90
Fisher Ideal, GM of (1) and (2)		100	125·85	100	114·5

The complete spliced run is given in Table 6.2. Before 1958, the two links just obtained (1954 as 125·85% of 1948 and 1958 as 125·85 × 1·145 = 144·1% of 1948) are taken and switched to 1958 as reference base. The 1948-based Paasche index is finally used for interpolation between 1948 and 1954 and the 1954-based index between 1954 and 1958.

TABLE 6.2

CONSUMER PRICE INDEX, FISHER IDEAL LINKS, 1948–72

Year	Index (1958 = 100)	Year	Index (1958 = 100)	Year	Index (1958 = 100)
1948	69·4	1957	97·4	1966	124·4
1949	71·7	1958	100	1967	127·8
1950	73·5	1959	100·7	1968	134·0
1951	79·5	1960	101·7	1969	141·4
1952	84·0	1961	104·9	1970	149·5
1953	85·7	1962	109·0	1971	161·7
1954	87·3	1963	110·55	1972	172·0
1955	90·4	1964	114·2		
1956	94·6	1965	119·6		

From *Blue Book* and Table 4.4

The run of Table 6.2 can be used to deflate consumers' expenditure at current prices to give a volume index of real consumption. Rather more roughly, the wages bill and other current price aggregates can be reduced to real terms in the same way. Further, the reciprocals of the index numbers of Table 6.2 give a good answer to the question of the declining purchasing power of the £ since 1948. Any reference base can be used; keeping 1958 and then switching to 1948:

Purchasing power of:	1948	1958	1968	1972
1958 £	—	£1	£0·746	£0·581
1948 £	£1	£0·694	£0·518	£0·403

By 1972 the 1948 £ is estimated to be 'worth' only 40·3p.

These are the advantages of the consumer price index. The index has some faults to be set on the other side of the scales. The spliced run is got by chaining at intervals of some five years or so and there is need not only to interpolate between successive bases (which is kept under control by the constraint of the Fisherian links), but also to extrapolate after the last base. The extrapolation is by use of the original Paasche index and so tends to run low. Further, the index is not derived from price quotations. It is implied by a constant-price valuation (real consumption) and the constant-pricing is achieved by a variety of devices including considerable use of unit values. To the extent that the consumer price index depends on unit values, it tends to include an element of quality appreciation and runs a little high as a pure price indicator. It is fortunate that these two factors work in opposite directions and so leave the balance of advantage in favour of the index.

The advantages and disadvantages of the retail price index tend to be the mirror image of those for the consumer price index. The index is always based quite firmly on price quotations and, since 1962, it is a chain calculated from annual links. Before 1962, earlier runs of the index need to be taken and spliced on. The earlier runs are of direct Laspeyres and the run from 1962 of chain Laspeyres form. However, of the three runs needed to cover the period 1948–62, only the third is of modern design, based on weights from a budget inquiry in 1953–4; the first two were interim index runs based on out-of-date budget material. Finally, none of the separate runs is carried back to years before the reference base. Consequently the spliced run from

TABLE 6.3

RETAIL PRICE INDEX, SPLICED LASPEYRES RUNS, 1948–72

Annual average	Interim Index		Index	Spliced run	
	June 1947 =100	Jan. 1952 =100	Jan. 1956 =100	Jan. 1962 =100*	1958 =100
1948	108			60·1	64·8
1949	111			61·2	66·0
1950	114			63·5	68·4
1951	125			69·6	75·0
Jan. 1952	132	100		73·494	
1952		102·6		75·4	81·3
1953		105·8		77·8	83·9
1954		107·7		79·2	85·3
1955		112·6		82·8	89·2
Jan. 1956		115·8	100	85·106	
1956			102·0	86·8	93·6
1957			105·8	90·0	97·0
1958			109·0	92·8	100
1959			109·6	93·3	100·6
1960			110·7	94·2	101·5
1961			114·5	97·4	105·0
Jan. 1962			117·5	100	
1962				101·6	109·5
1963				103·6	111·7
1964				107·0	115·3
1965				112·1	120·8
1966				116·5	125·6
1967				119·4	128·7
1968				125·0	134·7
1969				131·8	142·1
1970				140·2	151·1
1971				153·4	165·4
1972				164·3	177·1

From *Monthly Digest of Statistics*

* Continued with chain Laspeyres index, Jan. 1962 = 100.

1948 onwards is very much of Laspeyres type. It is shown in Table 6.3, first with the most-recent reference base of January 1962 and then switched to average 1958 as 100 for immediate comparison with the consumer price index of Table 6.2.

The coverage of the two index runs is somewhat different; the consumer price index covers all expenditure of all consumers whereas the retail price index is confined to nearly but not quite total expenditure of 'index' households. The main difference between the two, however, lies in the formulae used. The consumer price index of Table 6.2 is calculated from Fisherian links which may be expected to approximate fairly closely to the 'true' (constant-utility) index; there may be a little bias upwards because of the use of unit values and at the end of the run it is of Paasche form with a bias downwards. On the other hand, the retail price index has the upward bias of the Laspeyres form, undiluted from 1948 to 1962 and then moderated by the chain form. All this shows up in the spliced runs. From 1948 to 1962 the retail price index rose by 69 % as compared with 57 % on the other index; after the 1962 the chain usage of the retail price index does better giving a rise of 62 %, as compared with 58 % on the consumer price index, between 1962 and 1972.

The conclusion is that, for comparisons over many years, the spliced run of the consumer price index with Fisher Ideal links is to be preferred as a price deflator. For short-run comparisons since the chain form was introduced in 1962, the retail price index serves the purpose; it runs a little higher than the consumer price index but the differences are small. In the very short run, over months rather than years, there is no choice; the retail price index is the only one available and it is perfectly adequate.

6.4 Inequality of Incomes: Differential Price Changes

For all items (excluding housing), the British retail price index shows (3.6) that the price rise for pensioner households exceeds that for the main group of 'index' households in the ten years or so from 1962. The suggestion here is that, if the index could be calculated separately for a range of income levels, it would show the price rise decreasing as income increases. There would then be a differential price effect working against low-income families; such families would be more affected, by the direction their purchases take, by an inflationary increase in prices generally. This would have quite far-reaching implications on the inequality of income distributions in real as opposed to money terms.

The question to pursue is whether the differential price effect actually does exist. One way of answering is to take the index of retail prices in full detail of 92 sections and to re-weight with the distribution of expenditures, not by 'index' households as a group, but by various groups with specified ranges of income. A sequence of re-weighted index numbers is then obtained, each running monthly over a selected period, for a succession of increasing income levels. Muellbauer (1974a) quotes several studies of the kind indicating a differential price effect against low-income groups in post-war Britain. At the same time the inequality of *money incomes* has become less, offset to some extent by the differential prices effect to make the distribution of *real incomes* have a smaller improvement (if any at all) towards greater equality.

An alternative and preferable method is to estimate the constant-utility price index explicitly as a function of income, if this trick can be turned. On the assumption (2.8) of a utility function $u = u(q_1, q_2, \ldots)$ for consumer purchases $q_1, q_2, \ldots$, the constant-utility price index $I_{0t}(y)$ for price changes from time $t = 0$ to time t depends on the income level y taken for the constant utility. This only has empirical content if the utility function is specified or estimated. The utility function which suggests itself is that leading to the linear expenditure system of Stone (1954) and used by Muellbauer (1974a) in the present context. The function is that of Geary/Stone, written in the two-goods case to be pursued here for convenience of exposition:

$$u = (q_1 - \alpha_1)^{\beta_1}(q_2 - \alpha_2)^{\beta_2} \qquad (\beta_1 + \beta_2 = 1) \tag{1}$$

where α_1 and α_2 are positive parameters representing minimum purchases for $u \geq 0$ and where β_1 and β_2 are to be interpreted as slopes of Engel curves. Since utility is an ordered concept, any monotonic transform of (1) such as $u = \beta_1 \log (q_1 - \alpha_1) + \beta_2 \log (q_2 - \alpha_2)$ serves equally well and the 'standardisation' $\beta_1 + \beta_1 = 1$ is no real constraint.

The demand functions follow from the necessary conditions for maximum u given the prices p_1 and p_2 and the income y:

$$\frac{1}{p_1} \frac{\partial u}{\partial q_1} = \frac{1}{p_2} \frac{\partial u}{\partial q_2} \qquad \text{given } p_1, p_2 \text{ and } y = p_1 q_1 + p_2 q_2$$

This equation by logarithmic derivation of (1) is:

$$\frac{1}{p_1}\frac{\beta_1}{q_1-\alpha_1}=\frac{1}{p_2}\frac{\beta_2}{q_2-\alpha_2}$$

The two demand functions come from this and the budget equation for y:

$$q_1 = \alpha_1(1-\beta_1) - \alpha_2\beta_1\frac{p_2}{p_1} + \beta_1\frac{y}{p_1} \qquad (2)$$

and a similar expression for q_2. The demand functions in expenditure form are:

$$\begin{aligned} y_1 &= \beta_1 y + c_1 \quad \text{where } c_1 = \alpha_1(1-\beta_1)p_1 - \alpha_2\beta_1 p_2 \\ \text{and } y_2 &= \beta_2 y + c_2 \quad \text{where } c_2 = \alpha_2(1-\beta_2)p_2 - \alpha_1\beta_2 p_1 \end{aligned} \qquad (3)$$

where $y_1 = p_1 q_1$ and $y_2 = p_2 q_2$ and where the 'adding-up' condition $y_1 + y_2 = y$ is always satisfied since $\beta_1 + \beta_2 = 1$ is assumed and $c_1 + c_2 = 0$ follows. If the prices are given, then the c's as well as the β's are constants and (3) become linear Engel curves in total expenditures y with slopes given by the β's. Finally substitute (2) into (1):

$$\left.\begin{aligned} \text{Indirect utility function} \quad & u = \frac{y-a}{b} \\ \text{and Expenditure function} \quad & y = a + bu \end{aligned}\right\} \qquad (4)$$

where $a = \alpha_1 p_1 + \alpha_2 p_2$ and $b = \left(\frac{p_1}{\beta_1}\right)^{\beta_1}\left(\frac{p_2}{\beta_2}\right)^{\beta_2}$ $\qquad (5)$

At time $t = 0$, write p_{10} and p_{20} for the prices giving a_0 and b_0 for the constants of (5); at time t, write p_{1t} and p_{2t} giving constants a_t and b_t. Take the constant-utility level u and the corresponding y in terms of a_0 and b_0 by (4). The constant-utility price index is:

$$I_{0t}(y) = \frac{a_t + b_t u}{a_0 + b_0 u} \qquad \text{where } u = \frac{y-a_0}{b_0}$$

which simplifies to:

$$\text{Constant-utility price index } I_{0t}(y) = \left(\frac{a_0}{y}\right)\frac{a_t}{a_0} + \left(1-\frac{a_0}{y}\right)\frac{b_t}{b_0} \qquad (6)$$

Each of the two terms in (6) is a multiple of a particular price index:

$$\frac{a_t}{a_0} = \frac{\alpha_1 p_{1t} + \alpha_2 p_{2t}}{\alpha_1 p_{10} + \alpha_2 p_{20}} \qquad \text{and} \qquad \frac{b_t}{b_0} = \left(\frac{p_{1t}}{p_{10}}\right)^{\beta_1}\left(\frac{p_{2t}}{p_{20}}\right)^{\beta_2} \qquad (7)$$

The expenditure level y appears only in the multiples which combine (7) into $I_{0t}(y)$ in (6).

The extension to the general case of n goods is easily made. The Geary/Stone utility function (1) has n factors involving two sets of n positive parameters: $\alpha_1, \alpha_2, \ldots \alpha_n$ and $\beta_1, \beta_2, \ldots \beta_n$ where $\beta_1 + \beta_2 + \ldots + \beta_n = 1$. For given prices the Engel curves (3) become:

$$y_r = \beta_r y + c_r \qquad \text{where } \sum c_r = 0 \qquad (r = 1, 2, \ldots n)$$

This is the system of linear Engel curves taken by Allen and Bowley (1935) in classifying goods on a *scale of urgency* by the values of the intercepts c_r. At the top of the scale are the *necessary goods* $(c_r > 0)$ and the *luxuries* are at the bottom $(c_r < 0)$. Since (3) shows that the c_r depend on all prices, the scale of urgency varies with the prices. It is quite possible for (e.g.) butter to ascend the scale from a luxury to a necessary as prices change over time. The slopes β_r of the Engel curves are the constant parameters of the utility function. It is to be expected, though not absolutely certain, that β_r is small for a necessary since an Engel curve which starts high tends to rise slowly. Similarly β_r is likely to be large for a luxury.

The price index $I_{0t}(y)$ is still (6), the weighted average of two price indices (7) which are now to be extended and rewritten in our short-hand notation:

$$\frac{a_t}{a_0} = \frac{\sum \alpha p_t}{\sum \alpha p_0} \qquad \text{and} \qquad \log \frac{b_t}{b_0} = \sum \beta \log \frac{p_t}{p_0} \qquad (\sum \beta = 1) \qquad (8)$$

where p_0 and p_t are two price situations. The first index of (8) is a fixed-weighted arithmetic mean, the weights being the αp_0 values indicating minimum purchase for $u \geq 0$. The weights are also the main determinants of the intercepts of the Engel curves as in (3) and hence of the scale of urgency. A large α indicates a necessary good so that the index a_t/a_0 is heavily weighted with necessaries. The second index of (8) is fixed-weighted with the β parameters, the slopes of the Engel curves, and b_t/b_0 is a geometric as opposed to an arithmetic mean. A large β generally goes with a luxury so that the index b_t/b_1 is heavily weighted with luxuries.

Hence $I_{0t}(y)$ is a weighted mean of these two price indices and the total expenditure level y appears only, and explicitly, in the weights. As y increases, the index $I_{0t}(y)$ shifts because of a decline in the weight a_0/y of the first price index and a rise in the weight $(1 - a_0/y)$ of the second. This makes sense since the first index is dominated by necessaries and the second by luxuries and since rising expenditure transfers the emphasis from necessaries to luxuries. The shift in $I_{0t}(y)$ is quantified:

$$I_{0t}(y) = \frac{b_t}{b_0} - \frac{a_0}{y}\left(\frac{b_t}{b_0} - \frac{a_t}{a_0}\right) \qquad \text{and} \qquad \frac{d}{dy} I_{0t}(y) = \frac{a_0}{y^2}\left(\frac{b_t}{b_0} - \frac{a_t}{a_0}\right)$$

Hence the rate of increase of the 'true' price index with increasing expenditure y depends *directly* on the excess of the luxury-dominated index b_t/b_0 over the necessary-dominated index a_t/a_0, and *inversely* on the square of y. So, if b_t/b_0 is less than a_t/a_0, then the 'true' price index falls but at a declining rate as the expenditure level rises.

All this is a fortunate consequence of the Geary/Stone form of the utility function. The good fortune has practical relevance – only to the extent that the form of u is a reasonable approximation to the preferences of a typical consumer and only as long as problems of aggregation over groups of consumers are not serious. Within these constraints the 'true' index $I_{0t}(y)$ has been made empirical. A quick check whether necessaries (or luxuries) have increased more in price is often enough to determine whether the price differential rises against (or in favour) of the low-income groups. To *measure* the differential effect requires the computation of the two price indexes a_t/a_0 and b_t/b_0 and in its turn this means that the α and β parameters need to be estimated. It is 'on the cards' that these parameters can be estimated by getting the demand functions (2) from national income data.

Muellbauer (1974a) estimates the constant-utility price index (6) from British data by allowing for variable household composition by deflation of all expenditures by the number of 'equivalent adults' in the household. The number is assumed to be the same for all goods and independent of price/income levels, a simplification for which Muellbauer (1974b) finds some justification in the work of Barten (1964). The parameters α and β come from estimates made by Angus Deaton from *Blue Book* data for 1954–70 in nine categories of consumers' expenditure. Index numbers for 1970–72 on 1964 as 100 are derived. In these three years of rapidly rising prices the prices of necessaries increased even faster than the prices of luxuries. The gap that opened up between the indexes a_t/a_0 and b_t/b_0 then gave rise to a differential price movement against the low-income households. The 'true' price index in 1972 (1964 = 100) was 149 for households with half the mean income, but only 145 for those with more than twice

% of 1964	Price index		I_{0t} (y) at various levels* of y				
	$\dfrac{a_t}{a_0}$	$\dfrac{b_t}{b_0}$	$\tfrac{1}{2}\bar{y}$	$\tfrac{2}{3}\bar{y}$	$\bar{y}$	$2\bar{y}$	$4\bar{y}$
1970	129·6	127·8	129·9	129·6	129·0	128·4	128·1
1971	139·9	137·5	140·4	140·0	139·1	138·3	137·9
1972	148·1	144·3	149·0	148·2	146·9	145·6	144·9

* Levels at selected multipliers ($\tfrac{1}{2}$, $\tfrac{2}{3}$, 1, 2, 4) of 1964 mean expenditure $\bar{y}$ = £9·56 per equivalent adult per week.

the mean income, per equivalent adult per week. This is not a large differential but enough to affect the inequality of real income.

The question Muellbauer attempts to answer is: given a distribution of money incomes (per equivalent adult and over all households), how is it modified when deflated to real terms by use of a price index varying with income level? On the estimation summarised above, he finds that the inequality of *real incomes* was reduced by nearly 11 % between 1964 and 1970 but that the reduction in the inequality of *money incomes* was over 12 %. The overstatement in the use of money incomes, when some adjustments are made to correct for bias in the data, is put at about 15 %. This is the measure, in the period from 1964 to 1970, of the price differential against the low-income group.

6.5 International Comparisons of Real Income

The best-known work on inter-country comparisons of real income and purchasing power is that done in O.E.E.C. (Paris) by Gilbert and Associates (1958) in which eight countries in Western Europe are compared with each other and with the United States. The main comparisons are binary index numbers both of Laspeyres and of Paasche form for each European country on U.S. as base. The first two columns of Table 6.4 give the quantity index numbers for real consumption per head in 1950 using, first, base (U.S.) prices and then current (European-country) prices for weights. As they stand, these index numbers compare real consumption in one European country directly with the U.S. A comparison of real consumption between two European countries requires a switch of reference base, for example to the U.K. as 100:

Real consumption per head in France
Laspeyres quantity index

$$= \frac{52}{65} \ 100 = 80\% \text{ of U.K. real consumption} \tag{1}$$

TABLE 6.4

INTER-COUNTRY COMPARISONS OF REAL CONSUMPTION AND GNP PER HEAD

Countries	Binary Comparisons, U.S. = 100 Real Consumption per head, 1950		Comparisons with Average European Prices		
	Laspeyres (U.S. prices)	Paasche (European-Country prices)	Real Consumption per head, 1950 U.S. = 100	Real GNP per head, Av. Europe = 100	
				1950	1955
U.S.	100	100	100	274	242
Average Europe	—	—	—	100	100
U.K.	65	51	52	133	123
Denmark	64	51	53	136	111
Belgium	60	51	50	128	118
Norway	57	45	49	130	121
France	52	38	39	110	105
Holland	48	36	37	107	101
W. Germany	41	28	30	87	107
Italy	30	18	21	56	58

From Gilbert and Associates (1958)

Paasche quantity index

$$= \frac{38}{51} \ 100 = 74\frac{1}{2}\% \text{ of U.K. real consumption} \qquad (2)$$

The consumption levels of France and the U.K. are compared in the fixed-base form (1) by means of the fixed prices of the U.S. The comparison with (2) is more involved and the position is best cleared up in algebraic terms.

The algebra is that of the Laspeyres and Paasche forms but it is worth setting out afresh with the usual notation for the present spatial comparisons. Take U.S. as the base 0 and a selected European country as the current situation $r = 1, 2, \ldots 8$. Write Laspeyres index numbers and an implied (Paasche) quantity index:

$$P_{0r}(q_0) = \frac{\sum p_r q_0}{\sum p_0 q_0}; \ Q_{0r}(p_0) = \frac{\sum p_0 q_r}{\sum p_0 q_0}; \text{ and } Q_{0r}(p_r) = \frac{V_{0r}}{P_{0r}(q_0)}$$

where V_{0r} is the value comparison between the rth European country and the U.S. base. Switch reference base to s to compare two European countries (r with s):

$$\text{Laspeyres quantity index} \qquad = Q_{sr}(p_0) = \frac{\sum p_0 q_r}{\sum p_0 q_s} \qquad (3)$$

$$\text{Implied Paasche quantity index} = \frac{V_{sr}}{P_{sr}(q_0)} = \frac{\sum p_r q_r}{\sum p_s q_s} \frac{\sum p_s q_0}{\sum p_r q_0} \qquad (4)$$

The comparison (1) is an instance of the general form (3); the U.S. prices are used to make the quantity comparison between countries s and r. Similarly (2) is an example of (4) but now it is the pattern of consumption in the U.S. which comes in as well as prices and consumption in both countries s and r. Something better than this is to be sought.

Practice in the construction of index numbers over time provides a hint on what to do now. If one particular date is not regarded as suitable as a base, then it is usual to take an average over a period, e.g. budgets averaged over three years in the retail price index and commodity prices based on 1845–50 in *The Economist* index. By analogy, take average prices, $\bar{p}$ for a typical item, over all European countries in the comparison of real consumption of countries r and s:

Laspeyres quantity index $Q_{sr}(\bar{p})$

$$= \frac{\sum \bar{p} q_r}{\sum \bar{p} q_s} \quad (r \text{ and } s = 0, 1, 2, \ldots 8, r \neq s) \quad (5)$$

This gives a comparison either between two European countries or between one of them and the U.S. It is not difficult in practice, as described by Gilbert and Associates (1958), pp. 155–7. It is the formula suggested in Retail Prices Index Advisory Committee (1971) for inter-regional price comparisons in the U.K. by use of the national quantity pattern $\bar{q}$ in precisely the way that $\bar{p}$ is used in the quantity index (5).

The application of (5) to OEEC data gives the third column of Table 6.4 for real consumption per head in 1950 and the other two columns for real GNP per head in 1950 and 1955. All comparisons are with average European prices as weights and the reference base is taken as the U.S. in the first case and as a European average in the others. For example:

Real consumption per head in France

1950 $\frac{39}{52}$ $100 = 75\%$ of the U.K.

Real GNP per head in France

1950 $\frac{110}{133}$ $100 = 83\%$ of the U.K.

1955 $\frac{105}{123}$ $100 = 85\%$ of the U.K.

To extend the range of such comparisons of real income beyond a few developed countries requires data for other countries supplemented by more sophisticated techniques. Beckerman and Bacon (1970) use regression techniques on data from both developed and less developed countries. Write Y for the logarithm of real consumption per head and seek a regression of Y on various 'explanatory' variables, of which good ones turn out to be: $X_1 = \log$ newsprint consumption, $X_2 = \log$ number telephones. The regression calculated by Beckerman and Bacon with pooled data for 1955 and 1960 is:

$$Y = 5\cdot407 + 0\cdot2421\ X_1 + 0\cdot3023\ X_2$$

Given X_1 and X_2 in each of a range of 74 countries, they estimate real consumption per head in each country in 1954–5 and in

1962–3 and hence the inter-country inequality of real income (consumption). Using the Gini coefficient of inequality, scaled from zero for no inequality to a maximum of unity, they estimate the *inter-country* coefficient at 0·57 as compared with 0·39 for inequality *within* either the U.S. or the U.K. There is clearly great inequality of real income from one country to another.

To get price differences between countries to match the real-consumption estimates of Table 6.4, write an implied price index in a variant form which can be got from Gilbert and Associates (1958). The index is that implied by real GNP per head in a binary comparison of each European country on the U.S. and using either base (U.S.) or current (European) prices as weights. The index is a little more complicated than the ordinary run since there are various interlocking exchange rates involved in its calculation. The numerators of the index are purchasing-power equivalents of various currencies; some results are set out in Table 6.5 for 1950 and for 1955.

The Laspeyres calculation is to be interpreted as the changing purchasing power of the fixed U.S. pattern of consumption over the various currencies; e.g. £0·294 per U.S. $ from the U.S. pattern of consumer purchases when valued at £ and $ prices. To get an actual Laspeyres price index, divide by the official rate of exchange:

Laspeyres price index, U.K.

$$1950 \quad \frac{0\cdot294}{0\cdot357} \quad 100 = 82\cdot4\% \text{ of U.S. prices}$$

$$1955 \quad \frac{0\cdot319}{0\cdot357} \quad 100 = 89\cdot4\% \text{ of U.S. prices}$$

Further, the reciprocal of such an index has a particularly useful interpretation; for example, in 1950, the reciprocal of 0·824 is 1·21 to be interpreted as the fact the $1 converted into £'s and spent in the U.K. brings as much as $1·21 spent in the U.S. By 1955, the £ had a purchasing power rather nearer to the U.S. $; since 1·12 is the reciprocal of 0·894, $1 spent in £'s in the U.K. purchases as much as $1·12 in the U.S. The Paasche index gives similar comparisons of purchasing power on the alternative pattern of purchases, that in the local country. The complete set of price index numbers is shown in the table on p. 220.

The narrowing of the gap between the purchasing power of European currencies and the U.S. $ was a general picture of the period 1950–55.

TABLE 6.5

PURCHASING POWER EQUIVALENT, LOCAL CURRENCY PER U.S. $

Countries	Currency Unit	Official Exchange Rate	1950		1955	
			Laspeyres (U.S. quantities)	Paasche (European-Country quantities)	Laspeyres (U.S. quantities)	Paasche (European-Country quantities)
U.K.	£	0·357	0·294	0·219	0·319	0·272
Denmark	krone	6·91	5·58	4·32	5·94	4·57
Belgium	franc	50·2	45·0	37·0	44·9	37·6
Norway	krone	7·14	5·78	4·11	6·58	4·78
France	franc	350	312	223	394	287
Holland	florin	3·80	2·76	1·96	2·93	2·17
W. Germany	D-Mark	4·20	3·70	2·54	3·51	2·54
Italy	lira	625	577	330	605	337

From Gilbert and Associates (1958)

Price index	1950		1955	
(*U.S.*=100)	*Laspeyres*	*Paasche*	*Laspeyres*	*Paasche*
U.K.	82·4	61·3	89·4	76·2
Denmark	80·8	62·5	86·0	66·1
Belgium	89·6	73·7	89·4	74·9
Norway	81·0	57·6	92·2	66·9
France	89·1	63·7	112·6	82·0
Holland	72·6	51·6	77·1	57·1
W. Germany	88·1	60·5	83·6	60·5
Italy	92·3	52·8	96·8	53·9

The other gap disclosed in the table is that between Laspeyres and Paasche forms. As expected, the Laspeyres form is the greater but the differences are surprisingly large, a reflection of the quite different patterns of prices and consumption in Europe as compared with the U.S.

6.6 Real GDP based on Output Data

GDP aggregates, calculated annually and quarterly from the expenditure side, have been analysed sufficiently in Chapters 3 and 4 but once the emphasis shifts to short-run changes, e.g. monthly, then it is necessary to make estimates from the output side. Of the three measures of real GDP (**3.9**), it is that from the output side which is available with least delay and the only information published regularly on a monthly basis is on the main constituent of real GDP with the label: industrial production. Hence the technical problem is how to measure changes in real GDP as output, seasonally adjusted, in the short run. It is considered here, first, for a quarterly run of total real GDP and then (in **6.7**) for a monthly run of the index of industrial production.

It is in the problem of handling series published quickly and frequently that the difficulties arising from revision of the series from one publication date to the next become of critical importance. Some runs once published are never revised since their use depends on having definitive figures, e.g. the retail price index as used in various contractual arrangements. Other runs such as the wholesale price index (Department of Trade) or the index of average earnings of all employees (Department of Employment) are subject to regular but light revision. Still other runs, and particularly those derived from national income data, are revised regularly and substantially.

Table 6.6 gives a short run of GDP estimated from output data

TABLE 6.6

GDP BASED ON OUTPUT, ANNUALLY AND QUARTERLY (SEASONALLY ADJUSTED), 1968–73

Year and Quarter	GDP at current prices		Index numbers		Home costs per unit of output* 1963 = 100
	£mn	Index 1963 = 100	Laspeyres volume (real GDP) 1963 = 100	Implied Paasche price 1963 = 100	
Based on 1963:					
1963	26,825	100	100	100	100
1968	36,781	137·1	117·0	117·2	117·7
1969	38,805	144·7	119·5	121·1	121·8
1970	42,606	158·8	121·8	130·4	131·1
		1970 = 100	1970 = 100	1970 = 100	1970 = 100
Based on 1970:					
1970	42,845	100	100	100	100
1971	47,512	110·9	101·4	109·4	110·3
1972	53,139	124·0	104·1	119·1	121·6
1972 Q.1	12,515	116·8	101·4	115·2	117·6
Q.2	13,109	122·4	104·3	117·3	118·3
Q.3	13,444	125·5	104·3	120·3	121·4
Q.4	14,071	131·4	106·2	123·7	124·7
1973 Q.1	14,684	137·1	109·0	125·8	128·5
Q.2	14,858	138·7	108·6	127·7	130·0

From *Economic Trends*

* Implied Paasche price index from GDP at factor cost based on expenditure (Table 4.2).

based on 1970, annually from 1970 to 1972 and seasonally adjusted by quarters in 1972–3. The previous annual run based on 1963 is given for comparison. The Laspeyres index of real GDP is derived from the official constant-price valuations of output and the implied Paasche price index by deflation of the current-price valuations of output by the real GDP index. This particular implied price index is *not* published officially. Instead, the official tabulations rely on the implied price index got from the expenditure side and labelled 'home costs for unit of output'; see Table 4.2. Table 6.6 shows this published price index to complete the comparisons. Both the implied price index numbers are of Paasche form and cover all GDP; but one is from output and the other from expenditure data and they differ in make-up, e.g. in the treatment of import and export prices. Variations in the terms of trade affect them differently. The published index from expenditure data runs higher than the unpublished index from output data in Table 6.6; the 1970-based price index numbers

TABLE 6.7

REAL GDP BASED ON OUTPUT, QUARTERLY (SEASONALLY ADJUSTED), 1971–2

| Year and Quarter | Based on 1963 Economic Trends, 1972 | | | | Economic Trends, 1973 | | | 1963 series (July 1973) switched to 1970 = 100 | Based on 1970 Economic Trends Oct. 1973 |
	Jan.	Apr.	July	Oct.	Jan.	Apr.	July		
1971 Q.1	122·0	121·9	122·0	122·0	121·9	122·1	122·4	100·1	100·0
Q.2	123·8	123·8	123·9	123·8	123·8	123·9	124·1	101·5	101·3
Q.3	125·1	125·0	125·0	124·8	124·8	124·9	125·3	102·5	101·8
Q.4		124·8	125·0	125·0	125·0	125·1	125·6	102·7	102·3
1972 Q.1			123·6	124·2	123·9	123·8	124·3	101·7	101·4
Q.2				128·7	128·4	128·4	128·9	105·4	104·3
Q.3					129·3	129·4	129·9	106·3	104·3
Q.4						130·9	132·4	108·3	106·2

From *Economic Trends*

showed that a difference of about 2% had built up from 1970 to early 1973.

Table 6.7 provides an opportunity to look at the effect of revisions in successive publications of the same index: the seasonally adjusted quarterly run of real GDP as output. The estimates are taken from the issues of *Economic Trends* for January, April, July and October in 1972 and 1973, a period which saw some regular revisions in the 1963-based run and also, at the end, the introduction of the new 1970-based run. The table is designed to show both routine revisions in an established index and the periodic revisions consequent upon a rebasing of the index.

The routine revisions in the 1963–based index between January 1972 and July 1973 are quite small and not enough to raise difficulties in the ordinary usage of the index. The variations are, indeed, such that they could well be explained by revisions in the seasonal factors, estimated here (as in many official series) on a rolling basis which results in constant but usually small changes. There are larger differences between the last run of the 1963-based index (*Economic Trends*, July 1973) and the first run of the 1970-based index (*Economic Trends*, October 1973). They are shown in Table 6.7, on 1970 as a reference base, by quarters during 1971–2. The new index is seen to be a downward revision of the old. This is mainly because of the expected upward drift of the Laspeyres index of real GDP base-weighted on the increasingly remote year 1963. The new index, updated to 1970 weights, is a partial correction of the drift but it will itself tend to drift upwards in time. A chained run, e.g. with Fisher Ideal links, would do better in a longish run, but the Laspeyres run is acceptable as long as the change-over to a new base is not long delayed.

6.7 Industrial Production Index: Effect of Revisions

The monthly index of output described as covering industrial production is composed of the industrial groups: manufacturing, mining, construction and utilities (gas, electricity, water). The net output weight in total GDP in 1970 was 32.7% for manufacturing and 11.2% for the other three groups. On an annual basis, the monthly index of industrial production averaged over years can be compared with the *Blue Book* series of the corresponding constituents of GDP, and the (unpublished) price index implied by the comparison can also be written for the same constituents. These comparisons are made for manufacturing in Table 6.8. Manufacturing is chosen for the exercise since there is still another index so nearly comparable

TABLE 6.8

MANUFACTURING NET OUTPUT, 1968–72

| Year | Net output at current prices | | Index numbers | | |
	£mn	Index 1963 = 100	Laspeyres volume 1963 = 100	Implied Paasche price 1963 = 100	Index of wholesale prices* 1963 = 100
Based on 1963:					
1963:	8,953	100	100	100	100
1968	11,866	132·5	121·4	109·2	116·7
1969	12,666	141·5	125·6	112·6	120·9
1970	14,053	157·0	127·2	123·4	128·7
		1970 = 100	1970 = 100	1970 = 100	1970 = 100
Based on 1970:					
1970	13,936	100	100	100	100
1971	15,093	108·3	99·7	108·6	109·0
1972	16,645	119·4	101·6	117·6	114·8

From *Blue Book*, 1972 and 1973, and *Monthly Digest of Statistics*

* Department of Trade Index, home sales, all manufactured products.

that it can be thrown into the comparisons of Table 6.8: the Laspeyres index of wholesale prices published monthly by the Department of Trade, and averaged over the same years as the national income series in the table.

There is a twofold difference between the two price indicators. The index implied in the national accounts is of Paasche form as compared with the standard Laspeyres construction of the wholesale price index. The former has reference to net output prices whereas the latter uses gross prices inclusive of raw material/import content. The wholesale price index is to be expected to run the higher of the two, partly because of its Laspeyres form and partly because of rapidly rising materials prices in the period considered. This expectation is confirmed in Table 6.8 except for a divergence the other way in the last year (1972) for which the index numbers must be regarded as provisional.

Apart from fitting into the system of national income data, the index of industrial production has short-run uses of its own and it has a long history, both as the successor to historical index runs before 1938 and in its various rebasings since 1948. One of the more intractable problems in its construction is to decide whether the index should or could be devised to measure net output without duplication over the whole of industry or whether it need be confined to gross output of final products. This problem, considered at some length by Carter, Reddaway and Stone (1958) and later by Reddaway (1950) and others, is by no means resolved but the official index has come to be what can be fairly described as a good approximation to an indicator of net output.

The 1963-based index is described in detail in Central Statistical Office (1970). The subsequent run base-weighted on 1970 appeared for the first time annually in the 1973 *Blue Book* and monthly in the September 1973 issue of the *Monthly Digest of Statistics*, followed by a long historical run in *Economic Trends* of November 1973. There is no difficulty about the weights; they are the current-price valuations of net output by industrial groups from GDP estimates in the base year. All the problems arise in defining, and recording on a continuing monthly basis, the quantity relatives to be weighted. They are obtained for the most part from indicators of deliveries or sales by quantity or by revaluation at constant prices. Special calculations are needed when there is a long production period (engineering, construction), and input series of quantities of materials used are sometimes taken in default of output data. Earlier versions of the index contained some use of labour inputs (i.e. numbers employed) as substitute indicators. These are clearly very poor substitutes since they assume away productivity changes and understate output growth, and they have now been almost completely eliminated.

Two problems are considered here on this index of physical output changes, an index which is both much used and also much criticised. The first is the effect of revisions in the month-by-month publication of the index, and this is illustrated in Table 6.9 by reference to successive issues of the *Monthly Digest of Statistics* between May and December 1973. This short period saw two major revisions; first, some changes in the construction and engineering constituents of the 1963-based index, going back some time but only announced in June 1973 in a C.S.O. Press Release; secondly a rebasing of the index on 1970 weights and given in the *Digest* of September 1973. Table 6.9 shows the effect of the first in the 'before' and 'after' runs of the *Digests* of May and June 1973, an upward revision eventually

TABLE 6.9

INDEX OF INDUSTRIAL PRODUCTION,*
EFFECT OF REVISIONS, 1971–3

1973 *Digests*, issues of:

Date	May (1963 = 100)	June-Aug. 1963 = 100	Switched to 1970 = 100	Sept.-Nov. (1970 = 100)	Dec. (1970 = 100)
1971 Q.1	124·3	125·0	100·1	100·2	100·2
Q.2	125·1	125·8	100·7	100·9	100·9
Q.3	125·6	126·5	101·3	100·6	100·6
Q.4	124·6	125·8	100·7	100·4	100·4
1972 Q.1	121·7	123·0	98·5	98·0	98·0
Q.2	128·8	129·9	104·0	102·7	102·7
1972 July	129·7	130·4	104·4	101·8	101·8
Aug.	129·6	130·8	104·7	101·4	101·4
Sept.	131·1	132·7	106·2	103·9	103·9
Oct.	131·3	134·5	107·7	105·1	105·1
Nov.	132·2	135·5	108·5	105·7	105·7
Dec.	132·9	136·1	109·0	106·1	106·1
1973 Jan.	132·8	136·7	109·4	107·9	108·6
Feb.	135·3	138·4	110·8	110·3	110·7
Mar.	137·0	140·0	112·1	111·2	111·9
Apr.		140·6	112·6	109·7	110·0
May		141·3	113·1	110·1	109·9
June		140·7	112·7	111·0	111·1
July				111·3	111·5
Aug.				111·1	111·0
Sept.				111·9	111·6

From *Monthly Digest of Statistics*

* Seasonally adjusted.

pushing up the index of March 1973 from 137·0 to 140·0% of 1963. The table shows the effect of the rebasing by switching the last run of the 1963-based index to 1970 as reference base and it goes on to include the first regular revision of the new index in December 1973. The result is much the same as that found for the quarterly run of real GDP in Table 6.7 The rebasing on 1970 served as a partial correction of the upward bias in the previous run base-weighted on 1963. The subsequent routine revisions of December 1973 were small but generally upwards in 1973. Overall there was, in 1973, a considerable and disturbing seesaw movement in the published index; for example for January 1973:

Index	1973 *Digest of:*			
(1970 = 100)	May	June	Sept.	Dec.
Jan. 1973	106·3	109·4	107·9	108·6

TABLE 6.10

INDEX OF INDUSTRIAL PRODUCTION, REVISIONS AND SPLICED RUN, 1948–72

Year	Original Runs				Revised Runs				Spliced	
	1948 =100	1954 =100	1958 =100	1963 =100	1948 =100	1954 =100	1958 =100	1963 =100	1970 =100*	1948 =100
1948	100								50·5	100
1954	129·6	100			125·35	100			63·3	125·3
1955	136·6	105·1				104·90			66·4	131·5
1956	136·5	105·6				105·69			66·9	132·5
1957	138·4	107·5				107·58			68·1	134·8
1958		106·3	100			106·64	100		67·5	133·7
1959		112·6	105·1				105·04		70·9	140·4
1960		120·3	112·5				112·30		75·8	150·1
1961			113·9				113·63		76·7	151·9
1962			115·1				114·67		77·4	153·3
1963			119·0	100			118·07	100	79·7	157·8
1964			128·2	108·3				108·53	86·5	171·3
1965			131·9	111·7				111·79	89·1	176·4
1966			133·4	113·2				113·68	90·6	179·4
1967			133·3	113·9				115·06	91·7	181·6
1968				119·8				121·96	97·2	192·5
1969									99·9	197·8
1970									100	198·0
1971									100·5	199·0
1972									101·8	201·6

From *Annual Abstract of Statistics* and *Monthly Digest of Statistics*

* Continued from 1968 with 1970-based index, given 1968 link value of 97·2.

The second problem is the longer-run difficulty of splicing together a sequence of separate Laspeyres runs and of incorporating, at the same time, a variety of revisions. Table 6.10 gives for 1948, and then annually from 1954, the index of industrial production as originally published on a sequence of bases: 1948, 1954, 1958 and 1963. They all need to be adjusted to conform as far as possible with the new 1970-based index before being spliced together in a run capable of being continued by the 1970 index. The double process is described by Gardner, Brown and Francombe (1972) and the results given in Table 6.10. Among the adjustments are the carrying back of the amendments made to the construction and engineering indicators and the rearrangement of the whole complex of indicators into the 1968 Standard Industrial Classification. The splicing is made 'firm' by use of a three-year overlap each time and by taking the old index from its own base up to the 'splice' of the new index. So, between 1948 and 1954, the new (1954-based) series is spliced on over the period 1954–6 and the old (1948-based) index is allowed to run from 1948 until the 'splice' is made. There is one exception; the last (1970-based) series is spliced on in 1968 (with the aid of its value 97·2% of 1970 in that year) and not in 1970 or over 1969–71. The complete spliced run is, therefore, of forward Laspeyres form except between 1968 and 1970 when the backward Laspeyres form from 1970 to 1968 is equivalent to a forward Paasche index from 1968 to 1970.

The spliced run of Table 6.10 is first shown with 1970 as reference base and jobs back to a figure in 1948 of 50·5% of 1970. It is then switched to 1948 as reference base, to be read forwards effectively as a Laspeyres run chained at about five-yearly intervals. The overall growth in real output is 98%, or 3·1% per year cumulatively, from 1948 to 1970. The growth is fairly steady, with some slower stretches and some accelerations, but with only one actual 'dip', in 1958. At the end of the run the annual rate of growth declined, e.g. to less than 1% per year in the period 1969–72.

6.8 Employment and Unemployment

There are many definitions of employment and unemployment but statistical estimation is almost always based on simple counts of numbers. For any industrial group:

$$L = E + U$$

where the numbers in the labour force L are split into those employed E and a count U of the unemployed. The problem is often and rightly regarded as a matter of tracing the effects of unemployment in a social context. Changes in numbers are not a complete story here; other factors have social weight, e.g. changing distributions by age, sex and occupation, though there is an obvious dearth of relevant statistics.

The emphasis changes in an economic analysis where what is needed are some measures of the amounts of labour inputs and of the price of labour as a factor of production. The analysis must involve the employed labour and their earnings and the unemployed manpower and their loss of earnings. The numerical equation $L = E + U$ is not enough, since, as Peston (1972) demonstrates, the 'quality' of labour resources is as important as sheer numbers. Some grades of labour contribute more than others to the product of industry and (with qualifications on the supply side) get paid more, e.g. skilled as opposed to unskilled, adults as opposed to juveniles. The composition of L, E and U is constantly changing in these and other respects.

The economic problem is centred, as usual, on a value aggregate and its split into real and price components. Here it is the wages bill, changing from time $t = 0$ to time t with price and quantity components:

$$W_{0t} = P_{0t} \times Q_{0t}$$

By the same token, the problem is one of index numbers, not one of simple counting. The wages bill is a recorded value aggregate; one component is an index P_{0t} of the prices of labour and the other an index Q_{0t} of employment. A familiar question is whether to have changes in the 'quality' of labour (productivity) in the price index or in employment. The choice is between *wage rates* as 'pure' price quotations and average *earnings* as unit values. All wage rates can remain unchanged and earnings per head can still increase by shifts in the labour force towards adults or the more skilled. So, if P_{0t} is an index of wage rates, Q_{0t} shows changes in employment inclusive of the effect of quality changes; if P_{0t} is based on average earnings then quality changes are for the most part in P_{0t} rather than in Q_{0t}.

In economic models of production, the best bet is to opt for factor prices, including the price of labour, as 'pure' price quotations and so to take P_{0t} as an index of wage rates. The corollary is that

Q_{0t} is not a count of numbers; it is a weighted index allowing for all kinds of quality innovations. If P_{0t} is computed as a 'pure' price index, the obvious way is to take the implied quantity measure by deflation of the wages bill: $Q_{0t} = W_{0t}/P_{0t}$. And this is a practical proposition since index numbers of wage rates are available in base-weighted (Laspeyres) form. The appropriate measure of employment, to replace a number count, is the implied (Paasche) index. Specifically, the British index of wage rates (basic weekly wages) was, until 1972, a Laspeyres index base-weighted on the 1955 wage bill but with a reference base of January 1956:

$$P_{0t} = \frac{\sum w_0 \dfrac{p_t}{p_0}}{\sum w_0} = \frac{\sum p_t q_{55}}{\sum p_0 q_{55}} \quad \text{(where } w_0 = p_0 q_{ss})$$

The 1955 quantities q_{55} are the amounts of employment among the grades of labour with wage rates p_0 in January 1956. The practical estimation of w_0's however, is by updating the 1955 wages bill by the wage-rate rise from p_{55} to p_0. The current wages bill is $\sum p_t q_t$ to be deflated by P_{0t} to give the employment measure. For the purpose of relating the index P_{0t} to national income data based on 1958, the reference base is further switched to the average of 1958. Consequently, the Laspeyres index of wage rates and the implied (Paasche) index of employment become:

$$P_{58t} = \frac{\sum p_t q_{55}}{\sum p_{58} q_{55}} \quad \text{and} \quad Q_{58t} = \frac{\sum p_t q_t}{\sum p_{58} q_{58}} \bigg/ \frac{\sum p_t q_{55}}{\sum p_{58} q_{55}}$$

The employment index Q_{58t} involves, as it must, employment q_{55} of the base year 1955.

It is difficult to obtain even roughly consistent data from which to calculate the employment index. What can be done in the years 1958 to 1969 is to match the wage-rate index P_{58t} for manufacturing with the wages bill and the numbers of wage earners given for manufacturing industries in the 1970 *Blue Book*. One main difficulty with the data, set out in Table 6.11, is that they depend on the distinction between wages and salaries. This is overcome in the wage-rate index by simply specifying what rates of pay are wages. In the *Blue Book* data, the distinction is very much a matter of convention. Central Statistical Office (1968) comments that 'only a limited importance can be attached to the separation of wages from salaries in the national accounts. The distinction is necessarily arbitrary and no clear dividing line can be drawn, but it nevertheless has certain practical uses.' *Blue Books* later than that of 1970 have given up the attempt at the distinction so that Table 6.11 stops short in 1969.

TABLE 6.11

INDEX NUMBERS OF EMPLOYMENT,
WAGE EARNERS IN MANUFACTURING, U.K., 1958–69

Year	Wages bill* £mn	1958 = 100	Laspeyres index wages rates† 1958 = 100	Implied Paasche index, employment 1958 = 100	Numbers of wage earners* '000s	1958 = 100
1958	3,233	100	100	100	6,160	100
1959	3,372	104·3	102·5	101·8	6,150	99·8
1960	3,673	113·6	105·0	108·2	6,205	100·7
1961	3,870	119·7	109·2	109·6	6,170	100·2
1962	3,926	121·4	112·6	107·9	6,105	99·1
1963	4,015	124·1	115·9	107·1	6,065	98·5
1964	4,418	136·7	121·4	112·6	6,150	99·8
1965	4,819	149·1	126·0	118·3	6,245	101·4
1966	5,109	158·0	132·0	119·7	6,230	101·1
1967	5,057	156·4	137·2	114·0	6,040	98·1
1968	5,488	169·7	147·5	115·1	6,000	97·4
1969	5,976	184·8	155·6	118·8	6,060	98·4

From *Blue Book*, 1970, and *Monthly Digest of Statistics*

* Comparable data over time on Census of Production coverage from Table 18, *Blue Book*.

† Index of basic weekly wage rates, all workers in manufacturing, switched from January 1956 to average 1958 as 100.

The conclusion from these data is that numbers of wage earners in manufacturing understate the real rise in employment to such an extent that they provide no evidence of a rise at all between 1958 and 1969, just a fluctuation with no definite trend. The implied (Paasche) index of employment shows fluctuations around a sharply rising trend and even this may understate the situation if the Laspeyres wage-rate index runs as expected above the 'true' index of the price of labour. It is safe enough to estimate the increase in the trend of employment at about 20% between 1958 and 1969.

An alternative model is to incorporate all or most of the 'quality' changes in the labour force in an index of average earnings, i.e. by taking unit values instead of prices. The corresponding employment measure, stripped of most 'quality' changes, is then some average of numbers employed q_t industry by industry. In Laspeyres form:

$$Q_{0t} = \frac{\sum w_0 \dfrac{q_t}{q_0}}{\sum w_0} = \frac{\sum p_0 q_t}{\sum p_0 q_0} \quad \text{(where } w_0 = p_0 q_0 \text{)}$$

The weighting is by means of average earnings $p_0 = w_0/q_0$ in the base year. The index Q_{0t} is still not just a change in numbers; the weights in Q_{0t} are the relative wage bills in different industries and skilled workers carry a greater weight than the less skilled.

This alternative is less appropriate than the index of Table 6.11 as a measure of labour input but it is not obvious which is preferable in an attempt to measure unemployment instead of, or as well as, employment. In any case there may be no choice since it can easily happen that only the index base-weighted with average earnings can be calculated. Table 6.12 illustrates with an analysis by groups of manufacturing industries in Great Britain leading to measures of employment and unemployment among all employees (wages and salaries combined). The index numbers obtained in June 1972 and June 1973 in the last four columns are base-weighted with 1972 average earnings, the weights being reasonably good approximations (see footnote to table). They show no change in employment and a reduction of nearly 40% in unemployment between the two dates. Practically the same estimates are obtained from total numbers without weighting. This is accidental but perhaps not too unusual – there happens to be no correlation between the level of earnings and shifts (e.g.) in unemployment within manufacturing industry in the period.

Something more can be done with the data of Table 6.12. In any Laspeyres quantity index, e.g. one of real consumption, the numerator can stand on its own as a constant-price series and an indicator of quantity changes. So, here, the numerator of the index of employment represents earnings at constant rates of average earnings and the numerator of the index of unemployment shows loss of earnings at the same constant rates. They show employment or unemployment, measured from the economic angle as actual or potential earnings, and not just as numbers of bodies. The big advantage of their presentation is that the series can be related to each other to give (e.g.) percentage unemployment calculated with

TABLE 6.12

EMPLOYMENT AND UNEMPLOYMENT, ALL EMPLOYEES IN MANUFACTURING, GREAT BRITAIN, 1972–3

Industry	Average earnings (£)* June 1972	Employment ('000s)		Unemployment ('000s)		Actual and lost earnings (£mn)			
						Employment		Unemployment	
		June 1972	June 1973	June 1972	June 1973	June 1972	June 1973	June 1972	June 1973
Food, drink, tobacco	1,467	729·8	732·4	26·6	18·2	1,071	1,074	39·0	26·7
Chemicals	1,779	424·0	418·7	13·3	9·3	754	745	23·7	16·5
Metal manufacture	1,674	515·6	515·6	24·6	13·5	863	863	41·2	22·6
Engineering:									
Mechanical	1,545	963·0	942·4	38·2	21·0	1,488	1,456	59·0	32·4
Electrical, etc.	1,432	936·1	953·3	24·25	14·8	1,340	1,365	34·7	21·2
Shipbuilding	1,697	176·9	175·8	10·9	7·4	300	298	18·5	12·6
Vehicles	1,798	775·6	794·8	20·25	11·1	1,395	1,429	36·4	20·0
Metal goods	1,342	552·6	552·7	25·4	14·5	742	742	34·1	19·5
Textiles	1,272	558·0	550·7	21·6	12·4	710	700	27·5	15·8
Clothing, leather	986	470·7	452·1	12·3	7·7	464	446	12·1	7·6
Paper, printing	1,694	572·6	569·4	13·2	8·7	970	965	22·4	14·7
Other manufactures	1,469	938·4	946·1	33·7	21·8	1,378	1,390	49·5	32·0
Total		7,613·3	7,604·0	264·3	160·4	11,475	11,473	398·1	241·6
Index		100	99·9	100	60·7	100	100·0	100	60·7

From *Monthly Digest of Statistics* and Department of Employment *Gazette*

* Estimates for U.K. by division of wages and salaries in 1972 (from *Blue Book* 1973) by numbers of employees employed at June 1972, taken as approximate relative distribution of earnings by industry, G.B., June 1972.

proper weighting by earnings. For manufacturing in Great Britain, from Table 6.12:

June	Actual and lost earnings at 1972 rates, £mn			%
	Employment	Unemployment	Labour Force	Unemployed
1972	11,475	398·1	11,873	3·35
1973	11,473	241·6	11,715	2·06

On this basis unemployment fell from 3·35% to 2·06%. Here, again and by chance, the weighting makes no difference since the rate of unemployment fell from 3·36 to 2·07% when measured by total numbers.

This particular negative result need not be discouraging since the exercise which is *possible* on available data by industries is not the one which *should* be made. It is the occupational distribution, rather than the industrial, which is likely to influence the incidence of unemployment. The thesis to be tested is that posed by Peston (1972) and others: when unemployment is high, as in 1972, the proportion of adult skilled workers among the unemployed tends to be high. At low rates of unemployment, the unemployed are largely unskilled; the skilled only get unemployed, and increasingly so, as the rate of unemployment rises. To test the thesis, the exercise of Table 6.12 needs to be carried out on an occupational distribution, but the data are for the most part lacking. This is an instance of how published data are still inadequate for economic analysis.

6.9 Stock-Market Prices

There are several unofficial index numbers designed to show movements in share prices quoted on the London Stock Exchange and the best-known is the simplest: the *Financial Times* (FT) index computed daily for 30 market leaders among industrial ordinary shares. From its introduction in 1935 the index has had the object of providing a sensitive day-to-day indicator of the changing 'mood of the market' as reflected in the prices of leading industrial shares. It has never been intended, for example, to guide portfolio managers.

The FT index is an equi-weighted geometric mean of share-price relatives – so simple that it is calculated in practice in a few minutes several times a day. There is no need to perform calculations on data stored in a computer. All this depends a good deal on the well-known properties of an equi-weighted geometric mean. Write p_t for the typical share price, of the n shares in the index, at time t where $t = 0, 1, 2, \ldots$ are the successive periods at which the index is calculated (daily for $n = 30$ shares in the FT index). The n price relative p_t/p_0 are equi-weighted and the index GM_{0t} is the nth root of their product. It follows that GM_{0t} can be shown as the product of successive links of the same form, either for *every* period $t = 0, 1, 2, \ldots$:

$$GM_{0t} = \sqrt[n]{\left(\Pi \frac{p_t}{p_0}\right)} = \sqrt[n]{\left(\Pi \frac{p_1}{p_0}\right)} \sqrt[n]{\left(\Pi \frac{p_2}{p_1}\right)} \ldots \sqrt[n]{\left(\Pi \frac{p_t}{p_{t-1}}\right)}$$

$$= GM_{01} \times GM_{12} \times \ldots \times GM_{(t-1)t} \tag{1}$$

or for less frequent intervals. The result (1) permits the rebasing of the index on any other period r as 100 by simple switching. This follows since application of (1) gives:

$$GM_{0t} = GM_{0r} \times GM_{rt} \quad \text{for } 0 < r < t \tag{2}$$

and (2) can be rewritten to show how the reference base is switched:

$$GM_{rt} = GM_{0t}/GM_{0r}$$

Further, (1) allows for share-substitution at any time. Suppose that a share with price p' is substituted for one with price p at $t = 1$; all that needs to be done is to insert p'_2/p'_1 for p_2/p_1 in the second term of (1) and to continue with $p'_3/p'_2 \ldots$.

The calculation of GM_{0t} proceeds step by step from one period to the next, using the prices of whatever shares are included at the time, daily for the FT index with a varying collection of 30 shares. The selection of the shares is purposive and the index is not of the stochastic form envisaged for the geometric mean by Edgeworth (1.3). Even though the shares are far from a random selection, the fact that their prices are equi-weighted at all times does make the FT index an indicator of general price movements, not tied to any specific portfolio with predetermined weights. Nevertheless, it is possible to interpret the FT index approximately as a portfolio index – but only on a very odd investment strategy. This is established by Marks and Stuart (1971) following Rich (1948). The geometric mean (1) is a chain of daily links, each involving only small price changes, so that each geometric link can be approximated by an arithmetic link; see Marks and Stuart (1971) p. 319. The FT index is *precisely* a daily chain of equi-weighted *geometric* links and *approximately* a daily chain of equi-weighted *arithmetic* links. The arithmetic link from day t to day $(t+1)$ is the change in the value of a portfolio distributed equally by market value over the 30 shares at day t. To make up the chain, and approximate to the FT index, the portfolio is changed every day to keep it equi-weighted – by selling off some stock which has gone up more in price and replacing by purchases of shares which have gone up less in price. As Marks and Stuart put it, the FT index as an approximate portfolio index is based on the strategy: 'Hedge your bets continuously between the constituents of the index.' How sensible this is as a strategy to put in practice is seen in the computations made by Marks and Stuart and set out in Table 6.13.

The object of the exercise is to compare the FT index with two alternatives. One alternative is the direct arithmetic mean version $AM_{0t}=\frac{1}{n}\sum\frac{p_t}{p_0}$. The calculation of AM_{0t} is a major job if it is to use all the substitutions so easily made on result (1) but needing great care in the arithmetic version. The substitutions are very numerous as companies merge or disappear and as they issue bonus or rights shares. The calculations of Marks and Stuart are carried through on the original base (in 1935) and on other bases at end-years from 1935 to 1970. The work must be done afresh for each base r on the formula

$$AM_{rt}=\frac{1}{n}\sum\frac{p_t}{p_r} \tag{3}$$

and there is no simple switching formula such as (2). Table 6.13 shows one particular run: AM_{rt} for r as end-1950 and t from end-1951 to end-1970. This is the interesting period on the stock market; from 1935 to 1950 there were quite small movements in general share prices, even during wartime. The interpretation of AM_{rt} by (3) is a portfolio index of the simplest kind: keep the 30 shares as put together in an equi-valued portfolio at the base date r (end-1950 in Table 6.13).

The other alternative in Table 6.13 is a chain index of annual links. The link from end-year $(t-1)$ to end-year t is the equi-weighted arithmetic mean of 30 share-price relatives p_t/p_{t-1}. The whole chain at end-year t on end-year r as base is:

$$AM'_{rt}=AM_{r(r+1)} \times AM_{(r+1)(r+2)} \times \ldots \times AM_{(t-1)t} \tag{4}$$

This is the standard chain Laspeyres form; the annual links are base-weighted on an equal distribution of shares by market value.

TABLE 6.13

FT INDEX OF PRICES OF INDUSTRIAL ORDINARY SHARES, GM AND AM VERSIONS, 1951–70

End-year	Geometric mean FT index switched to end-1950=100	Arithmetic mean Marks and Stuart index end-1950=100	
		Direct	Chain
1951	105·4	105·6	105·6
1952	100·1	101·3	101·1
1953	113·0	115·8	115·3
1954	159·0	166·0	163·3
1955	173·2	184·9	179·1
1956	154·5	169·1	161·6
1957	142·9	155·2	153·6
1958	194·9	220·0	222·5
1959	292·5	323·5	334·4
1960	263·9	291·7	302·3

End-Year	Geometric mean FT index switched to end-1950=100	Arithmetic mean Marks and Stuart index end-1950=100	
		Direct	Chain
1961	263·4	290·3	304·7
1962	244·7	277·2	287·9
1963	301·0	345·0	364·0
1964	289·5	331·6	352·3
1965	293·6	332·5	359·3
1966	268·2	307·5	331·3
1967	336·4	392·9	430·1
1968	437·7	514·0	561·6
1969	352·1	426·3	462·2
1970	294·4	364·2	396·6

From Marks and Stuart (1971), Tables 3 and 5

Marks and Stuart do not calculate (4) but it is constructed by chaining the links in their Table 3. The chain index of Table 6.13 here is (4) with r as end-1950 and t from end-1951 to end-1970.

The FT index run of Table 6.13 is to be looked at in two ways. It is *precisely* the geometric mean GM_{rt} of the same share-price relatives as used in the direct arithmetic mean AM_{rt}. The relation of the two is given approximately by a formula quoted by Marks and Stuart:

$$\frac{GM_{rt}}{AM_{rt}} = 1 - \tfrac{1}{2}\frac{\sigma_p^2}{AM_{rt}^2} \text{ where } \sigma_p^2 = \frac{\text{variance of price relatives}}{p_t/p_r} \tag{5}$$

In particular, except in the trivial care where all price relatives are equal, the geometric mean version is always less than the arithmetic mean. The second view of the FT index is as an *approximation* to a chain Laspeyres index of form (4) but with daily links. It follows that this approximate FT index GM_{rt} is similar to the annual chain AM'_{rt} in showing from one period to the next the changing value of a fixed portfolio equi-distributed by market value at the outset. The period is daily for the FT index but annually for AM'_{rt}.

On these two views, it is appropriate to take the ratio of the geometric version and the chain arithmetic version to the direct arithmetic version. At two dates when stock-market prices were at or near peaks, Table 6.13 gives:

End-year	% of direct arithmetic index Chain arithmetic index	Geometric index	Coefficient of variation (%) of price relatives
1959	103·3	90·4	43·8
1968	109·3	85·2	54·5

The coefficient of variation in the last column is σ_p/AM_{rt} and it is found from (5). The spread of share-price relatives is large at both dates, the standard deviation being about 50% of the mean. The great diversity of movements of share prices, even among the market leaders, is clearly the reason for the gaps between the geometric FT index and the direct and chain arithmetic versions, and hence for the difficulty in estimating the general movement of share prices at all accurately.

The steady drift of the FT index, as an approximation to a daily chain index, below the direct arithmetic version fits in with the result of **5.5** above on the chain/direct ratio as a product of factors.

The factor at day t depends on the correlation between p_{t+1}/p_t and the quantity change from the base to day t. The peculiar portfolio strategy of the daily chain index, approximating to the FT index, is such that the quantity change is inverse to the price change up to day t. What of the short-run subsequent price change from day t to day $(t+1)$? The expectation is that a price which has had considerable rises in the past will continue to rise over one day ahead. Hence the correlation of the result of **5.5** tends to be negative; the *daily* chain (and the FT index) is to be expected to drift below the direct arithmetic version. This does no more than confirm (and explain) that the geometric form always lies below the arithmetic.

In the longer run, there may be an inverse relation between price changes of the past and those of (say) a year ahead, particularly at times when a 'bear' market is giving way to a 'bull' market or conversely. It is to be expected, therefore, that the *annual* Laspeyres chain index may sometimes fall below the direct arithmetic version but equally (as in 1959 or 1968) rise above it. Table 6.13 confirms this expectation. Indeed the annual chain index not only drifts but jumps ahead of the direct index in the 'bull' market of 1958–9, an upward movement which is reinforced in the next 'bull' market of 1967–8. By end-1968 the annual chain index is nearly 10% above the direct arithmetic version and some 30% above the geometric FT index.

It remains to compare the FT index and its arithmetic version with one or other of the index numbers related to portfolio management and particularly with those weighted by market capitalisation. The most useful comparison is with the daily index published by *The Times* since 1964, shown in total and for two subgroups of shares separately. One subgroup comprises the shares of the 50 largest industrial companies; the other relates to a sample of 100 companies capitalised at under £60 mn in 1964. *The Times* index is relevant to the management of a fixed portfolio of shares of larger companies, or of small companies, or of any combination of the two.

Table 6.14 is taken straight from Marks and Stuart (1971) Table 8 and compares *The Times* index runs, based on 2 June 1964, with both the original (geometric) version and the direct arithmetic version of the FT index with reference base switched to 2 June 1964. The differences between one index and another are large and variable over the seven years from 1964 to 1970, particularly in the 'bull' market of 1967–8 and the subsequent collapse in 1969–70. This is

TABLE 6.14

FT AND *THE TIMES* INDEX NUMBERS COMPARED,
2 JUNE 1964 = 100, 1964–70

| End-year | FT Index | | The Times *Index* | | |
	Geometric mean*	Arithmetic mean†	Larger companies	Smaller companies	Main index
1964	99·5	100·2	96·57	95·77	96·41
1965	100·9	102·7	99·92	103·67	100·62
1966	92·2	94·9	88·89	92·00	89·47
1967	115·6	124·7	116·32	121·60	117·35
1968	150·4	166·5	168·69	155·11	166·04
1969	121·0	140·1	143·01	132·71	140·91
1970	101·2	119·7	133·94	113·69	129·85

From Marks and Stuart (1971), Table 8

* Switched to 2 June 1964 as 100.
† Marks and Stuart index based on 2 June 1964 as 100.

surprising since most of the 30 FT index shares are also among the 50 shares of *The Times* larger-companies index. The fact that even the arithmetic version of the FT index differs from this component of *The Times* index illustrates that the weighting of a portfolio index can make a lot of difference in volatile stock markets.

A few broad conclusions stand out. Portfolio indices are many and various, and differences in their investment strategies are reflected in quite different performance, particularly in the boom and slump of the late 1960s. The geometric FT index remains what it was intended to be: a sensitive, short-run indicator of the mood of the market. It must lie below its arithmetic version; any portfolio manager should be able to 'beat' it.

7 Further Index-Number Problems

7.1 Sampling Aspects: Price Quotations

There are many problems which have been only partially solved in the theory and in the practice of index numbers and some of them can be conveniently considered in this last chapter. The first problem is that of the influence of sampling and other errors, first raised in **1.7** and in need of further examination. As an opening gambit we can quote Hofsten taking a 'hard line' on the British retail price index:

> Like any other statistics, the accuracy of an index number should be given in terms of its variance. . . . So far nobody seems to have attempted to produce any theory for index numbers in such terms, and it seems doubtful whether any such theory could be of any practical use. . . . The concept of an accurate index should be given up. Statisticians should not be forced to behave as if it were possible to make the index very accurate, if only much money is spent on its construction. If government policy requires great confidence in the index, the statisticians should not permit themselves to be used as hostage. Hofsten (1956), pp. 8, 14

What Hofsten is objecting to, in an index of prices at retail, is the *purposive* selection both of the commodity items to be priced and of the retail outlets for the pricing. In fact there is quite general agreement that a price index should be related to a specific aggregate such as consumers' expenditures and hence that the selection of *items* should be purposively directed at the aggregate. A comprehensive probability sample of items would be meddlesome and place in jeopardy the concept of a price index as (e.g.) the cost of maintaining some consumption level. The selection of *outlets* is something quite different and there is a strong case for a probability sample of outlets (e.g.) stratified by area and type. In an earlier publication

Hofsten seems to agree with this diagnosis:

> The selection of items . . . based on common sense and not on proper sampling methods . . . is no serious drawback. There is another sampling problem involved, the selection of retail outlets where the prices shall be collected. . . . To be satisfactory the price collection should be based upon an efficient sample of retail outlets. The construction of such a sample cannot be too difficult. Hofsten (1952), p. 42

True, as some countries (e.g. Sweden) have demonstrated. Nevertheless purposive selection of outlets, as well as of items, is still the rule rather than the exception. There is room for considerable improvement in the design of price index numbers.

For purposes of exposition, the following analysis relates to a monthly retail price index of direct or chain Laspeyres form, and the British retail price index described in Central Statistical Office (1967) is used as illustration. It takes up the story of the 'guidelines' laid down in **1.7**, and a clearly defined terminology will help here and later. An all-items price index can be disaggregated into more detailed indices at various levels: first for *groups* such as food or housing, then for *subgroups* such as dairy produce or vegetables, and finally for *sections* such as butter or margarine. Index weighting is taken down usually to section level but not further. The British index is weighted over 92 sections and below this level there are *items* specified in detail but not weighted, e.g. New Zealand butter, Danish butter. As a further elaboration, with particular reference to the definition of quality changes, take a *commodity* either as a whole section with its assigned weight (e.g. butter) or as a subdivision with no more than a rough weight (e.g. sausages in a section covering sausages, pies, canned meat and other meat products). A commodity then comprises many specific items only some of which are selected for pricing. An item subject to change in specification is termed a *variety* or a *quality*. The essential feature here is the specification and its alteration, which may be a switch as from New Zealand to Irish butter or a technical change as a pork sausage from 50 to 60% meat content.

An extensive analysis of the sampling problem in index-number construction is in a Staff Paper by P. J. McCarthy in Stigler (1961), following earlier work by Mudgett (1951), Adelman (1958) and Banerji (1959). The general recommendation is that more use should be made of probability sampling in practice, perhaps at the design stage, but certainly in the continuing price collection which keeps the index running. Purposive selection can hardly be avoided at this stage in getting the commodity make-up of the index down to section level, but there are possibilities of probability sampling worth exploration in the selection of specified-in-detail items for pricing. There would be difficulties in sampling design, e.g. on stratification of items by such factors as substitutability, but they are not insurmountable. In the continuing price collection, the initial selection of retail outlets for reporting needs to be supported by precise provision for substitution over time as 'births' and 'deaths' of outlets occur. Despite the rather lazy position many countries adopt, it is here that probability sampling can be used to great effect. Retail outlets are easily stratified by (e.g.) area and type, certainly enough for a stratified random sample of a fairly elaborate kind. Any good census of distribution or a comprehensive system of registration (e.g. for VAT) provides the essential frame.

Once probability sampling is used, a good part of the error in a price index calculation comes under control and a measure of precision for sampling variation can be attached to the index. It is only a matter of getting the sampling distribution, and its variance, for the estimator used (e.g. a price relative). The following results are taken from Cochran (1962). Write p_0 and p_t as the base and current price reported by a particular outlet for a specified item. Assume that a random sample of n outlets is drawn from an infinite frame and that the reported price quotations from each outlet are adjusted for quality changes (see **7.5–7.8**). Write $\bar{p}_0$ and s_0 in base period, and $\bar{p}_t$ and s_t currently, for the mean and standard deviation of prices over the n outlets. Then the best *estimator* of the price relative for the item from the sample of outlets is:

$$R_{0t} = \bar{p}_t / \bar{p}_0 \tag{1}$$

and for large n (say $n > 100$) the sampling distribution of R_{0t} is approximately *normal* with *sampling variance* given approximately by:

$$\text{var } R_{0t} = \frac{R_{0t}^2}{n} \left(\frac{s_0^2}{\bar{p}_0^2} + \frac{s_t^2}{\bar{p}_t^2} - 2\rho \frac{s_0 s_t}{\bar{p}_0 \bar{p}_t} \right) \tag{2}$$

when ρ is the correlation coefficient between p_0 and p_t over the outlets. In practice, price collections give all the data needed for (1) and (2) except (usually) for the value of ρ. The sample design is such that ρ is certainly positive and quite large; in the absence of other information, take $\rho = \frac{1}{2}$ in order not to understate the sampling variance. Then the 95% confidence interval for the (approximately) normal distribution of R_{0t} can be written from (1) and (2) as:

$$R_{0t} \pm 1 \cdot 96 \ SE \qquad \text{where } SE^2 = \text{var } R_{0t}$$

It is to be stressed that the best estimator (1) is the *ratio of sample means*. The alternative estimator as the *mean of sample ratios*, i.e. mean (p_t/p_0) over the n outlets, is known to have bias and often markedly so; it is *not consistent* in the sense that it does not tend to the population price relative (being estimated) as the sample size is increased indefinitely. On the other hand, the ratio (1) under certain (quite usual) circumstances is the best linear unbiased estimator of the population price relative.

For many of the food items in the price collections for the British retail price index the means and variances of the price quotations over all outlets are published and some of them are taken in Table 7.1 for illustration of the application of (1) and (2). It is no more than an illustration since the British index is based neither on

TABLE 7.1

FOOD PRICE QUOTATIONS: MEAN AND STANDARD
DEVIATION, 1973–4

Item	Number of quotations*	Mean price (p per lb)		Standard deviation (p)	
		Jan. 1973	Jan. 1974	Jan. 1973	Jan. 1974
	n	$\bar{p}_0$	$\bar{p}_t$	s_0	s_t
Butter, N.Z.	730	22·7	21·3	1·9	1·4
Danish	768	25·1	24·5	1·7	1·6
Margarine, standard	152	12·2	15·6	0·75	0·85
lower-priced	133	10·4	13·6	0·7	0·7
Lard	811	8·9	14·6	1·5	1·7

From Department of Employment *Gazette*

* Average of numbers used at the two dates.

probability samples of retail outlets nor on the ratio-of-means estimator (1). The price relatives to be estimated from Table 7.1 are of form $R_{0t} = 100 \ \bar{p}_t/\bar{p}_0$ for $t = $ January 1974 on the base January 1973, i.e. the last monthly price relative in the 1973/4 Laspeyres link in the chain index. The applications of (1) and (2) are set out in Table 7.2 where the estimates are built up into three sectional

TABLE 7.2

SAMPLING VARIANCE OF PRICE INDEX: BUTTER, MARGARINE AND LARD

Item and Section	Price relatives $R_{0t}=\dfrac{p_t}{p_0}100$	var R_{0t}	Section weights† Jan. 1973 w	Products $w\,R_{0t}$	w^2 var R_{0t}
Butter, N.Z.	93·8	0·0702			
Danish	97·6	0·0549			
Section: Butter*	95·7	0·0313	0·6	57·42	0·01127
Margarine, standard	127·9	0·3659			
lower-priced	130·8	0·4779			
Section: Margarine*	129·4	0·2110	0·2	25·88	0·00844
Section: Lard	164·0	0·7405	0·2	32·80	0·02962
Subgroup: Butter, margarine and lard			1·0	116·10	0·04933

From Table 7.1

* R_{0t} for section $=\frac{1}{2}$ sum of two individual price relatives; var $R_{0t}=\frac{1}{4}$ sum of two individual variances.

† Weights of retail price index.

index numbers and then by sectional weighting into the subgroup for butter, margarine and lard. The assumption, not always appropriate in practice, is made that the samples for different items are *independent*, bringing in the result that the variance of a weighted sum, with *given* weights w such that $\sum w = 1$, is the sum of the separate variances weighted with w^2. Of the three sections, one contains only a single item but the other two have pairs of items aggregated with equal internal weights ($w=\frac{1}{2}$ for each item). For the subgroup in the end:

Price index $\sum w\,R_{0t}$ $=116\cdot1$
Variance $\sum w^2$ var $R_{0t}=0\cdot049$
Standard error $\sqrt{\text{variance}}$ $=0\cdot22$

The best estimate of the index in January 1974 is 116·1% of January 1973 and the 95% confidence interval is $116\cdot1\pm1\cdot96\times0\cdot22=116\cdot1\pm0\cdot43$, so that we are 95% confident that the index is in the range from about 115·7 to about 116·5. A good approximation is about 116.

The precision of the all-items index can be built up in this way; it allows for *sampling errors* in the selection of outlets. There is, in addition, a great variety of *non-sampling errors* which have traditionally been treated by survey statisticians in the context of errors of response and non-response. It was not until Hansen,

Hurwitz and Bershad (1959) that an attempt was made to treat sampling and response errors together, to construct a model of their combined variances. The model has since been extended to give conditions for minimum mean-square error of all kinds. The general idea, rapidly becoming practicable, is to 'trade off' such non-sampling errors as those arising from inaccurate response against the well-documented sampling errors; see Fellegi and Sunter (1973) and Jabine and Tepping (1973).

7.2 Sampling Aspects: Weights

The main result on the effect of errors in weights, briefly summarised in **1.7,** is due to Bowley (1897, 1912) and it can be set out simply:

Given: a set of n observations on a variable x giving mean $\bar{x}$ and standard deviation s_x and on an associated weight w giving mean $\bar{w}$ and standard deviation s_w.

Assume: each x comes from an independent sample from its own population but with common variance, var x; similarly for w and the common variance, var w; and no correlation between x and w.

Then: the sampling distribution of the weighted mean:

$$y = \sum wx / \sum w \tag{1}$$

is approximately normal for large n and under certain (quite usual) circumstances has the approximate variance:

$$\left.\begin{array}{l} \text{var } y = A \text{ var } x + B \text{ var } w \\ \text{where} \quad A = \frac{1}{n}\left(1 + \frac{s_x^2}{\bar{x}^2}\right)\left(1 + \frac{s_w^2}{\bar{w}^2}\right) \text{ and } B = \frac{1}{n}\frac{s_x^2}{\bar{x}^2}\left(1 + \frac{s_w^2}{\bar{w}^2}\right) \end{array}\right\} \tag{2}$$

The mean or index (1) is in the usual shorthand notation. The interpretation of (2) proceeds for convenience in terms of a Laspeyres price index (1) where x is the price relative of a typical item and w is its expenditure weight. First note that $A > B$ in all cases, so that the errors in weights (var w) have *less* effect on y than the errors in price relatives (var x). Next, the critical factor in var y is seen to be the coefficient of variation $s_x/\bar{x}$ of the price relatives. If the price movements show a wide dispersion from the base to the current period, the coefficient is large and both terms in var y in (2) are substantial. Errors in weights have some effect, though less than those in price relatives. Finally, if price movements are not widely dispersed, then the coefficient $s_x/\bar{x}$ may be sufficiently small for B to be negligible compared with A in (2). It is under these circumstances that errors in weights can be neglected.

The whole result fails, however, if there is correlation between weights and price relatives. This can happen if there are one or two preponderant weights or (more usually) if items with large weights have marked price changes either way.

Two things must be checked in practice before it is safe to neglect errors in weights. One is the absence of substantial correlation between weights and price movements. If there is such a correlation it need not be fatal; it is an indication to proceed with caution. The other is that the dispersion of prices since the base period is not great. When some prices go up fast and others hardly move (or go down), then errors in weights can have some effect (though always less than errors in prices) on the precision of the price index. These cautionary comments can be illustrated in some actual cases.

The first case to look at is the highly simplified calculation of Table 7.2 where there is one dominant section (butter) with a price fall as opposed to price rises in the other two sections. The subgroup index is very sensitive to changes in the relative weight of butter. For example, if the true weight of butter is 70%, with 15% on each of the other sections, then a recalculation in Table 7.2 gives the true subgroup index as 111·0 and the estimated 116·1 is nearly 5% out. Fortunately, troubles of this kind, even when they arise, get lost in the calculation of the all-items index.

A less extreme case of the same kind is seen in the attempt in Table 3.3 to reconstruct a price index for retail sales by simply changing weights in the retail price index. Nothing can be done if the group price indexes are not appropriate but it is possible to run a check on the effect of errors in weights in view of the warning signal that there is one large group (food) with rapidly rising prices. Take the index in 1973 (1971 = 100) for illustration and calculate it with different sets of weights:

Group weights	Food	Alcoholic drink	Tobacco	Durables	Clothing	Miscellaneous goods
Cases: (a)	48·6	3·2	6·9	11·8	16·9	12·6
(b)	49	3	7	12	17	12
(c)	54	—	—	13	19	14

Here (a) is the case taken in Table 3.3, for present purposes assumed accurate. Of the alternatives, (b) just rounds off the weights and (c) assumes that no drink and tobacco are sold through the outlets of the retail sales index. Recalculating as in Table 3.3:

PRICE INDEX FOR RETAIL SALES,
1973 (1971 = 100)

Weights:	(a)	(b)	(c)
Non-food sales	110·7	111·0	112·5
All sales	117·8	117·9	119·4

This is the kind of situation where the accuracy of weights does matter – there is a strong correlation between weights and price changes, larger weights going with larger price increases. Even the omission of food, with the largest weight and price increase, does not stabilise the index. The conclusion of **3.3** to drop the index is confirmed.

A more straightforward case of a quantity (rather than a price) index provides a final example: the index of employment

$$Q_{0t}(p_0) = \frac{\sum p_0 q_t}{\sum p_0 q_0} = \frac{\sum w_0 \dfrac{q_t}{q_0}}{\sum w_0} \qquad (w_0 = p_0 q_0) \tag{3}$$

used in **6.8** with the data of Table 6.12. The q's here are numbers and the p's average earnings in various industries. The weights w_0 are approximate but errors in them should have little effect since changes in employment are seen in Table 6.12 to have only modest dispersion and a weak correlation with the weights. This can be tested by making two (rather extreme) variations in weights. First, put $p_0 = 1$ in (3) so that Q_{0t} becomes $\sum q_t / \sum q_0$, the change in numbers, making the index of employment 99·9 instead of the original 100·0 (Table 6·12). Next, put $w_0 = 1$ in (3) and Q_{0t} becomes the equi-weighted mean $\frac{1}{n}\sum q_t / q_0$, not shown in Table 6.12 but quickly calculated:

Industry	Employment, June 1973 (June 1972 = 100)	Industry	Employment, June 1973 (June 1972 = 100)
Food, drink, tobacco	100·4	Vehicles	102·5
Chemicals	98·8	Metal goods	100·0
Metal manufacture	100·0	Textiles	98·7
Engineering:		Clothing, leather	96·0
Mechanical	97·9	Paper, printing	99·4
Electrical, etc.	101·8	Other	100·8
Shipbuilding	99·4		
		Total	1,195·7

Hence the equi-weighted $Q_{0t} = 1,195 \cdot 7/12 = 99 \cdot 6$, again little different from the original $100 \cdot 0$. The fact that the original (weighted) index is slightly greater is the result of the fact that what correlation there is between quantity relatives and weights is positive.

7.3 Best Linear Index: Two-situation Case

The analysis of **4.7** of the discrepancy between the Laspeyres and Paasche runs suggests that a run be sought which is a 'best fit' to the data in some sense or other. The following development, which is perhaps of more theoretical than practical importance, takes up the suggestion. In the case of two years 0 and 1, the 2×2 value matrix transforms by division by the leading entry into a 2×2 matrix **D**:

$$\begin{bmatrix} \sum p_0 q_0 & \sum p_0 q_1 \\ \sum p_1 q_0 & \sum p_1 q_1 \end{bmatrix} \text{ giving } \mathbf{D} = \begin{bmatrix} 1 & Q \\ P & V \end{bmatrix} = \begin{bmatrix} 1 & Q \\ P & PQ(1 + \rho) \end{bmatrix}$$

where V is the value change, P and Q index numbers of Laspeyres form and ρ the discrepancy between the Paasche and Laspeyres forms. Pose the question: is ρ as small as possible? If so, P and Q are the indexes of best fit to the data. If not, two other forms are to be sought to make ρ a minimum and so to fit better than P and Q.

Put up price and quantity index numbers p and q to fit to the data as given by **D**. A perfect fit and satisfaction of the factor-reversal test ($pq = V$) require **D** to equal

$$\mathbf{D}^* = \begin{bmatrix} 1 & q \\ p & pq \end{bmatrix}$$

Since **D** and **D*** in fact differ, write the difference matrix:

$$\mathbf{E} = \mathbf{D}^* - \mathbf{D} = \begin{bmatrix} 0 & q - Q \\ p - P & pq - PQ(1 + \rho) \end{bmatrix}$$

and the usual measure of difference as the sum of squares of the entries in **E**:

$$d^2 = (p - P)^2 + (q - Q)^2 + \{pq - PQ(1 + \rho)\}^2 \tag{1}$$

The *Best Linear index numbers* are p and q for minimum d^2.

Note that, if $p = P$ and $q = Q$ are optimal, then $d = PQ\rho$ and so ρ is a minimum. But this won't do since ρ is not generally minimal. The necessary conditions for minimum d^2 are that the partial derivative of (1) with respect to p and q are both zero for given P, Q and ρ:

$$(p - P) + q\{pq - PQ(1 + \rho)\} = (q - Q) + p\{pq - PQ(1 + \rho)\} = 0 \quad (2)$$

Only approximate solutions of (2) are possible and the one to pursue arises when ρ is small enough to enable p and q to be written approximately in ρ, ignoring ρ^2. For this, try $p = P(1 + \alpha\rho)$ and $q = Q(1 + \beta\rho)$ when α and β are independent of ρ. To anticipate, if α and β turn out to be proper fractions, then p and q fall between the Laspeyres and Paasche forms: $P < p < P(1 + \rho)$, $Q < q < Q(1 + \rho)$ if $\rho > 0$. On substituting for p and q in (2) and dropping ρ^2 and higher powers:

$$P\alpha + PQ^2(\alpha + \beta - 1) = Q\beta + P^2Q(\alpha + \beta - 1) = 0$$

giving $\quad \alpha = \dfrac{Q^2}{1 + P^2 + Q^2} \quad$ and $\quad \beta = \dfrac{P^2}{1 + P^2 + Q^2}$

and these are proper fractions as required.

The conclusion is that, though the Best Linear index is *not* either the Laspeyres or the Paasche form, it *does* lie between them in the two-situation case. This is a comforting thought but of limited value; the case of practical utility is that of a run of index numbers.

7.4 Best Linear Index: General Case

Consider price/quantity data in a closed period of $(k + 1)$ years $t = 0, 1, 2, \ldots k$, and seek two index runs of best fit to the whole block of data:

$$\left.\begin{array}{ll} \text{Price:} & p(0), p(1), p(2), \ldots p(k) \\ \text{Quantity:} & q(0), q(1), q(2), \ldots q(k) \end{array}\right\} \quad (1)$$

When found, these optimal runs will be of index numbers which depend on *all* years, both earlier and later than the year of the index. Note that the runs (1) are not expressed in terms of any reference base; they are akin to constant-quantity runs of price and constant-price runs of quantity. They match, not **D**, but the original value matrix:

$$\mathbf{V} = \begin{bmatrix} \sum p_0 q_0 & \sum p_0 q_1 & \cdots & \sum p_0 q_k \\ \sum p_1 q_0 & \sum p_1 q_1 & \cdots & \sum p_1 q_k \\ \cdots & \cdots & \cdots & \cdots \\ \sum p_k q_0 & \sum p_k q_1 & \cdots & \sum p_k q_k \end{bmatrix}$$

and if (1) provides a perfect fit V will also equal:

$$\mathbf{pq}' = \begin{bmatrix} p(0)q(0) & p(0)q(1) & \ldots & p(0)q(k) \\ p(1)q(0) & p(1)q(1) & \ldots & p(1)q(k) \\ \ldots & \ldots & \ldots & \ldots \\ p(k)q(0) & p(k)q(1) & \ldots & p(k)q(k) \end{bmatrix}$$

where $\mathbf{pq}'$ in the matrix notation is the product of the price run as a column vector $\mathbf{p}$ and the quantity run as a row vector $\mathbf{q}'$. The matrices V and $\mathbf{pq}'$ differ in practice and the object of the exercise is to choose $\mathbf{p}$ and $\mathbf{q}$ of (1) to minimise:

Sum of squares d^2 of entries in $\mathbf{E} = \mathbf{V} - \mathbf{pq}'$ (2)

The optimal vectors $\mathbf{p}$ and $\mathbf{q}$ are the *Best Linear index runs*.

The solution of the problem requires some well-known but advanced linear algebra and the notation and results assumed below are to be found in a text such as that of Yaari (1971). First, d^2 of (2) is the sum of the diagonal elements, the *trace* tr, of the matrix $\mathbf{EE}'$, i.e. the minimum sought is of:

$$d^2 = \text{tr } \mathbf{EE}' \qquad \text{where} \qquad \mathbf{E} = \mathbf{V} - \mathbf{pq}'$$

On expansion: $d^2 = \text{tr } \mathbf{VV}' - 2\mathbf{p}'\mathbf{Vq} + \lambda^2$

when λ^2 is the product of $\mathbf{p}'\mathbf{p}$ and $\mathbf{q}'\mathbf{q}$, each a sum of squares. The necessary conditions for min d^2 are that the partial derivatives with respect to $\mathbf{p}$ and $\mathbf{q}$ are both zero, reducing to $\mathbf{Vq} - (\mathbf{q}'\mathbf{q})\mathbf{p} = \mathbf{V}'\mathbf{p} - (\mathbf{p}'\mathbf{p})\mathbf{q} = 0$ and finally yielding:

$$\mathbf{VV}'\mathbf{p} = \lambda^2 \mathbf{p} \qquad \text{and} \qquad \mathbf{V}'\mathbf{Vq} = \lambda^2 \mathbf{q} \qquad (3)$$

It remains to interpret (3) from which the Best Linear index runs $\mathbf{p}$ and $\mathbf{q}$ are to be derived. The results needed from (e.g.) Yaari (1971) relate to the *characteristic equations* of the given square matrices $\mathbf{VV}'$ and $\mathbf{V}'\mathbf{V}$, both real, symmetric and of order $(k+1) \times (k+1)$. The characteristic equation of $\mathbf{VV}'$ is $\mathbf{VV}' - \lambda^2 \mathbf{I} = 0$, giving a root λ^2 as an *eigenvalue* of $\mathbf{VV}'$ and an *eigenvector* $\mathbf{p}$ such that $(\mathbf{VV}' - \lambda^2\mathbf{I})\mathbf{p} = 0$. Since this is the first equation of (3), λ^2 is to interpreted as the λ^2 of (3) and $\mathbf{p}$ as the Best Linear price index. The other best-fitting index $\mathbf{q}$ follows similarly as an eigenvector of $\mathbf{V}'\mathbf{V}$ which corresponds to the same eigenvalue λ^2. All this holds together since $\mathbf{V}$ given by the data provides matrices $\mathbf{VV}'$ and $\mathbf{V}'\mathbf{V}$ having the same diagonal elements with a positive sum; so there is at least one positive eigenvalue and λ^2 is taken as the largest of them.

This theoretical result does not give a general formula for the Best Linear index runs; it is a computational procedure from which the runs are estimated in any numerical example. It does, however, provide the general assurance that the runs do exist. The theory sketched here is due to Theil (1960) with some links back to earlier work by Stuval (1957). There are later developments in the work of Kloek and de Wit (1961), Banerji (1961, 1963) and others.

The derivation of the Best Linear index runs from actual price/quantity data over a period of quite modest length is a matter of heavy computation with iterative procedures. It is certainly not a practical proposition for an index published regularly but it is feasible in an econometric study of a given period when a computer programme is already set up for estimation of macro-economic relations. Illustrative examples are available in the literature; Kloek and de Wit (1961) applied the technique to Dutch trade statistics in 1921–36 and, more recently, Jazairi (1971) has given an application to Egyptian trade in the post-war period (1954–63). In the course of this work the Best Linear index runs were found to display bias and, to overcome this deficiency, a variant was developed and described as the Best Linear Average Unbiased (BLAU) index runs.

7.5 Quality Changes: Prices versus Unit Values

The last problem taken up here is a very wide one: the treatment of changes in the varieties or qualities of goods available on the market and the related changes in tastes of consumers as represented in shifts in their preference scales. For expository purposes the main case considered is a temporal price index, and the corresponding implied quantity index, subject to a continuous process of change over time in which one variety is replaced by another. All that is said applies to comparisons between groups, regions or countries, indeed with even greater force in view of the wide dispersion often found between the Laspeyres and Paasche forms, e.g. in inter-country comparisons (6.5).

Something has already been said on one aspect of the problem: whether to use price quotations or unit values in a price index, e.g. of import and export prices or of wage rates and average earnings. To make a practical 'go' of a pure price index based on actual quotations requires a nice balance between items specified in over-elaborate detail and rather vague instructions to price reporters. At one extreme the specification is so 'tight' that reporting breaks down even in an index chained annually; at the other extreme a good deal of quality change is allowed to creep into the price index. To the extent that a price index is successfully constructed from price quotations, the corresponding implied quantity index, e.g. of real imports and exports or of employment, incorporates the quality changes. Since the two index numbers multiply to the value change, if quality variations are kept out of the price index, they must 'pop up' in the quantity index.

This is surely the result to be desired in general. But it is possible and sometimes desirable to incorporate some or all of the quality changes in the price factor, specifically through the use of unit values instead of price quotations. If all quality changes are in prices, then the implied quantity index measures volume in a narrow sense, e.g. employment by numbers at work. In any case unit values are tempting substitutes for prices; they are often easily obtained from the data and look like prices, e.g. in the same units such as £ per ton or p per head per hour. In using them, however, it must always be explicitly recognised that they reflect both changes in quoted prices and shifts in the varieties bought and sold. How widespread the quality changes are in the unit-value index depends on the fineness of the commodity classification; quality changes are included only in so far as they occur within the categories of the classification.

The best-known examples of a unit-value index, either as a proxy for a price index or in its own right, are in the statistics of external trade (3.7). The quality changes which are swept into the index numbers are circumscribed by the degree to which the standard classification (SITC) is taken down to fine categories. In Table 3.15, for example, quality changes *within* a category such as 'motor spirit' or 'kerosene, etc.' are carried over into the unit-value index of fuel imports or exports; only shifts *between* such categories are reflected in the corresponding volume index. This is perhaps not at all bad in practice.

A less obvious example is in the analysis of economic measures of employment (6·8). If the quantity index is based on numbers employed, then the matching price index is one of average earnings rather than wage rates. For these to be generally acceptable in an economic context, if not in other connections, the industrial/occupational classification would need to be much finer than is usual in practice (see Table 6.12).

7.6 Quality Changes: Technical Factors

It is evident that quality changes are much too complex in nature to be left to a simple matter of accepting or rejecting a unit-value index. A less superficial analysis is needed, and one based firmly on economic-statistical theory. The treatment which follows concentrates attention first on technical aspects of quality change before passing on to the economic-theoretic approach by means of household production theory. It will be limited to quality changes involving any *substitution* of one item for another within a commodity category. This may be no more than a pork sausage with 60% meat for one with only 50% meat, or a seat in a selected ABC cinema for one in an Odeon. It may also be a new product or model coming in to replace an old one, e.g. a detergent for a soap powder or a colour TV set for a black-and-white one. There are related problems not covered by the treatment, e.g. extending an existing list of commodities in an index by adding new ones without knocking out old ones, an adjustment which is best undertaken when the index is rebased. The related matter of changes in consumer tastes, however, is left over for later consideration (7·8).

The classical approach to the problem of adjusting a price index for quality changes is that of Hofsten (1952) and his methods have been widely adopted by official statisticians and developed in practice (e.g.) by Nicholson (1967).

Take the case when one item 'a' priced in a commodity group is replaced at time t by a new item 'b', requiring adjusted price relatives to bridge the gap from time $(t-1)$ to time $(t+1)$ opened up by the change at time t. The old item provides the price relative up to $(t-1)$ and the new one from $(t+1)$; something needs to be done in between. Hofsten took the reaction of consumers (according to their preference scales) into account, but he had in mind more the objective or technical aspect and specifically an indicator of quality, measuring the various amounts of service provided by a range of varieties of the commodity. Even so, a change from item a to item b is a complex affair influencing the prices and purchases of a wide range of commodities on the market. The Hofsten case simplifies the situation by assuming that the item substitution is a quality improvement (deterioration) expressed as an increased (decreased) service to be got from the item and equivalent to a reduction (increase) in the price of the item and in no other prices. The second of these constraints can be quite serious.

Hence, a technical coefficient g is sought, a constant independant of all prices and purchases, so that one unit of the new item b is equivalent, on the single criterion of quality assumed, to g units of the old item a. The coefficient g is an *index of quality*; $g > 1$ indicates an improvement and $g < 1$ a deterioration. Further, if $g > 1$, the quality improvement is equivalent to a corresponding price reduction in the new item and to no other price changes, and similarly for a deterioration ($g < 1$). For example, if $g = 2\cdot0$, the new item is twice as good as the old and twice the price.

Write $p_a(t)$ and $p_b(t)$ as the prices of the two items at time t, whether or not they are actually quoted on the market. Then by equivalence in the Hofsten case:

$$p_b(t) = g p_a(t) \tag{1}$$

and the run of successive price relative for the commodity item from one time to the next is:

$$\cdots \quad \frac{p_{t-1}}{p_{t-2}} = \frac{p_a(t-1)}{p_a(t-2)}; \quad \frac{p_t}{p_{t-1}} = \frac{p_b(t)}{g p_a(t-1)}; \quad \frac{p_{t+1}}{p_t} = \frac{p_b(t+1)}{p_b(t)} \quad \cdots \tag{2}$$

The result (2) shows how this particular item is handled in the price index when the substitution of b for a is made at time t. The price relative p_t/p_{t-1} at the change-over point can be interpreted in familiar index-number terms as the straight change in unit value $p_b(t)/p_a(t-1)$ deflated by the quality index g. The application of (2) to a direct index on a base 0, often remote, requires that allowance be made for several substitutions on the way. If there are k substitutions, if the base item had price p_0 and if the current (kth) item has price $p_k(t)$, then the price relative is:

$$\frac{p_t}{p_0} = \frac{p_k(t)}{g_1 g_2 \cdots g_k p_0}$$

for this particular commodity item in the direct index.

The practical question is: how to get an estimate of g from market data? In a perfectly competitive market, the conditions for equilibrium require that three ratios are made equal: the ratio of prices of two commodities available on the market, the ratio of their marginal costs to the producer and the marginal rate of substitution to the consumer. In practice, markets are not perfectly competitive and the two items substituted may not even be quoted together at any one time. There are three practical possibilities to consider and they are taken in turn.

(i) *Splicing*. This is a method applicable when both items a and b are available on the market and the time t is that judged to be one of equilibrium. The quoted prices $p_a(t)$ and $p_b(t)$ are equivalent, in the sense that their ratio equals the marginal rate of substitution to the consumer, and the index g is given directly by (1). The method in practice is the standard one of splicing. The entry in (2) for time t, on substituting from (1), becomes simply $p_a(t)/p_a(t-1)$ and leap-frogging over the change-over:

$$\frac{p_{t+1}}{p_{t-1}} = \frac{p_t}{p_{t-1}} \times \frac{p_{t+1}}{p_t} = \frac{p_a(t)}{p_a(t-1)} \times \frac{p_b(t+1)}{p_b(t)}$$

Hence, *before* the substitution the commodity price relative is given by the old item a and *after* the change the price changes in the new item b are spliced on.

This is the method commonly adopted by official statisticians, provided only that market prices are available for both items being substituted, and subject to their judgement that the prices are in equilibrium, the items being 'equally attractive' to purchasers. Many examples could be quoted of appropriate use of the method. A simple case is when a manufacturer introduces a new detergent package but keeps the old product on the shelves alongside the new for a limited period. A more sophisticated example could arise in booking theatre seats. It may be that the original seat price used in a price index is the price in the upper circle but that the theatre is planning to reconstruct this part of the house. A switch is made to the seat price in the stalls and the quality index g is just the ratio of stalls to upper-circle seat prices in what is judged to be a 'normal' relation at the time t of change-over. (g can vary and still be 'normal' over time, e.g. about 2 in London in the 1950s but nearer 3 in the 1970s). The method is clearly more applicable to non-durables than to consumer durables, such as refrigerators, bought infrequently by any one consumer. Nicholson (1967) shows that the splicing method can be very rough and ready for durables and that the price index tends to have an upward bias for this reason.

(ii) *Cost changes*. The index g may be estimated from the supply side as the ratio of the marginal cost of item b to that of item a, whether or not this is consistent with consumer preferences in an imperfectly competitive market. This method is not infrequently used by official statisticians as the easy way out when the substitution of item b for item a is made without an overlap. Formula (1) is then not available and the cost-estimate of g is substituted straight into (2) and so into the price index.

The method is immediately applicable to a wide range of items for which producers' costs can be obtained, e.g. proprietary foodstuffs or consumer durables subject to rapid model changes. The Bureau of Labor Statistics has used the method for some items in the U.S. consumer price index, and noted – and not with approval – by Stigler (1961) as implying an equivalence between quality and production costs. Many authorities have raised objections, e.g. Griliches (1961) who comments that costs may overstate an improvement in quality by accepting as 'improvements' whatever costs more, irrespective of consumers' views, and Nicholson (1967) who has remarked on the peculiar difficulty of allowing for changes in fashion items on a cost criterion. Such objections are reinforced if, as does happen, average costs are used in estimating g instead of marginal costs.

(iii) *Quality indicators.* Most in line with the Hofsten case is the determination of the index g as a single proxy indicator of quality. The 'quality' of varieties of a commodity is not directly measurable but certain *characteristics* $z_1, z_2, z_3, \ldots$ can be picked out which are both measurable and correlated with 'quality', e.g. the characteristics of durability and reliability. The Hofsten case assumes that one characteristic z is enough and that the quality index $g = z_b/z_a$, the ratio of the amounts of the characteristic possessed by items a and b. This is supported by writing equivalent prices $p_a(t)$ and $p_b(t)$, whether or not quoted on the market, as having the same ratio g. The implication here is that there is at time t a *quality price* $c(t)$ attached to the characteristic z so that

$$p_a(t) = c(t)z_a; \quad p_b(t) = c(t)z_b; \quad \text{and so} \quad \frac{p_b(t)}{p_a(t)} = \frac{z_b}{z_a} = g \tag{3}$$

Consequently (1) holds: $p_b(t) = gp_a(t)$ not in market prices but in equivalent prices implied by the amounts of the quality characteristic z possessed by the items.

There are many cases in practice where the one-characteristic method works well enough, e.g. the meat content of a pork sausage or the number of matches per box. The index $g = 1\cdot2$ in (3) then implies, for example, a raising of the meat content from 50 to 60%, or the number of matches from 75 to 90 per box, and a similar increase in the equivalent price per lb of sausages or per box of matches. There may even be more fanciful applications. Consider a price which is the admission charge to the ground of a selected football club, say Queen's Park Rangers. Suppose the club is promoted in year t to the First Division of the Football League. There is a quality improvement which may well be measured by a single characteristic: ground attendance. The index g can then be estimated as the ratio of average attendances in year t at First and Second Division matches.

The stage is now set for an extension of the method to allow for several and not just one indicator of quality. Result (3) needs to be developed to give a relation of the *market price* of a variety to the *quality prices* of the various characteristics which describe the variety. The concept of quality prices as 'shadow' prices behind the prices of items on the market was introduced by Houthakker (1952). But the idea of their statistical derivation by regression techniques has a longer history from Court (1939) and Stone (1956) to recent work by Griliches (1961), Adelman and Griliches (1961) and others.

Take m characteristics of the quality of varieties of a given commodity and write p for the market price of a variety with a particular combination of characteristics. The relation assumed as an extension of (3) is then written:

$$p = c_0 + c_1 z_1 + c_2 z_2 + \ldots + c_m z_m \quad \text{at time } t \tag{4}$$

where $z_1, z_2, \ldots z_m$ is the bundle of characteristics possessed by the variety and where $c_1, c_2, \ldots c_m$ are the quality prices. All prices, the c's and the p's, vary over time. There are many examples of commodities for which the relation (4) needs to be taken, particularly among consumer durables. The commodity could be a colour TV set and there are many varieties actually or potentially available on the market, distinguished by and with prices dependent on such characteristics as $z_1 =$ quality of image (by number of lines); $z_2 =$ screen size (in square inches); $z_3 =$ quality of the sound (on some technical measure); and so on through quality of colour, durability and reliability.

Multiple-regression techniques applied to cross-section data on prices and characteristics of varieties at time t serve to estimate the quality prices, $c_1, c_2, \ldots c_m$, in (4). The 'state of the art' is described in Griliches (1971). There are two ways of using (4), estimated from the data, to adjust a price index for quality changes. One is to estimate the quality index g for the substitution of item a by item b at time t. From the bundles of characteristics possessed by a and by b, (4) gives $p_a(t)$ and $p_b(t)$, and hence $g = p_b(t)/p_a(t)$. The adjusted sequence of price relatives for the commodity is then given by (2) for insertion in the price index. The other use of (4) is to estimate a price relative p_t/p_0 for the direct price index base-weighted on year 0. This is in the spirit of a base-weighted index; the bundle of characteristics of the item selected in year 0, with price p_0, is specified and substituted in (4) to give the current price p_t of an unchanged item. The estimate avoids any reference to quality changes which may occur between the base year and time t.

Another application of (4) can be noticed in passing. A regression estimation of (4) can be made from a combination of time-series and cross-section data provided that 'dummy' variables are added to the equation to sweep in changes in p over time, taken here as from year to year from annual data. A quality-adjusted run of annual price relatives for the commodity item considered then drops out of the regression equation as the sequence of coefficients of the 'dummy' variables (all quality characteristics z_1, z_2, ... z_m held constant). This application derives the run of price relatives, adjusted for all quality changes, at one 'go' and it avoids the estimation of g for formulae such as (1) and (2). Griliches (1971) gives an example in his Table 3.4 for prices of passenger cars, from U.S. data over the period 1954–60. Estimation of a whole run from one block of data in this way is subject to the same limitations in practice as the Best Linear index of **7.4**.

These uses of the regression model (4) put us at some risk of running ahead too fast. In particular the adjustment of a price index for quality changes is done separately item by item; every time an item has a quality change, the appropriate quality index g is estimated in order to correct its price relative. It is just assumed that there are no changes either in other prices or in the weights of the index. This is far too restrictive an assumption in any practical situation; there are bound to be indirect and cross-effects of any quality change. Progress can only be made, however, by laying a more elaborate and economic-theoretic basis for analysis and an attempt to do this is made below. In the end, it will appear that the one-price adjustment for quality change is really valid only in one simple case.

7.7 Quality Changes: Household Production Theory

A closer link is needed between the quality-adjustment of a price index and the preference scale of a consumer or household than the expected equality between the index g and the marginal rate of substitution under competitive conditions. The position reached, at the end of **7·6**, can be developed by making a clear-cut separation between *market commodities* and their varieties on the one hand and the *quality characteristics* which actually meet the household needs on the other hand. The theoretical model now developed has two corresponding and quite separate pieces: the *budget constraint* imposed on the household purchases of market commodities out of a given income, and the ordinal *utility function* expressing the household preferences for the *quality characteristics* in meeting household needs. The two pieces need to be linked together and a convenient way of achieving this is to take household consumption as an economic activity, similar to industrial production, in which inputs of market commodities purchased give rise to the satisfaction of needs as outputs. The technical relation between inputs and outputs must be specified and it can be described as the *household production function*. This function is similar to (e.g.) the production function of a manufacturing firm; whereas the firm transforms inputs into outputs on the factory floor, the household makes the transformation from purchase of commodities into satisfaction of needs in the home, e.g. in the preparing and cooking which goes on in the kitchen.

A household production model of this kind was first formulated by Lancaster (1966) and Muth (1966) and it is worth while quoting their own general descriptions:

> We assume that consumption is an activity in which goods . . . are inputs and in which output is a collection of characteristics. . . . The personal element in consumer choice arises in the choice between collections of characteristics only, not in the allocation of characteristics to the goods. Lancaster (1966), p. 133.

> Commodities purchased on the market by consumers are inputs into the production within the household . . . characterised by a conventional production function. The (qualities) produced, in turn, are arguments of a conventional utility function of the household. Muth (1966), p. 699

In a formulation of a static model at a given time t, write $x_1, x_2, \ldots$

x_n for purchases of n market commodities at market prices p_1, $p_2, \ldots p_n$ and yielding amounts $z_1, z_2, \ldots z_m$ of m quality characteristics. Denote household income and expenditure by y, taken as equal with saving assumed away. The model is then:

Household production function
$$F(x_1, x_2, \ldots x_n;\ z_1, z_2, \ldots z_m) = 0$$
Budget constraint $\qquad p_1 x_1 + p_2 x_2 + \ldots + p_n x_n = y$
Utility function $\qquad u = u\,(z_1, z_2, \ldots z_m)$

As a special case, the one mainly pursued here, break the relation of household production into m separate functions, one for each characteristic:

$$z_1 = f_1(x_1, x_2, \ldots x_n);\ z_2 = f_2(z_1, x_2, \ldots x_n);\ \ldots \qquad (1)$$

which implies non-substitutability between quality characteristics. It is no great constraint to assume that, when inputs increase in a given proportion, so do outputs. The functions are then homogeneous of degree one. Lancaster goes on to take $f_1, f_2, \ldots$ in (1) as linear in the x's, the *Lancaster Linear Model*. Muth, however, was more interested in the case when the arguments of $f_1, f_2, \ldots$ are non-overlapping sub-sets of the x's.

It is to be stressed that the model is so set up that the x's are purchases of *commodities*, not of varieties, and *quality change* is now a technical matter to be sought in a shift in the form of the production function. For example, the x's include various consumer durables (refrigerators, TV sets and so on) in whatever models are available on the market at the prices given by the p's. The household production function translates them into quality characteristics; if there is a quality change, the function is altered in form.

The following exposition takes for simplicity the case of three market commodities (x_1, x_2 and x_3) and two characteristics (z_1 and z_2). The extension to the general case is easily made. The model of the household as a utility-maximiser is then to be expressed in programming terms: given total expenditure y and market prices p_1, p_2 and p_3, determine purchases x_1, x_2 and x_3 to convert into characteristics for maximum utility:

$$\left. \begin{array}{ll} \max u = u(z_1, z_2) & \text{subject to} \quad y = p_1 x_1 + p_2 x_2 + p_3 x_3 \\ & \text{and} \qquad\qquad F(x_1, x_2, x_3;\ z_1, z_2) = 0 \end{array} \right\} \qquad (2)$$

The programme is best solved in two stages.

Stage (i): take z_1 and z_2 as given objectives and fix x_1, x_2 and x_3 to minimise expenditure y at given prices p_1, p_2 and p_3:

$$\min y = p_1 x_1 + p_2 x_2 + p_3 x_3 \quad \text{subject to } F(x_1, x_2, x_3; z_1, z_2) = 0 \quad (3)$$

The necessary conditions are that the ratios $\dfrac{\partial F}{\partial x_1} : \dfrac{\partial F}{\partial x_2} : \dfrac{\partial F}{\partial x_3}$ are made equal to the given price ratios $p_1 : p_2 : p_3$ and with (3) they give the x's and minimum expenditure:

$$\text{Expenditure function} \quad y = y (p_1, p_2, p_3; z_1, z_2) \quad (4)$$

If y is given, (4) can be interpreted as a relation between optimal z_1 and z_2 in the sense that these quality characteristics are got with minimum expenditure equal to the given expenditure. The relation can be shown as the *frontier curve AB* in the two dimensions of Fig. 7.1. The curve is a 'frontier' in the sense that it encloses all the

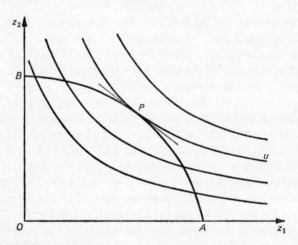

FIG. 7.1 Frontier curve

points representing combinations of z_1 and z_2 which can be achieved, given prices and total expenditure. It can be assumed to be concave to the origin. Since F is assumed to be homogeneous of degree one, it follows that (4) is also homogeneous of degree one in z_1 and z_2 so that by the well-known Euler's Theorem:

$$y = z_1 \frac{\partial y}{\partial z_1} + z_2 \frac{\partial y}{\partial z_2} \quad (5)$$

The ratio of $\dfrac{\partial y}{\partial z_1}$ to $\dfrac{\partial y}{\partial z_2}$ is the slope of the tangent at the relevant point P on the frontier curve AB. It is to be noticed that the position and slope of this curve depends not only on the market prices but also on the form of F. Hence quality changes, which are expressed through alterations in F, are shown by a shifting frontier curve AB.

Stage (ii): the programme (2) is completed by fixing z_1 and z_2 in the expenditure function (4) to maximise the utility level at given prices and total expenditure:

$$\max u = u(z_1, z_2) \quad \begin{aligned} &\text{subject to } y = y(p_1, p_2, p_3; z_1, z_2) \\ &\text{and given } p_1, p_2, p_3 \text{ and } y \end{aligned} \Bigg\} \tag{6}$$

The necessary condition is that the marginal rate of substitution $\left(\text{the ratio } \dfrac{\partial u}{\partial z_1} : \dfrac{\partial u}{\partial z_2}\right)$ equals the ratio $\dfrac{\partial y}{\partial z_1} : \dfrac{\partial y}{\partial z_2}$. The optimal position in stage (ii) and hence for the whole programme is best shown in the diagrammatic terms of Fig. 7.1. The marginal rate of substitution is the slope of the tangent to the indifference curve at some utility level u. The ratio $\dfrac{\partial y}{\partial z_1} : \dfrac{\partial y}{\partial z_2}$ is the slope of the tangent to the frontier curve AB. The optimal position occurs at the point P when the curve AB touches one of the indifference curves. The properties of the optimum are then clear: z_1 and z_2 are given by the co-ordinates of P in terms of the given values of the market prices p_1, p_2 and p_3 and of expenditure y. Hence u is so given, as the *indirect utility function* $u = u(p_1, p_2, p_3, y)$, and its inverse is the *expenditure function*:

$$y = y(p_1, p_2, p_3, u) \tag{7}$$

which simply give the minimum expenditure to get to the utility level u at given market prices.

To apply all this to the anlysis of quality changes, it is necessary to introduce one further concept: the *quality prices* as 'shadow' prices of quality characteristics behind the observed market prices. The ratio of quality price $\pi_1 : \pi_2$ represents the equilibrium value of the marginal rate of substitution between z_1 and z_2 and this is found as $\dfrac{\partial y}{\partial z_1} : \dfrac{\partial y}{\partial z_2}$ at stage (ii). The relation (5) then shows that π_1 can be taken as $\dfrac{\partial y}{\partial z_1}$ and π_2 as $\dfrac{\partial y}{\partial z_2}$ (and not only proportional) giving on substitution into (5) the result:

$$y = \pi_1 z_1 + \pi_2 z_2 \tag{8}$$

showing that the quality prices are such that total expenditure is split into 'expenditure' on the quality characteristics at the quality prices. Hence, from the point of view of quality changes in a price index, the relations to be used are *not* those on the commodity market; but they are concerned rather with quality characteristics and quality prices as represented in Fig. 7.1. A quality change shifts the position of the frontier curve AB and hence shifts the point P and the corresponding values of z_1, z_2, π_1 and π_2.

A quality-adjusted price index is then to be derived on the lines of the constant-utility price index of **2.8**, but with reference to quality characteristics and prices. Fix an initial utility level u_0 so that by (7) the expenditure is $y_0 = y(p_{10}, p_{20}, p_{30}, u_0)$ in terms of initial *market* prices but also by (8) as $y_0 = \pi_{10} z_{10} + \pi_{20} z_{20}$ in terms of the initial *quality* prices and the optimal values of the quality characteristics. Take, in another situation, different sets of prices and, in particular, new quality prices π_{11} and π_{21}. Define the minimum expenditure y_1 to remain at the utility level u_0 at the new prices and hence the quality-adjusted price index $I_{01}(u_0)$ at the u_0 level. Exactly as in **2.8**, and finally making the extension to any number of characteristics, in the usual shorthand notation:

$$I_{01}(u_0) = \frac{y_1}{y_0} < \frac{\pi_{11} z_{10} + \pi_{21} z_{20}}{\pi_{10} z_{10} + \pi_{20} z_{20}}$$

and generally:

$$I_{01}(u_0) < \frac{\sum \pi_1 z_0}{\sum \pi_0 z_0} \quad \text{of Laspeyres form} \tag{9}$$

The problem in the application of (9), apart from that of aggregation over a group of consumers (which is always with us), is to specify characteristics as a technical job and then to estimate the quality prices. The answer would seem to lie with a regression estimate as in **7.6**, giving coefficients to be interpreted as quality prices; this is the method followed in recent work by Griliches (1971) and others. There is one snag: whereas the *market* prices used in the corresponding analysis of **2.8** are the *constants* of a budget *line* tangential to an indifference curve, the *quality* prices in Fig. 7.1 come from the point P where a *curve AB* touches an indifference curve and so are *variable* with $z_1, z_2, \ldots$. The regression equation, however, estimates the quality prices as constants.

There is no difficulty in one special case, that of the *Lancaster Linear Model* where the household production functions (1) are linear in all x's. In our expository case:

$$z_1 = z_{11}x_1 + z_{12}x_2 + z_{13}x_3 \text{ and } z_2 = z_{21}x_1 + z_{22}x_2 + z_{23}x_3 \qquad (10)$$

where z_{rs} (for $r = 1, 2$ and $s = 1, 2, 3$) is a constant to be interpreted in such a way that x_1 units of the first commodity possesses $z_{11}x_1$ and $z_{21}x_1$ amounts of the two quality characteristics, and similarly for other commodities. Hence stage (i) is a linear programme

$$\min y = p_1x_1 + p_2x_2 + p_3x_3 \quad \text{subject to (10)}$$

and the curve AB of Fig. 7.1 is converted into a polygon form such that the quality price ratio $\pi_1 : \pi_2$ is constant along one line segment. In other words, the regression estimate can proceed, giving constant quality prices, as long as only one linear segment of the frontier curve is taken. Notice that, at stage (ii), the programme becomes non-linear in that the indifference map is composed of curves. Ironmonger (1961, 1972) carries the linear assumption one step further by taking the indifference curves also of polygon form and reducing the whole exercise to the application of the well-known linear programming technique.

Consequently, as long as we can assume the linear model, we are home and dry. The technique of **7.6** for quality adjustment is under-pinned by household production theory; regression techniques estimate quality prices and provide the quality index g. The results are by no means as simple in the general case of the household production function.

7.8 Changes in Tastes and in Qualities

The development of the constant-utility price index in **2.8** depends on the assumption that the consumer has unchanged tastes so that his preference map is the same in the price situations compared. Something can be done, in purely practical terms, to overcome the difficulties created by the fact that tastes do change. Certainly the difficulties must not be exaggerated. Suppose that the price index calculated is of Laspeyres form base-weighted on year 0 and at the utility level u_0. The theoretical basis of the Laspeyres index in year

t is the constant-utility form $I_{0t}(u_0)$ with the Laspeyres index as an upper bound. This index does *not* answer the question: how much more income does the consumer need today to remain as well off as yesterday? Any change in tastes confuses the issue. The index *does* answer a different question: how much more income would the consumer have needed yesterday if the prices yesterday had been different, and specifically if they had been the prices ruling today? This is a hypothetical question and if the 'yesterday' is a remote time in the past it may also be regarded as irrelevant to today's situation at today's very much changed tastes. The remoteness and irrelevance is much diminished in practice by chaining the true and Laspeyres index numbers e.g. on an annual basis. The comparisons are still hypothetical and tastes still change, but once a year the index is brought up to date and applicable to today's tastes.

A similar analysis applies to the constant-utility price index $I_{0t}(u_t)$ based on the utility level of year t and its lower bound, the Paasche form. The hypothetical question answered is then: how much less income would the consumer need today if prices were as yesterday instead of what they are today? One reason why some authorities, such as Mudgett (1951) and Fisher and Shell (1972), prefer the Paasche to the Laspeyres form lies in this interpretation; they would rather hypothetical questions relate to the here and now. There is, however, much less weight to this preference if the choice is between chain index runs.

The situation on changing tastes, however, is not altogether satisfactory and some theoretical support may well be sought. The household production function of **7.7** succeeds in getting *quality changes* separated off by the frontier curve *AB* of Fig. 7.1 but it still leaves the theory at the mercy of *changes in tastes* as reflected in quality characteristics rather than market purchases. It is possible to develop some theory which allows for changes in tastes and in qualities in parallel, but generally in useful shape only when confined to the special case of changes described as 'quantity-augmenting' for taste changes and as 'repackaging' for quality changes. The early work on this theory in the 1950s grew out of a short note by Ichimura (1951) with advertising expenditure in mind. Ichimura defined an isolated change in tastes in one commodity x by a shift parameter k such that the marginal rate of substitution of x against each of the other commodities is changed in the ratio k:1 while all other marginal rates are unchanged. The theory has since been greatly developed by Fisher and Shell (1968), by Muellbauer (1973) and by others.

The following analysis follows the notation of **2.8**, again for expository purposes in the case of two market commodities and for an individual consumer. The tastes of the consumer are now taken as changing over time and the change is *quantity-augmenting* if

$$u = u(gq_1, q_2) \quad \text{at time } t \tag{1}$$

is the utility function for purchases q_1 and q_2, where g is a parameter (which varies over time) indicating the tastes change. Take $g = 1$ at the base date $t = 0$ and $g > 1$ at time t in (1). If the prices at $t = 0$ are p_{10} and p_{20} and the utility level attained u_0, then the expenditure function can be written $y = y(p_{10}, p_{20}, u_0)$ as in **2.8** where it is used to define the constant-utility price index $I_{0t}(u_0)$ for unchanging tastes. The effect of a quantity-augmenting tastes change is precisely the same as that of a labour-augmenting technical progress in macro-economic theory. The technical-progress case is handled by measuring quantities and prices in efficiency units; see Allen (1968), p. 238. So, here, the first good (but not the second) is converted into efficiency units by writing the quantity $q^*_1 = gq_1$ and the price $p^*_1 = p_1/g$. Consequently, at time t, the expenditure function becomes of the form:

$$y = y(p^*_{1t}, p_{2t}, u) = y\left(\frac{p_{1t}}{g}, p_{2t}, u\right) \tag{2}$$

as a consequence of the tastes change. The utility level u in (2) is at choice. If it is set at u_0, then the constant-utility price index, at this constant-utility level, but adjusted for change in tastes, can be written:

$$I_{0t}(u_0) = y\left(\frac{p_{1t}}{g}, p_{2t}, u_0\right) \Big/ y(p_{10}, p_{20}, u_0) \tag{3}$$

Muellbauer (1973) calls this the *cardinal index* of price changes, adjusted for variation in tastes confined to the first commodity. He contrasts it with an alternative price index

$$C_{0t}(u_0) = y\left(\frac{p_{1t}}{g}, p_{2t}, u_0\right) \Big/ y\left(\frac{p_{10}}{g}, p_{20}, u_0\right) \tag{4}$$

which he describes as the *current-tastes ordinal index* for the same price changes since the comparison uses the augmented tastes for the first commodity at time t. The case of $g > 1$ at time t corresponds to an increased preference for the first commodity as compared with the base date. So the adjusted price p_{10}/g is less than the original price p_{10} and, since y is an increasing function of prices,

$$y\left(\frac{p_{10}}{g}, p_{20}, u_0\right) < y(p_{10}, p_{20}, u_0).$$

So $I_{0t}(u_0) < C_{0t}(u_0)$ (for $g > 1$)

and the cardinal index, as the 'regular' adjustment for tastes-augmentation, is less than the index based on current tastes.

Fisher and Shell (1968) obtain their results by the use of (4) rather than (3). They show, for example, that an increased (quantity-augmented) preference for a price-elastic commodity implies that the price index needs adjustment by reducing the weights of com-plementary goods and raising the weights of substitutes. This is the kind of situation met when a commodity is introduced at a high price and is then price-elastic. Muellbauer (1973) obtains explicit forms of the cardinal index (3) and of the ordinal index (4) by taking the particular Geary/Stone utility function (**6.4**):

$$u = (q_1 - \alpha_1)^{\beta_1} (q_2 - \alpha_2)^{\beta_2} \ (\beta_1 + \beta_2 = 1)$$

where the parameters α_1 and α_2 indicate quantity-augmenting taste changes in the first and the second commodities respectively. If α_1 decreases, then u increases for given q_1 and q_2 and the preference for the first commodity is greater. It is found that the cardinal form (3) of the tastes-adjusted price index decreases with α_1 but that the index of type (4) may go either way.

The use of the parameter g in the utility function (1) applies equally to quality changes of the quantity-augmenting type and described by Fisher and Shell (1968) as *simple repackaging*. This label is appropriate since the quality improvement is such that the new quality is the same as the old except that there is more of it, e.g. more matches per box or a new TV set which gets bigger or better after its first introduction on the market. The analysis of such repackaging changes is simplified and extended by Muellbauer (1973), using an adjustment of form (3), found to have the usual Laspeyres upper bound. The main point is that quality adjustment is then in one price only by a quality index g, the case of **7.6**.

There is more to it than this. Fisher and Shell obtain, and Muell-bauer establishes more simply, the following necessary and sufficient result: a quality change in one commodity can be corrected by adjusting its price by a factor g, independently of all other prices and of all purchases, if and only if the quality change is of the quantity-augmenting (simple repackaging) type. The necessary part is of particular interest since it implies that adjustment by means of formula (1) or (2) of **7.6** is valid *only if* the quality change is of the simple repackaging kind. All other uses, and particularly the regression method applied to a variety of quality characteristics, ignore indirect effects and are at best approximate.

We are back where we were at the beginning of **7.6**. In a complicated problem such as the adjustment of a price index for changes in quality or tastes, it is all too easy to come round in a full circle. Much remains to be done on the problem both in theory and in practice.

Bibliography

Adelman, Irma, 'A New Approach to the Construction of Index Numbers', *Review of Economics and Statistics*, **40** (1958) 240–9.

Adelman, Irma, and Griliches, Z., 'On an Index of Quality Change', *Journal of the American Statistical Association*, **56** (1961) 535–48.

Afriat, S. N., 'The Theory of International Comparisons of Real Income and Prices', in *International Comparisons of Prices and Output*, ed. D. J. Daly (New York, 1972).

Allen, R. G. D., 'Index Numbers of Volume and Price', in *International Trade Statistics*, ed. R. G. D. Allen and J. Edward Ely (New York, 1953).

— 'Price Index Numbers', *International Statistical Review*, **31** (1963) 281–301.

— 'Sampling for Current Economic Statistics', *Journal of the Royal Statistical Society*, A, **127** (1964) 76–88.

— *Macro-economic Theory* (London, 1968).

Allen, R. G. D., and Bowley, A. L., *Family Expenditure* (London, 1935).

Banerji, K. S., 'Precision in the Construction of Cost of Living Index Numbers', *Sankhya*, **21** (1959) 393–400.

— 'A Unified Statistical Approach to the Index Number Problem', *Econometrica*, **29** (1961) 596–601.

— 'Best Linear Unbiased Index Numbers and Index Numbers Obtained through a Factorial Approach', *Econometrica*, **31** (1963) 712–18.

Barten, A. P., 'Family Composition, Prices and Expenditure Patterns', in *Econometric Analysis for National Economic Planning*, ed. P. E. Hart (Colston Papers, **16**, Bristol, 1964).

Beckerman, W., *An Introduction to National Income Analysis* (London, 1968).

Beckerman, W., and Bacon, P., 'The International Distribution of Incomes', in *Unfashionable Economics*, ed. Paul Streeten (London, 1970).

Bortkiewicz, L. von, 'Zweck und Struktur einer Preisindexzahl', *Nordisk Statistisk Tidskrift*, **1** (1922) and **3** (1924).

Bowley, A. L., 'Relations between the Accuracy of an Average and that of its Constituent Parts', *Journal of the Royal Statistical Society*, **60** (1897) 855–66.

— 'The Measurement of the Accuracy of an Average', *Journal of the Royal Statistical Society*, **75** (1912) 77–88.

— *Elements of Statistics*, 5th ed. (London, 1926).

— *Wages and Income since 1860* (Cambridge, 1937).

Brown, J. A. C., and Deaton, A., 'Models of Consumer Behaviour: A Survey', *Economic Journal*, **82** (1972) 1145–1236.

Brown, R. L., Cowley, A. H., and Durbin, J., *Seasonal Adjustment of Unemployment Series*, Studies in Official Statistics, Research Series, no. 4 (HMSO, 1971).

Carter, C. F., Reddaway, W. B., and Stone, Richard, *The Measurement of Production Movements* (Cambridge, 1948).

Central Statistical Office, *Method of Construction and Calculation of the Index of Retail Prices*, Studies in Official Statistics, no. 6, 4th ed. (HMSO, 1967).

— *National Accounts Statistics, Sources and Methods*, 2nd ed. (HMSO, 1968).

— *The Index of Industrial Production*, Studies in Official Statistics, no. 17 (HMSO, 1970).

Cochran, W. G., *Sampling Techniques*, 2nd ed. (New York, 1962).

Cost of Living Advisory Committee, *Report*, Cmnd. 3677 (HMSO, 1968).

Court, A. T., 'Hedonic Price Indexes with Automotive Examples', in S. L. Horner *et al.*, *The Dynamics of Automobile Demand* (New York, 1939).

Craig, J., 'On the Elementary Treatment of Index Numbers', *Journal of the Royal Statistical Society*, C, **18** (1969) 141–52.

Divisia, F., 'L'Indice monétaire et la théorie de la monnaie', *Revue d'Economie Politique*, **39** (1925) 980–1008.

Dorfman, R., Samuelson, P. A., and Solow, R. M., *Linear Programming and Economic Analysis* (New York, 1958).

Durbin, J., and Murphy, M. J., 'Seasonal Adjustment Based on a Mixed Additive-multiplicative Model', *Journal of the Royal Statistical Society* (1975, forthcoming).

Edgeworth, F. Y., *Papers Relating to Political Economy*, vol. I (London, 1925a).

— 'The Plurality of Index Numbers', *Economic Journal*, **35** (1925b) 379–388.

Engel, E., 'Die Productions- und Consumptions-Verhältnisse des Konigreichs Sachsen', reprinted in *Bulletin de l'Institut International de Statistique*, **9**, Appendix (1857, 1895).

Fellegi, I. P., and Sunter, A. B., 'Balance between Different Sources of Survey Errors', *Bulletin of International Statistical Institute*, **45**, III (1973) 334–54.

Fisher, F. M., and Shell, K., 'Tastes and Quality Change in the Pure Theory of the True Cost-of-Living Index', in *Value, Capital and Growth: Papers in Honour of Sir John Hicks*, ed. J. N. Wolfe (Edinburgh, 1968).

— *The Economic Theory of Price Indices* (New York, 1972).

Fisher, Irving, *The Making of Index Numbers* (Boston, 1922).

Fowler, R. F., *Some Problems of Index Number Contruction*, Studies in Official Statistics, Research Series, no. 3 (HMSO, 1970).

— *Further Problems of Index Number Construction*, Studies in Official Statistics, Research Series, no. 5 (HMSO, 1973).

— 'An Ambiguity in the Terminology of Index Number Construction', *Journal of the Royal Statistical Society*, A, **137** (1974) 75–88.

Frisch, Ragnar, 'The Problem of Index Numbers', *Econometrica*, **4** (1936) 1–38.

— 'Some Basic Principles of Price of Living Measurements', *Econometrica*, **22** (1954) 407–21.

Gardner, J. W., Brown, R. L., and Francombe, K., 'Historical Series of the Index of Industrial Production', *Economic Trends*, **223** (1972).

Geary, R. C., 'A Note on a Constant-utility Index of the Cost of Living', *Review of Economic Studies*, **18** (1950) 64–6.

Gilbert, Milton, and Associates, *Comparative National Products and Price Levels*, O.E.E.C. (Paris, 1958).

Griliches, Z., 'Hedonic Price Indexes for Automobiles', in Stigler (1961) and reprinted in Griliches (1971).

— *Price Indexes and Quality Change* (Cambridge, Mass., 1971).

Haberler, G. von, *Der Sinn der Indexzahlen* (Tübingen, 1927).

Halsbury, Lord (chairman), *Report of the Committee of Enquiry on Decimal Currency*, Cmnd. 2145 (HMSO, 1963).

Hansen, M. H., Hurwitz, W. N., and Bershad, M. A., 'Measurement Errors in Censuses and Surveys', *Bulletin of International Statistical Institute*, **38**, II (1959) 359–74.

Hicks, J. R., *Value and Capital*, 2nd ed. (Oxford, 1946).

— *A Revision of Demand Theory* (Oxford, 1956).

Hofsten, E. von, *Price Indices and Quality Changes* (Stockholm, 1952).

— 'Witchcraft and Index Numbers', *Malayan Economic Review*, **1** (1956) 6–14.

Houthakker, H. S., 'Compensated Changes in Quantities and Qualities Consumed', *Review of Economic Studies*, **19** (1952) 155–64.

Ichimura, S., 'A Critical Note on the Definition of Related Goods', *Review of Economic Studies*, **18** (1951) 179–83.

Ironmonger, D. S., *New Commodities and Consumer Behaviour* (unpublished thesis, 1961, and Cambridge, 1972).

Jabine, T. B., and Tepping, B. J., 'Controlling the Quality of Occupation and Industry Data', *Bulletin of International Statistical Institute*, **45**, III (1973) 360–88.

Jazairi, N. T., 'An Empirical Study of the Conventional and Statistical Theories of Index Numbers', Oxford Institute of Economics and Statistics *Bulletin*, **33** (1971) 181–95.

Kendall, M. G., 'The Early History of Index Numbers', *International Statistical Review*, **37** (1969) 1–12.

Keynes, J. M., *A Treatise on Probability* (London, 1921).

— *A Treatise on Money*, Vol. I (London, 1930).

Klein, L. R., and Rubin, H., 'Constant Utility Index of the Cost of Living', *Review of Economic Studies*, **15** (1948) 84–7.

Kloek, T., and de Wit, G. M., 'Best Linear and Best Linear Unbiased Index Numbers', *Econometrica*, **29** (1961) 602–16.

Konüs, A. A., 'The Problem of the True Index of the Cost of Living', Institute of Economic Conjuncture *Economic Bulletin*, nos. 9–10 (Moscow, 1924).

Lancaster, K., 'A New Approach to Consumer Theory', *Journal of Political Economy*, **74** (1966) 132–57.

Laspeyres, E., 'Hamburger Warenpreise 1850–1863', *Jahrbücher für Nationalökonomie und Statistik*, **3** (1864) 81 and 209.

Leser, C. E. V., 'Forms of Engel Functions', *Econometrica*, **31** (1963) 694–703.

Marks, Peter, and Stuart, Alan, 'An Arithmetic Version of the Financial Times Industrial Ordinary Share Index', *Journal Institute of Actuaries*, **97** (1971) 297–324.

Marshall, Alfred, *Money, Credit and Commerce* (London, 1923).

Maunder, W. F. (ed.), *Bibliography of Index Numbers* (International Statistical Institute, 1970).

McKenzie, L., 'Demand Functions without a Utility Index', *Review of Economic Studies*, **24** (1957) 185–9.

Mitchell, B. R., *Abstract of British Historical Statistics* (Cambridge, 1962).

Moroney, M. J., *Facts from Figures* (London, 1951).

Mudgett, B. D., *Index Numbers* (New York, 1951).

Muellbauer, J., 'Household Production Theory, Quality and the Hedonic Technique' and 'The Cost of Living and Taste and Quality Change', Birkbeck College *Discussion Papers* (London, 1973).

— 'Prices and Inequality: the United Kingdom Experience', *Economic Journal*, **84** (1974a) 32–55.

— 'Household Composition, Engel Curves and Welfare Comparisons between Households', *European Economic Review*, **5** (1974b) 103–122.

Muth, R. F., 'Household Production and Consumer Demand Functions', *Econometrica*, **34** (1966) 699–708.

Nicholson, J. L., 'The Measurement of Quality Changes', *Economic Journal*, **77** (1967) 512–30.

Paasche, H., 'Über die Preisentwicklung der letzten Jahre', *Jahrbücher für Nationalökonomie und Statistik*, **23** (1874) 168.

Peston, M., 'Unemployment: Why We Need a New Measurement', *Lloyds Bank Review*, **104** (1972) 1–7.

Prais, S. J., and Houthakker, H. S., *The Analysis of Family Budgets* (Cambridge, 1955).

Reddaway, W. B., 'Movements in the Real Product of the United Kingdom, 1946–1949', *Journal of the Royal Statistical Society*, A, **113** (1950) 435–55.

Retail Prices Index Advisory Committee, *Proposals for Retail Prices Indices for Regions*, Cmnd. 4749 (HMSO, 1971).

Rich, C. D., 'The Rationale of the Use of the Geometric Average as an Investment Index', *Journal Institute of Actuaries*, **74** (1948) 338–9.

Richter, M. K., 'Invariance Axioms and Economic Indexes', *Econometrica*, **34** (1966) 739–55.

Roy, R., 'Les Index économiques', *Revue d'Economie Politique*, **41** (1927) 1251–91.

Ruist, Erik, 'Index Numbers, Theoretical Aspects', *International Encyclopaedia of the Social Sciences*, Vol. 7 (New York, 1968).

Sauerbeck, A., 'Prices of Commodities and the Precious Metals', *Journal of the Royal Statistical Society*, **49** (1886) 581.

Stigler, G. J. (chairman), *Report on the Price Statistics of the Federal Government*, National Bureau of Economic Research, General Series, no. 73 (New York, 1961).

Stone, Richard, 'Linear Expenditure Systems and Demand Analysis', *Economic Journal*, **64** (1954) 511–27.

— *Quantity and Price Indexes in National Accounts*, O.E.E.C. (Paris, 1956).

Stuval, G., 'A New Index Number Formula', *Econometrica*, **25** (1957) 123–31.

Theil, H., 'Best Linear Index Numbers of Prices and Quantities', *Econometrica*, **28** (1960) 464–80.

Ulmer, M. J., *The Economic Theory of Cost of Living Index Numbers* (New York, 1949).

Walsh, C. H., *The Measurement of General Exchange Value* (New York, 1901).

Wood, G. H., 'Real Wages and the Standard of Comfort since 1860', *Journal of the Royal Statistical Society*, **72** (1909).

Yaari, M. E., *Linear Algebra for Social Sciences* (Englewood Cliffs, N.J., 1971).

Index